AF283984

Georgian
CHELTENHAM

Fulwar Craven, 1845.

Georgian CHELTENHAM

Edith Humphris & Captain E. C. Willoughby

The History Press

First published 1928
This edition published 2008

The History Press Ltd
The Mill, Brimscombe Port
Stroud, Gloucestershire, GL5 2QG
www.thehistorypress.co.uk

Copyright © in this edition The History Press, 2008

All rights reserved. No part of this book may be reprinted
or reproduced or utilised in any form or by any electronic,
mechanical or other means, now known or hereafter invented,
including photocopying and recording, or in any information
storage or retrieval system, without the permission in writing
from the Publishers.

British Library Cataloguing in Publication Data.
A catalogue record for this book is available from the British Library.

ISBN 978 1 84588 606 6

Typesetting and origination by The History Press Ltd
Printed in Great Britain

Contents

List of Illustrations

Foreword

As one who has many associations with Cheltenham I have been asked to explain by way of preface certain circumstances connected with the authorship of *Georgians in a Georgian Town*.

Captain E. C. Willoughby, whose name appears on the title-page with that of Miss Edith Humphris, had not quite completed his portion of the work when the Great War broke out.

Fired by an impulse of patriotism he at once volunteered for active service, and though his record justified an application for a commission, he preferred to join the ranks, so as to be able, as he expressed it, to see everything that appertained to the life of a soldier. Recognition of his merits soon brought him promotion; he obtained the rank of Captain when he embarked with his regiment for Gallipoli. There, while leading his Company in the advance on Chunak Bahr, he fell wounded, and was soon to be carried off to what was supposed to be a place of safety.

Since then nothing has been heard of him. His name still lingers on the list of our "missing" heroes.

It was known to be his wish before he left England that this work should be given to the public even if he himself should not be here to finish it.

Captain Willoughby was well qualified to write on the social life of Cheltenham. During the last century many members of his family resided from time to time in the town and neighbourhood. He himself was educated at Cheltenham College, and after practising at the Bar married and settled in the town, becoming Editor and Managing Director of the leading local newspaper.

Miss Humphris, who collaborated with Captain Willoughby, also belongs to an old-established Cheltenham family, and has always taken an active interest in local customs and traditions, on the subject of which she has published some attractive writings.

Readers will gather for themselves that this is in no sense a mere formal narrative of the fortunes of Cheltenham long prominent and still celebrated as a Spa.

The authors have endeavoured, and I venture to suggest with conspicuous success, to paint a picture of Georgian customs and early Victorian manners, in the suitable frame of a health resort.

The sketches of life in these conditions will supply the collector of historical incidents with interesting material; and satisfy those to whom social curiosity appeals as a fascinating indulgence.

Nor are these sketches wholly detached from the absorbing themes of to-day. The chapters which carry us back to the Napoleonic Wars and describe the doings of the interned prisoners, the anxiety for news, the criticisms and complaints, and the visits of the Duke of Wellington on one occasion fresh from Waterloo reproduce phases and incidents with which many of us are familiar to-day.

Like Brighton and Weymouth, Cheltenham, as the introductory chapters remind us, has "basked in the sunshine of Royal favours," and while it may be a matter for conjecture as to the precise extent to which it was indebted to the patronage of George III for the rapid rise from the "Summer Village of all that is fashionable" to its present position of a considerable and populous town, it would be ungrateful to that illustrious personage and contrary to accepted local traditions to minimise the obligation thus conferred. But given the fullest recognition of the value of the Royal patronage bestowed in distant years, Cheltenham may claim to-day that her reputation as a town does not rest exclusively on the fame of her mineral springs.

Since the far-off period described in this volume of Georgian history when royal and other visitors of distinction gathered under the elm-trees of the old Well Walk, two institutions have grown into existence, each of which has added materially to the prestige of Cheltenham.

The Cheltenham College has contributed to the Church, the Army and the Law some of their brightest ornaments.

The Ladies' College, from small beginnings sixty-two years ago, has, mainly through the organising skill and indefatigable industry of the late Dr Dorothea Beale, the first Principal, attracted the countenance and support of the late Princess Royal of England, the Empress Frederick, and achieved a European reputation.

A further charm is added to Cheltenham by its soothing climate, the beautiful scenery of the surrounding country and the reposeful character of the town itself. Sheltered from the north and east by the Cotswold range and situated on the fringe of the Severn valley, with wide well-kept streets and broad avenues rich in foliage and flower, the Cheltenham of to-day endeavours to retain the attractiveness of the Georgian epoch; and by combining that which is pleasing to the eye and healthy to body and mind; justifies the motto adopted by the Municipality: SALUBRITAS ET ERUDITIO.

J. T. Agg-Gardner

Introduction

The Georgians are not quite things of the past. If we strain our eyes we may haply catch a glimpse of the skirts of their garments as they pass into the twilight which precedes history. In the following pages are a series of pictures, loosely strung together, of former *habitués* of Cheltenham Spa and its neighbourhood.

The town itself would still in many ways suit the Georgians who made it, could they come to life again and saunter through the streets and walks as of old. A great deal of Cheltenham has altered little since George IV was King, and many of the houses retain their old powdering-rooms.

There were until lately one or two old residents who remembered the long seat by the old Assembly Rooms, which stood in Rodney Road, where part of Lloyds Bank stands to-day. On it would sit, "with his feet stuck out, Fulwar Craven, The Last of the Dandies, in his canary-coloured waistcoat, and another man who seemed to be a king among them all, in a white hat, with beaver half an inch long." This last was, perhaps, Colonel Charretie making bets about everything on the earth and off it.

Our grandfathers or great-grandfathers remembered all the Georgian *beaux*. There was a stout old gentleman with a kindly face who was the Duke of Gloucester, that beloved if not too intellectual prince who was one of the makers of Cheltenham Spa. He arrived in the town usually just in time for a race meeting, and enjoyed himself so much that he came every year for twenty-nine years, and sometimes stayed so long that he was almost looked upon as a resident.

Then there were Colonel Berkeley of Berkeley Castle and Craven and Grantley and all the Berkeleys of that ilk; tall and splendidly made and very masculine men, with an engaging innocence of face which sometimes strangely belied their real characters, except, perhaps, in the case of Moreton Berkeley, that very perfect knight, who probably looked exactly what he really was.

There was Colonel Hamerton, limping from his old wound; and Corry, the brilliant Irishman, Tom Moore's great friend; Dr Boisragon, beloved of children and princes; and Sir Josiah Coghill, the rollicking sailor, with his laugh that could be heard from Pittville to Leckhampton, his boundless charities, his strange seafaring language, and his witty wife who "worked mesmerism" with Bulwer Lytton. Colbecks, also, the last of the old Macleods of Lewis, Colonel Riddell with his life-restoring powders; and countless others, not forgetting that old chronicler of the times he lived in, Major Pryse Lockhart Gordon, who artlessly confesses in his memoirs that he laid down his sword when he met a rich widow. Worse luck, he laid down his pen also, when he came to Cheltenham.

Here, too, is Berkeley Craven, beautiful and dangerous as Satan fallen from Heaven, Lord of the Manor of Prestbury, and son of the "Princess Berkeley," by her first husband, Lord Craven. These people tell the story of Cheltenham in their diaries and letters and newspapers, and we glean yet more from the stories of the older inhabitants.

Here the Georgians flirted and loved, rode marches, fought duels and gambled. Big men they were for the most part, with big sins and sometimes great repentances, but they were most of them generous and kind-hearted. Hard riders and harder swearers, maybe; yet often free from the petty meannesses of smaller men. They sat on that long seat outside on sunny days and in the summer evenings, and in bad weather stayed inside their old Assembly Rooms, which they kept up as a sort of club, having their meals carried across there from The Plough. They troubled their homes, hotels and lodgings but little and their wives a good deal at times. Most of them had their redeeming features, even the splendid Prince Regent, Colonel Berkeley's friend and Grantley Berkeley's godfather, who remembered old friends when they fell on evil days, and would also go over evidence for hours before he signed a death-warrant, searching for any excuse to set aside the cruel sentences of his time. There was none like him among his subjects; like Saul he towered above them in charm, in brilliancy and devilry. You can see him to-day in his Garter robes in the Wallace Collection; a king, every inch of him.

When most of his company had passed away one of the survivors, Grantley Berkeley, thus describes Cheltenham, as he knew it in his later years:

Cheltenham, like Brighton, very soon began to stretch out its arms to the surrounding lanes, and to turn what used to be the pretty by-ways into streets and roads. The market was no longer held in the High Street, shops spread themselves in all directions, magnificent promenades and convenient places for drinking the water arose, and from a little neat and rather hungry-looking town it became in size almost a city.

I remember one night, after a very hard day in the Broadway country, long after dark, coming on my hack in company with General Berrington and Colonel Berkeley to the summit of the hills. When we first commanded a view of the town after the substitution of gas for the dim lamps that at such a distance used to resemble glow-worms, we pulled up to look at the unwonted brilliancy. Soon afterwards schools and a large college were established, and more staid visitors arrived; not so much for the amusement afforded by the splendid establishment of hounds, or for the lively society in the evening as for the education of their sons.

And so Cheltenham had new lamps for old. The Gas Company and the schools came, and the Georgians ceased to hunt in the Cotswold country and revel in The Vale. And, perhaps, time had been kinder to them than they deserved, for we are apt to remember their splendid clothes and fine horsemanship and to forget the poor crying for bread; the scaffolds reeking with blood; the women hanged for stealing handkerchiefs or loaves of bread; the immorality, gambling, drunkenness.

Many of the incidents related in this book may be "small beer," such as routs, balls, assemblies and other festivities, but they help us to reconstruct life at the fashionable Spa, and, when related in the high-flown language of contemporary scribes, the stories are not lacking in mild humour. However, drama was not often absent in Cheltenham, outside the theatre as well as within its walls, and it is really remarkable how eventful for many of the distinguished visitors to the Spa was their sojourn in Cheltenham.

The curtain rises and the characters will now be presented in turn. But let there be a note of warning. The entertainment, if entertainment it proves to be, is sometimes of the variety-show sort, with little—if any—connection between the various turns, though a short sketch of the general history of the town has been given.

"In and out, above, around, below,
'Tis nothing but a magic shadow Show;
Laid in a box, whose candle is the sun,
Round whom these phantom figures come and go."

I

Cheltenham

*Before AD 48 to AD 1714—Cheltenham in the British, Roman and Saxon
Periods;—and from the Norman Conquest to the reign of Queen Anne.*

It has been said that Tennyson had the two-mile-long High Street of Cheltenham
in his mind when he wrote the lines:

> "There rolls the deep where grew the tree,
> O earth, what changes hast thou seen!
> There where the long street roars hath been
> The stillness of the central sea."

And from the fossil remains discovered there it seems more than likely that at one
time Cheltenham formed part of the bed of the sea.

At Belas Knap on Cleeve Hill remains of prehistoric men, women and children
have been found, but not much is now known of these early Cheltonians.

Some of the earlier chroniclers have told us of the limpid Chelt meandering like
a silver riband through the emerald green valley from its source at Dowdeswell,
three miles out of Cheltenham, to where it joins the Severn at Wainlode's Hill.
Later, when the High Street came into existence—most likely on the cattle
tracks of the ancient Britons—the little river still wandered along the middle of
the street, while jewelled kingfishers and leaping silvery fish broke the calmly-
rippling crystal-clear stream up into a thousand diamond splinters of spray. It was
the garden of the Lord well watered, and even when Cheltenham had become a
spa, the Chelt was still crossed by stepping-stones, and shaded near The Plough
Inn by a huge tree, with spreading branches.

The British camps were in a line on the brow of the Cotswolds and—after the
Roman Emperor, the kindly Claudius, with his general, Plautius (whose Christian
wife is said to have been in Gloucester in AD 43), conquered the British tribe of
the Dobuni in AD 43 and took possession of Cheltenham and its surroundings,

which he governed so well that the aborigines worshipped Claudius as a god—the Roman fortresses were formed on the site of the British camps and some of them can still be seen, while the Roman roads, with their beautiful names, are also more or less with us still. In AD 50, tradition says that the Apostle Paul himself first preached Christianity in the neighbourhood. Lysons brings arguments in support of this theory and says that Gloucestershire was probably the first county in England to embrace the Gospel.

The Roman power in Britain gradually declined, largely on account of the migration of the people homewards to defend Rome from foreign foes. The Saxons took advantage of the defenceless state of the country, thus left almost to its own devices, made attacks at different times, and took possession of portions of land, until by degrees they became masters of the whole of the island. It appears that this part of Britain was conquered in the sixth century, when in 577 Ceawlin and his brother Cutha defeated the Romans in a great battle at Dyrham then Deorham in Gloucestershire, and obtained possession of the three great Roman cities of Glevum, Corinium and Aquae Sulis, which became known to the Saxons by the respective names of Gleoceaster (Gloucester), Cyrenceaster (Cirencester) and Akemanceaster (Bath). The last named is still famous for the warm baths from which it gets its Roman and Saxon names. "To our contact with the Roman power," says Lysons, "we are indebted for an earlier amount of civilisation than perhaps any other part of England." After the battle of Deorham the Romans practically disappeared for ever. England was now cut up into a Heptarchy whose largest and most important kingdom was the western one, which included this part of the country.

A church had, it is said, been built and endowed in Cheltenham prior to the Heptarchy, and soon after the conversion of the Saxons to the Christian Faith buildings must have been erected here for divine service. The Saxons first took a fancy to Cheltenham because, as Fosbroke remarks, they always built their towns "in bottoms surrounded by hills." These invaders occupied the place for almost four hundred years, and made their mark on it. In 584 the first Saxon king ruled over the towns of the Mercian kingdom, including Cheltenham, which town occupied a central position between the two Mercian royal places of Gloucester and Winchcomb.

The name Cheltenham may have meant "The abode of the Celts," but some authorities think that the town got its name from the Saxon words Chilt (a spot rising to an eminence) and ham (a monastery or village).

It is thought that vineyards were first planted in Gloucestershire in the year 280, and here the Romans cultivated willows for binding their vines. In Saxon times the countryside was in a very high state of cultivation, and its vineyards had already become quite famous. The mention of "selected places for vineyards" appears in the earliest Saxon charters. In about 790 a priory of Benedictine monks was founded at Cheltenham, on the site subsequently occupied by houses Nos 403 and 404 High Street, just at the left-hand corner of Cambray, where it branches off from the High Street. In the year 903, at a synod held at Cloveshoe, there were great discussions about Cheltenham Priory. Cheltenham seems to have escaped the notice of the Danes and, in a quiet way, it continued to prosper. King Edward the Confessor began to reign in 1042, and for twenty-four years he, as Lord of the Manor, was the owner of all Cheltenham, to which place he granted a charter.

Most of the inhabitants of Cheltenham under Edward the Confessor were more or less bondmen, though all of these were not called slaves.

The Domesday Book says that the town in Saxon times was "Terra Regis," and that King Edward the Confessor held "Chintenham." There were eight hides and a half, Reinbald (the priest) "holds an Hide and an half, which belongs to the Church. There are two mills of 11s 3d. In the time of King Edward it paid £9 5s 0d and three thousand loaves for the Dogs." It is thought that the priest was Reinbald or Rumbald, Dean of the Collegiate Church of Cirencester, and Chancellor of England in 1065. He witnessed the Charter given to Westminster Abbey. On his gravestone in his Church at Cirencester were inscribed the words, "Rumbald lies here."

Two noblemen closely connected with Gloucestershire were indirectly the causes of the Norman Invasion of England. The first of these, Earl Godwin, had a great deal of property in England, and had bestowed on his disapproving wife Gytha land at Woodchester, as she refused that at Berkeley, of which he had despoiled the Church, and where, by his orders, his men seized the nunnery, and outraged the abbess and several of her nuns, whose ghosts are still supposed to walk and shriek in the neighbourhood. Godwin quarrelled with King Edward, and fled to the Court of William of Normandy, whose interest in the fair realm governed by the Confessor was thus intensified.

The second was Brihtric of Gloucester, Lord of the Manor of Tewkesbury. He had been sent by King Edward on an embassy to the Court of Baldwin, Count of Flanders, and while there won the love, which he did not reciprocate, of Baldwin's beautiful daughter, the fair-haired Matilda. Brihtric was later to feel the truth of the saying, "Hell hath no fury like a woman scorned." The history books of our youth tell us how William, Duke of Normandy, son of Duke Rollo by Arlette, the tanner's daughter of Falaise, came to Bruges as a suitor for the hand of the Count's daughter, but was coldly received by the haughty and lovesick maiden. The Duke of Normandy is said to have horsewhipped the Princess Matilda through the streets of her father's capital, and thus to have won her respect, if not her heart. As Duchess of Normandy, Matilda had the whip-hand of Brihtric, for in 1066 she became Queen of England. Her husband, the Conqueror, seized Brihtric's lands at Tewkesbury and Gloucester and gave them to his Queen, who held them until her death, while the unfortunate Saxon languished in prison at Winchester and was, some say, murdered by the Queen's orders. At any rate, he never regained his freedom.

In 1066 the Conqueror himself became Lord of the Manor of Cheltenham.

The King became very fond of Gloucester, and generally spent Christmas there. It was at the Parliament held in this city in 1080 that William gave orders for the wonderful survey of England known as the Domesday Book, and in 1084 and 1085 the King again held Court in this neighbourhood. At a synod held in 1084 mention was made of a priory and also of a church and its chapels at "Chintenham."

Amongst the knights who had accompanied the Duke of Normandy to England was the Prince Hardinge, son of Sueno, King of Denmark, who married Eva, the Conqueror's niece, and settled at Bristol. His son, Robert, took the name of Fitzhardinge, became a canon of Bristol Cathedral and founded St Augustine's Abbey, now part of the Cathedral, where he was buried in 1170. In 1068, Fitzhardinge, at his house in Baldwin Street, Bristol, entertained with great splendour the King of Leinster and a suite of sixty persons, who passed through the city with the captive wife of the rival prince of the Breffini. Maurice, Fitzhardinge's son, married the daughter of Roger de Berkeley, a Gloucestershire lad who was related both to Edward the Confessor and to the Conqueror. His former name was plain Roger, and he lived at Dursley, but after the Conquest William I gave him the Manor of Berkeley, from which he took his surname. He was, in his latter years, one of the monks of the Priory of Leonard Stanley, which he endowed richly. There had been considerable political rivalry between the Fitzhardinge and Berkeley families, but this was ended when Fitzhardinge's son married Roger Berkeley's daughter and Berkeley's son married Fitzhardinge's daughter. Eva, the Norman wife of Prince Hardinge, or Fitzhardinge, founded, after her husband's death at Bristol, a nunnery in which she lived for the rest of her life, while her son, Maurice, founded two hospitals near Berkeley. Robert, the elder son of Maurice, bequeathed the greater part of his property towards the endowment of churches and priories. From this time, throughout the history of Cheltenham up to within the memory of perhaps a few of the older people, the Berkeley family identified itself more or less with Cheltenham, and ruled the town, until that masterful priest, the Reverend Francis Close (later Dean of Carlisle), wrenched the sceptre from the iron grip of William Berkeley, Earl Fitzhardinge.

In 1087 William Rufus ruled in England in his father's place. He too loved the old cathedral city where his father and the Saxon kings and the Roman Emperor Claudius had held court and summoned Parliaments. Probably the Red King's staghounds hunted deer at Deerhurst, for hunting was his chief pleasure in life. After Lanfranc's death it became necessary to choose a new Archbishop of Canterbury. William II was keeping Christmas at Gloucester at the time, while Anselm, the learned and revered Abbot of Bec in Normandy (whose famous abbey's name survives in Tooting Bec), was staying at the convent at Arle, just outside the town of Cheltenham. The shrewd Norman King at once bethought himself of the best man, probably, that he had ever known, and remembered that he was about six miles away. Messengers were sent to request Anselm to come to Gloucester, where the King desired to make him primate of all England, but the holy Abbot refused to come. The King's messengers, however, would stand no nonsense and the pious and protesting priest was taken by main force and dragged before the King, where in the midst of the Christmas revelry Anselm received an unsought piece of preferment with the remark: "You have yoked together a poor feeble old sheep and a fiery ox," which doubtful compliment to his appearance and disposition the Red King calmly ignored. The princes of this house knew their own minds. On the statue at Rouen of the robber, Rollo, is inscribed the remark which that pirate prince made when he first beheld his future domain of Normandy: "*J'y suis. J'y reste.*"

In all the glorious old Cathedral at Gloucester, the most attractive thing to some of us has always been the lifelike and almost contemporary painted bog-oak effigy on the tomb of the eldest son of the Conqueror, Robert, Duke of Normandy. Half-leaning on his elbow, the blue-eyed heir to his father's throne lies wakeful on his tomb, clad from head to heel in grey chain-mail armour, grasping his good cross-handled sword and with his legs crossed Crusader-fashion. Some say that cruel Rufus put out his brother's eyes in Cardiff Castle and then had him murdered. At any rate, the unfortunate Robert died in captivity, and was buried in the great Cathedral, whose Norman nave is to Gloucestershire men and women the most beautiful thing in the world in the way of architecture. Was it a judgment on Matilda that in the city which she stole from Brihtric her favourite son lies, done to death by his own brother, and buried by the charity of the local monks?

In 1100, Henry I succeeded the Red King, who had been shot in Hampshire, in the country which he had laid waste in order to make the New Forest his happy hunting-ground. Nothing very startling happened in the royal Manor of Cheltenham in this reign, but in 1133 the rectory of St Mary's Church was given to Cirencester Abbey, and two years later the King died, and Stephen, son of the Conqueror's sister Adela and of the Count of Blois, became King of England, and Lord of the Manor of Cheltenham, which he held until his death in 1154. Henry II, son of the Empress Maud and Geoffry Plantagenet, gave Cheltenham to Queen Eleanor as part of her dowry, but resumed possession of it when he quarrelled with his wife.

In 1154, Walter de Hereford took the manor on lease, and held it until 1156. The vineyards are again mentioned in 1154. These gradually increased and improved until at length a great deal of wine was exported, and it was thought to be little inferior to the wines of France. In 1370, Thomas Lord Berkeley had a large vineyard at Cheltenham, which he tended with great care. A good many old vines may be found about Cheltenham but the grapes do not seem to ripen very well nowadays. The Vineyards Hill recalls the merry days on the Cotswolds when the little foxes had a chance to spoil the vines.

In 1199 King John exchanged the Manor of Cheltenham for other lands with the famous Henry de Bohun, Earl of Hereford, upon whose attainder the manor reverted to the Crown. In 1219 Henry III gave Cheltenham to the great Earl of Salisbury, William Long Espée, elder son of Henry II and Fair Rosamond. This lady, Jane, daughter of Walter Lord Clifford of Frampton-on-Severn, had for her incomparable loveliness been given the name of Rosa Mundi—hence Fair Rosamond. She died, by the orders, it is said, of the jealous Queen, at the age of thirty-seven in the nunnery of Godstow. Lord Clifford endowed the nunnery for ever with the rental of a meadow and a mill out of his manor at Frampton. Fair Rosamond's elder son, Long Espée, the new Lord of the Manor of Cheltenham, was connected by marriage with the Despencers, some of whom are buried in Tewkesbury Abbey. William Long Espée appears to have favoured his grandfather, the founder of the nunnery of Godstow, rather than his royal father and his beautiful mother. He was so pious that when he was dying at Salisbury he insisted that he must kneel on the ground on his bare knees to receive the Last Sacrament, which the famous Earl of Salisbury moistened with an abundance of penitential tears. William, son of Long Espée, left the Kingdom without the King's leave in order to take part in the expedition against the Saracens. This gave the reigning monarch, Henry III, an excuse to seize his estates, including the fat Manor of Cheltenham, with its loaves and wine. He gave the manor to the Bishop of Hereford, but in 1247, as his custom was, took back his gift, and exchanged Cheltenham with the Abbot of Fécamp in Normandy for the towns of Winchelsea and Rye in Sussex; after which John Limel, Esq. (who died in 1309), held the manor on lease of that religious foundation.

Cheltenham prospered quietly under her foreign lords. The chief local excitement during the next few reigns seems to have been the knighthood granted on 21st August 1346 on the field of Crécy to Sir Richard de la Bere, for saving the Black Prince's life in that battle. One of the then fashionable ostrich feather coats of arms was also granted to this gallant and fortunate soldier. Several members of the Berkeley, Trye, Dutton and Hicks families, all well known in Cheltenham, had come over with the Conqueror and now fought under the Prince of Wales at Crécy and were suitably rewarded, and a body of Gloucestershire volunteers under Maurice Lord Berkeley was included in the victorious army, when the valour of these Gloucestershire men was highly praised. Indeed, to judge from the local trinkets collected on the field, the battle appears to have been mainly won by the Royal Gloucestershire Yeomanry.

Doubtless Cheltenham had heard much about the tragedy of Edward II. In the absence of the reigning Lord of Berkeley the unhappy King was conveyed a prisoner to the castle and the surrounding country rang with his agonised shrieks when the King of England was barbarously done to death by the orders of his wife and of her lover. Once before, the doors of Gloucester Cathedral had swung open to admit a mournful procession, when the eldest son of the Conqueror and Matilda of Flanders had died obscurely in captivity at Cardiff Castle. Now it was the actual and basely murdered King of England to whom the Gloucester monks, fearless as Anselm of old, did not hesitate to give honourable sepulture. In later days the Cathedral was enriched by gifts offered by pilgrims at Edward's gorgeous and gilded shrine.

The grant by Henry III to the Abbey of Fécamp of the Manor of Cheltenham was confirmed by an Act passed to Edward III. The manor was subsequently sold to the Norman Abbey of Montburg, but in consequence of the dissolution of alien priories, Cheltenham once more became the property of the Crown.

During this period the Parish Church of Cheltenham, dedicated to the Blessed Virgin Mary, was becoming more and more beautiful. A church is known to have existed here at the time of the Domesday survey, but no part of the present structure, with the possible exception of part of the base of the tower, is earlier than the twelfth century; St Mary's Church is a cruciform edifice with a central tower, and the first impression of a stranger on entering it would probably be a feeling of admiration for its exquisite proportions.

"The north transept," says Mr T. Overbury, FRIBA (a member of the firm of Messrs Healing & Overbury), in his book on *The Parish Church, Cheltenham,* from which he has kindly allowed quotations to be made: "was the chapel of St Katharine of Alexandria, with a chantry. The very fine wheel window in the eastern wall is probably symbolical of this saint, while in the north gable is another circular window ... The south transept was the chapel of the Blessed Virgin Mary, with a rich chantry, and the restored Early English piscina and aumbry in its south wall would seem to indicate that it was built earlier than the geometric windows ... The architectural features of the Chancel are now almost entirely of fourteenth-century date. The side windows are Decorated, the central one on the south side being modern. The late Mr Francis Bond considered that the style of architecture was due to the Gloucester Abbey influence, and that in such cases the windows are absolutely contemporaneous and date between 1330 and 1360 ... The piscina, built in the eastern jamb of the southernmost window, is most uncommon, with openings to the west and north, having cusped and crocketed ogee arches, battlemented cornices and mutilated figures in the spandril of the arches ... The western wall of the nave is Norman, of the first half of the twelfth century, and outside has two characteristic Norman buttresses, with the billet mould string carried round them, and right across the west end ... The south wall of the nave has been doubtless rebuilt ... In my opinion the north wall of the nave is the original Norman wall propped up and with the arches inserted." The rood-loft disappeared at the Reformation or soon afterwards, the ancient stone altar and font were also cleared away, as were the carved figures which were originally over the high altar. In the north transept and in the north wall of the north aisle are tomb recesses with ball-flower decorations, and the north porch, now used as a baptistery is, says Mr Overbury, "a fine example of Perpendicular work, its Berne vaulting and Tudor rose bosses being very good … Opening out of the north side of the chancel is the sacristy, rebuilt on old foundations, and in the window is the only old glass, well worth seeing."

The broach spire of St Mary's Church is 155 feet in height and the lower part of the tower was probably built about 1150 or earlier, the middle stage in about 1200, the upper part and spire in about 1300.

Rudder tells us that Horton, the renowned sacrist, who, in the fourteenth century, began to build the beautiful cloisters and who rebuilt the high altar, aisle and other parts of Gloucester Cathedral, was ordained in the Parish Church. "He received the benediction at Cheltenham from the Bishop of Hereford, by leave of the Bishop of Worcester."

The lease of the Manor of Cheltenham was purchased in 1466 by Maurice Lord Berkeley. With this event the direct connection of the town with the Berkeley family began. Up to 1468 Cheltenham returned two members to Parliament, but the practice was discontinued in consequence of a petition from the inhabitants to Queen Elizabeth, in which they complained fretfully that their members were a great *expense* to them.

On 3rd May 1471, Edward IV passed through Cheltenham on the eve of the battle of Tewkesbury, with an army consisting of 3000 infantry and a large body of cavalry. He stayed for "a little refection" and caused his people to "do the like." While in the town the King had certain knowledge that his enemies were already come to Tewkesbury, and after his hastily snatched meal Edward marched on and stayed the night in a field, probably at Elmstone Hardwick or Tredington, not more than three miles from Queen Margaret and her army.

In the ensuing battle, fought in what have ever since been called The Bloody Meadows, at Tewkesbury, Edward of York utterly routed the Queen's forces, and the vanquished Margaret of Anjou was soon, like her husband Henry VI, an inmate of the Tower of London. Their young son, "Edward ye Prince fleeing to ye townwarde" after the battle, was slain, it is said by Richard Duke of Gloucester, afterwards Richard III, and his followers.

Richard Crookback subsequently married Anne Neville, daughter of the Kingmaker, and widow of that Prince of Wales with whose death Richard is credited. The monks of Tewkesbury Abbey were not behind those of Gloucester in reverence for the unfortunate dead, for they buried two murdered princes, the poor young Prince of Wales, and also Humfrey Duke of Gloucester, who is said to have been drowned in a butt of Malmsey wine. Sir Maurice de Berkeley, brother of the fifth Lord Berkeley, fought for Edward of York at the Battle of Tewkesbury, and greatly distinguished himself.

In 1466 Edward IV had granted the Manor of Cheltenham to the Nunnery of Sion in Middlesex. The rulers of that monastic institution possessed the manor until 1540, when they were deprived of it by virtue of the Act which abolished all monasteries.

Fourteen years after the battle of Tewkesbury the day of retribution came for
Richard III; he was slain fighting valiantly at Bosworth Field, clad in the selfsame
suit of polished armour in which he had fought, and perhaps killed, the Prince
of Wales at Tewkesbury. The crown of England was found hanging on a thorn
bush. Henry Earl of Richmond, a Welshman, son of a Red Rose Princess and
Owen Tudor, who had been one of Margaret's supporters at Tewkesbury, took
the crown up and put it on his own head. He afterwards married Elizabeth the
White Rose Princess of York, daughter of Edward IV and Elizabeth Woodville,
and sister of the Princes who had been slain in the Tower. It is now known that
Richard Crookback, far from being a monster of deformity, had one shoulder
only slightly higher than the other, and was a powerfully built man with a face
of exquisite beauty, and of singular fascination of manner. His alleged murder of
Prince Edward seems not to have been completely proved, though local tradition
is strongly against him.

A well-known family in the old days of Cheltenham was that of Smith. Some
of them were doctors and others merchants, and subsequently members of the
family kept the Fleece Hotel in the High Street. An almost prehistoric Smith
is said to have killed an enormous sea-serpent, which had been washed ashore
when the Severn overflowed its banks, and became a terror to the county round
Deerhurst and Walton, where it poisoned people and destroyed cattle. When
Smith killed the serpent he was given an estate on Walton Hill.

After the Reformation, Henry VIII took possession of Cheltenham and the town
was reduced to poverty. It was many years before the old prosperity returned.

On Henry's death in 1547 the Manor of Cheltenham was held by Edward VI,
and in 1553, by Queen Mary, who granted it in the following year to Catherine
Buckler and her brother Roger Lygon for their joint lives. These were relatives by
marriage of Judge Greville, whose brass inlaid monument is in the Parish Church
at Cheltenham. After the death of Queen Mary in 1558, Queen Elizabeth was Lady
of the Manor. In the sixteenth year of her reign she granted a lease of it for the
term of thirty-one years to Sir John Woolley, who, after the deaths of Catherine
Buckler and Roger Lygon, came into possession. In 1555 the first entry in the
present Manor Roll had been made. It was in 1578 that Richard Pates founded
the Elizabethan Grammar School at Cheltenham. It is said that Queen Elizabeth
visited the Cheltenham Grammar School and was so pleased that she gave to Pates
part of the property with which he endowed it. He left some land also for charities
in Cheltenham and Gloucester, and also to Corpus Christi College, Oxford.

Richard Pates was the friend and correspondent of the famous Sir Humphrey
Gilbert, brother-in-law of Sir Walter Raleigh. The Raleighs were really
Gloucestershire people; some of Sir Walter's descendants married into the family
which then owned Sandiwell Park. "Sir Walter Raleigh's friendship with Richard
Pates probably led to the establishment in 1565 of the Cheltenham tobacco
plantations, the first on English ground.

Shakespeare seems to have known his Vale of Evesham well, and very likely he used to come over and poach in this part of the country, when he had made Stratford too hot to hold him. A local proverb was embodied by the Stratford poet into his writings—"As thick as Tewkesbury mustard"—and some writers, at least, believe that the lad who indulged his sporting tastes at the expense of the Lucys of Charlecote also took part in the "coursing on Cotsal"—a favourite sport then as now on those "high wild Hills whose rough uneven ways draw out our miles and make them wearisome." Only a sportsman well acquainted with the Cotswold Hills could have written Shakespeare's plays. The Harts of Tewkesbury, descended from Shakespeare's favourite sister, Joan, lie buried in the churchyard of Tewkesbury Abbey. An old lady who was a member of this family died in about 1890 in Gloucester. She was Mrs Fletcher, head of a firm of cutlers, and she owned Shakespeare's jug, and other relics. There were legends of Shakespeare's old theatrical clothes, in which some of the Hart children or their descendants used to dress up.

On 27th February 1597, the Rectory of Cheltenham was leased to Francis Bacon, afterwards Lord Chancellor, the great statesman and philosopher, who subsequently, when Lord Verulam, farmed out the curacy of Cheltenham and Charlton Kings for the whole term of forty years to Mrs Badger or Baghott, who had paid him 1000 marks for the lease. The avaricious lady "mother of both the Higges" was clearing £600 a year, but was not fulfilling certain obligations which she had undertaken. Bacon's letter of remonstrance to Mrs Badger ends: "Your loving friend, Fra. Verulam. From Yorke House, the 19th Nov. 1620."

The Cheltenham rectory was subsequently granted to Sir Bagshot Hicks, on condition that he should allow a yearly stipend of £40 a year to the officiating minister. Sir Bagshot delegated the power of electing the minister to Jesus College, Oxford, and twenty-three Welsh Bachelors of Art held the living from that time up to the appointment of the Rev. R. Foulkes in 1799.

We must now return for a moment to the history of the Parish Church, on a tablet in which it is recorded that Ludowick Packer, Gent., gave in 1603 the third bell to this parish. At the foundry of the famous Rudhalls of Gloucester in 1697 all the old bells of St Mary's were re-cast and made into eight.

These bells were in use until about 1844, when, after a lapse of two centuries the great Rudhalls finally melted them down at the same establishment.

In the tower is preserved a sanctus bell of ancient form, called the Saints' Bell, once used as a fire-bell, and a little tablet facing the marigold window says that Lord Gage gave a fire-engine to the town.

An old mural monument is that put up to the memory of Joseph Arkell, who died in 1699, and of "Frances his wife, daughter of Henry Blomer of Cowly, gentleman." Henry Blomer was perhaps the son of Giles Blomer, who died at Cowley, in 1624. Mr Arkell was a member of a family said to be descended from Flemish princes, but to-day scattered over the Cotswold country in almost every walk of life.

Mrs Thrale, Dr Johnson's friend, came as a child to Cheltenham and wandered about the church where she was interested in Dr English's monument to his wife, with its curious inscription.

Captain Henry Skillicorne's monument is a marvel. At the end of an inscription about two yards long there are squeezed in words to the effect that Mrs Elizabeth Skillicorne, his wife, was buried in the Quakers' Graveyard.

In 1628 John Dutton of Sherborne, Gloucestershire, bought the Manor of Cheltenham of the Prince of Wales for £1200. After this transaction the manorial rights were vested in the Dutton family for two hundred and fifteen years. Dutton's ancestor, Odart, had come over, with his five valiant brothers, with William the Conqueror and was Steward to Neale, Constable of Hugh Lupus, Earl of Chester. The family became possessed of the Manor of Dutton in Cheshire, from whence they took their name; and one of the Duttons, Ralph, acquired further fortune as a reward for his services to Ranulph, sixth Earl of Chester, when he was attacked at Chester Fair by the Welsh.

During the Civil Wars Cheltenham was most deeply engaged, chiefly on the royal side. On 14th February 1643, Charles I wrote from Oxford to John Stubbes of Charlton Kings and asked him for the loan of twenty pounds, or his plate. One of the siege pieces struck out of unalloyed gold at Oxford at this time was dug up in June 1861 in Charlton Kings. The road from Stow on the Wold then passed by the Hewletts, and along the back of the town of Cheltenham. The armies of both parties, therefore, had to march through the place on their way to Gloucester, when it was in a state of siege. The following vivid account is taken from "A true relation of the late Expedition of his Excellency, Robert Earl of Essex, ordered by the Commons, 7th October 1643."

"On the 4th of September (1643) near Stow on the Wold, a smart skirmish happened with Prince Rupert, who attacked Essex with about 4000 horse, and still appeared before the Parliament's Army as they marched on, for many miles together. On the 5th September, Lord Essex advanced to Prestbury Hills, where he drew up his whole army in view of the city of Gloucester, and discharged four pieces of great ordnance to give them notice of his approach; soon after we discovered the enemy's quarters on fire, for upon our advance, they deserted the siege and marched away all that night in fear and disorder, the rearguard of our army, some ordnance and ammunition, stayed on the top of the hills by reason of the steepness thereof, darkness of the night, and tempestuousness of the weather, whereby, besides the famine, the whole army had, for the three days' march before, extremely suffered through accounting that the enemy had already destroyed; and that night through the violence of cold and rain, divers of their horses died. His Excellency, with the rest of the army, quartered that night below the hill at Prestbury. The next day, being Wednesday, his Excellency marching to Cheltenham, the enemy fell into the quarters of Colonel Dalbeirs regiment, but having the alarm, soon retired with little loss. The next day, being Thursday, the enemy beat up the quarters of Col. Beere's and Col. Goodwin's regiment; the loss was not considerable, only Major Bora charging the enemy very bravely, to make retreat for the rest. His Excellency stayed at Cheltenham till Friday, and then marched with his whole army to Gloucester, where he continued until Sunday, furnishing the town with ammunition, money and other necessaries. In all these removes since our army came down the hills, the enemy avoided quartering near us, lying at Sudeley when we were at Gloucester; and when we came to Tewkesbury and advanced with part of our forces to Upton, they marched with their army to Evesham, and towards Worcester, ten miles, at least from us; whereby it appears that they pursued ten days to seek battle. On Friday morning his Excellency arose with his whole army from Tewkesbury, intending to quarter that night at Cheltenham, but upon advertisement that a body of the enemies were then in Cirencester, our want of necessaries and victuals still increasing upon us, his Excellency made a long march with the vanguard of the army to fall upon them, which he did about one o'clock of the night, sending a party of horse to seize upon the sentinels and guards, while we, with the rest of the horse, begirt the town. We took there forty loads of victuals, which, under God's providence, was the preservation of the army till the day we fought the great battle of Newbury: there were taken six standards, all the officers except the two colonels, who were absent, with divers other gentlemen of quality, above three hundred common soldiers and four hundred horse."

Skeletons were found in the Cheltenham High Street, in St James's Square, St George's Square and Grove Street, and also on the sites of the Bethel Chapel and the old Roman Catholic Chapel. A pistol was also found, with a curious revolving wheel attached to it. It seems that this must have been the scene of some considerable engagement of the Civil Wars.

A letter from Henrietta Maria written to her husband in 1646 is quoted by Prinn in the Cheltenham Manorial Rolls, a tart and discouraging document, at the end of which Her Majesty remarks:

"I send you this man express, hoping that you will not have passed the militia bill. If you have, I must think of retiring for the present into a convent, for you are no longer capable of protecting anyone, not even yourself."

One can only hope that she was a more indulgent wife to Henry Jermyn, Earl of St Albans, if she really married him.

On 6th December 1643 (and again in 1644), Charles I visited Sir Charles Pope, created Earl of Downe, at his seat at Cubberley, Gloucestershire, the royal army being in 1643 stationed in the neighbourhood of Cheltenham. Several members of the Dutton family lost their estates because they were royalists. Sir Baptist Hicks set fire to his house on the Cotswolds lest it should shelter the Republican Army.

Colonel Henry Norwood of Leckhampton, Captain Conway Whithorne of Charlton Kings, Sir Thomas and Sir John Byron, Sir R. Ducie of Woodchester, the Marquess of Worcester and Sir R. Lawrence, a member of the family who owned The Greenway, Shurdington, were on the King's side, though the inhabitants of Gloucester and Tewkesbury sided with Cromwell. In 1643 the wife of Dr English, Incumbent of Cheltenham, died of a broken heart on account of her husband's persecution and imprisonment by the Puritans, while Mrs Henry Fowler, wife of the Rector of Minchinhampton, was turned out with her children on to the Common in the snow. Her husband was almost killed by the soldiers. W. Fowler, who bought the manor of Stonehouse in the reign of Queen Elizabeth, Edward Fowler, Bishop of Gloucester, the Fowlers who settled in Cheltenham, and these Minchinhampton Fowlers appear to have all come from the same stock, and their coat of arms is the same, while the Cheltenham Fowlers claim descent from the persecuted Rector of Minchinhampton, and they also think that they are related to the Bishop of Gloucester, an author against whom John Bunyan wrote, though the Bishop did not care a tinker's curse for his critic, and retaliated with a pamphlet, of which the title was something like "Dirt to be wip'd out". Henry Fowler (of Queen's College, Oxford) of Co. Gloucester, gent., took his BA degree, aged about twenty-one, on 10th November 1591. He may have been Rector of Minchinhampton in 1611 or 1612. Henry Fowler of Co. Gloucester, and of Magdalen College, Oxford (BA, 17th April 1605; MA, 4th February 1607-8), was about twenty-two years of age in 1605, and was Rector of Minchinhampton from the year 1618, and he, it was who was ill-treated by the Puritan soldiers. His son Henry Fowler of Minchinhampton, matriculated at Oriel College, 1st April 1636, aged seventeen, and graduated 14th December 1639. "After he had been a graduate he served very faithfully in his Majesty's Army, during the Grand Rebellion begun by the Godly Party, and afterwards betook himself to the study of Physick, which he did with good success in his own county." The date on which Henry Fowler was licensed as a medical practitioner is given as 13th March 1678, but this seems more likely to be the date of his death. John Walker, DD, in his *Sufferings of the Clergy*, gives a dramatic account of the happenings at Minchinhampton Rectory on New Year's Day, 1643, and on a later occasion in the same year. On New Year's Day the Rector was sitting by his fireside, apparently in his study, when a party of soldiers, sent by one Captain Buck of the Parliamentary Army, burst into the room, seized the unfortunate clergyman, held the point of a sword against his breast, presented pistols at him, and shook a "poll-axe" over his head, "railing at him for Reading Common Prayer and His Majesty's Proclamations, calling him Mass Priest, Rogue, Rascal, with other contumelious language, as 'Sirrah! you can Furnish the King with a Musquet, a Corselet, and a Light-Horse; but Thou old Knave, thou canst not find anything at all for the Parliament.'" They fell on the lame man, and pole-axed him, so that he was left bleeding, permanently crippled and deaf from injuries to his head. "His wife and children on bonded knees entreated mercy and compassion for him, but all in vain; for instead of that some of the kindred and friends of Captain Buck, who had sent them on this errand, stood by, jeering and clapping their hands for joy." A great many members of the Buck family are buried in Minchinhampton Churchyard, and the Captain appears to have been a Minchinhampton man, well known to the Rector, for whom and for his family he felt the bitterest hatred. Some months after the attack on Mr Fowler, when Mrs Fowler and one of the girls seem to have been alone in the Rectory, Captain Buck "comes in person to Mr Fowler's house; breaks open the window of his son's study, who was a physician; enters the house that way; and destroys several things of great value in the way of Physick; as Extract of Pearl, *Aurum Potabile*, Confection of Amber, Pearl in Boxes, Bezoar-stone, Compound Waters, etc., upon which, one of Mr Fowler's daughters telling Buck he might be ashamed to spoil such things, he presently called her Whore, and knock'd her down with his Poll-axe; and being risen again, knock'd her down a second time, and after that a third time, and would no doubt a fourth, had she been able to rise again. Upon which Mrs Fowler asking him if he thought 'twas possible for her to stand by and see her Child murdered, Buck presently, without any regard either to her Age or Sex, caught her by the throat, knock'd her down and when down, kick'd her, and trampled on her with his Feet. After which, he and his Rabble Plundered the House, and so departed. If this monstrous Barbarity exceeds Belief, let it be known that August the 18, 1643, it was deposed upon Oath before Sir Robert Heath, Lord Chief Justice of the King's Bench." Not much seems to be known of Henry Fowler, Rector of Minchinhampton, his son, Henry, the physician (four times Mayor of Gloucester), and his other children, though one would like to know more of the girl who stood up to Captain Buck. The Fowlers who eventually settled in Cheltenham were descended from Henry Fowler, the doctor, but the first of them who comes into the story of Cheltenham is William Fowler, of Dursley or Stonehouse in the County of Gloucester, and of St John's, Westminster. He and his wife, Hester, *née* Jackson, were the parents of the Rev. Henry Bond Fowler, born in 1753, who married Mary, daughter of Edward Webb, Esq, of Minchinhampton, and Mr Fowler was the nephew, as his wife was the niece, of the Rev. William Bond, who had a school at "St Chloe's, Nailsworth," locally pronounced "Sinkleys." Edward Webb belonged to a family which is said, perhaps in jest, to have come over with the Conqueror and peopled the valleys of Stroud. A member of this prolific family had a persistent lover who came and stayed at her parents' house for six weeks until she married him to get rid of him! Another Webb had eight children, to each of whom he left one of his eight mills. Amongst the Webb monuments and tombs in the district is one at Horsley to "Edward Webb, Esq, Clothier."

Henry Fowler, a doctor, son of the Rev. H B Fowler, and great-great-grandson of Dr Henry Fowler of Minchinhampton married, in 1815, at Avening Church, Anne Day, daughter of Jeremiah Day of Woodchester and his wife Fanny, who had

been a Miss Remmington, a relative, and possibly a sister of John Remmington of
Barton End House, Horsley. It is indeed probable that both John Remmington and
Fanny, were the children of Samuel Remington or Remmington, of Woodchester,
whose wife, Anne, "daughter of John and Mary Vick of this town," died on 6th
June 1763, and lies buried under the reading-desk at Minchinhampton Church.
Mary, the wife of John Vick, junior, daughter of Charles Smith of Horsley,
gentleman, died 22nd July 1942, and "Frances Vick, sister of the aforesaid Anne
Remington, died October 7th, 1809 in the eighty-second year of her age." It
is likely that John Remmington inherited Barton End House from the above-
mentioned Charles Smith of Horsley. The Remmingtons were a Jacobite family,
and Fanny Remmington gave to her granddaughter, the daughter of Dr Henry
Fowler of Cheltenham, two miniatures, one of Prince Charlie, mounted in gold,
and the other of a man in a flowing brown wig, thought by some to be Hyde, Earl
of Clarendon. Both were kept together, evidently as great treasures, but in the old
days they were hidden away.

John Remmington, so it is said, had three daughters who went out together to
India, and who all became engaged during the voyage. They were subsequently
either Mrs Mary Tombs (mother of Sir Henry Tombs, VC), or another daughter,
Mrs Moore and Mrs Skinner. Another daughter was Frances Vick Remmington,
who married Hickey's acquaintance, Colonel George Wood of the Bengal Army,
while there was also a son, Samuel Remmington. There is a legend that one of the
Tombs family, an officer in the army, completely disappeared during a campaign
or in a battle in Afghanistan, and that his fate could never be ascertained. Sir
Harry Tombs's father was Major-General John Tombs, but who the lost officer
was, history does not relate. Members of the Tombs family are said to have hidden
the then fugitive Charles II at their house at Long Marston.

The Minchinhampton and Cheltenham Fowlers descend from the Fowlers of
Foxley, Co. Bucks, one of whom, Richard, was a Crusader, under Richard I, and
roused the Christian camp in time to ward off a night attack by the Saracens, for
which service Coeur de Lion gave him the Vigilant Owl for a crest, instead of
the Hand and Lure. Thomas Fowler was Esquire of the Body to Edward IV, and
Richard Fowler, a soldier, was, in that reign, Chancellor of the Duchy of Lancaster.
Edward Fowler lived at Bromhill in Norfolk, and was on active service in Scotland
in the reign of Henry VIII. He married Sibyl or Cecilia Leghe or Lee, sister of
the then Bishop of Lichfield who, in October 1539, got St Thomas's, Stafford, as a
family possession, and settled one of the Fowlers, his nephew, there as a country
gentleman, whence the latter's son or grandson, Richard, came to Gloucestershire,
and lived at Biggs' Place or Brimscomb House in the parish of Bisley. Born in 1539,
he married the daughter of John Shewell or Armstrong of Ferris' Court, Bisley,
died in 1623, aged eighty-four, and was buried at Minchinhampton. His children
were Henry Fowler, Rector of Hampton Rood or Minchinhampton (born in
1579, died 1643), who married Mary, daughter of John Griffin of Stroud. The

Rector had a brother, Roger, who died unmarried, and sisters, amongst whom were Tacie (Mrs Robert Freame of Lypiat), Joan (Mrs John Butler of Oakridge), and Mrs Wadley? of Worcestershire. Of the Rev. Henry Fowler's own children, Henry, the physician, born 1619, married Martha Dean of "Minchinghampton," Richard, born 1629, married Miss Butt of Bisley, Roger is not known to have married, Elizabeth, perhaps the one "knock'd down" so much by Captain Buck, married John Fleetwood of the north of England, whilst her younger sisters, Mary, Beata, Anne and Sarah, died unmarried.

St Chloe's school, of which the Rev. William Bond was head master, may have had some connection with St Mary's Mill which Rudder describes as a former chapel, situated in Minchinhampton parish, and famous for a room in it called Friar Bacon's study, because Roger Bacon is said to have been educated in it. He tells us that Nathaniel Cambridge of Nailsworth gave a thousand pounds which was laid out in the purchase of Saintloe Farm in the parish of Minchinhampton, and that in 1690 or 1699 a school was there erected.

Of this old place, now called St Loe's House, Amberley, Mary Macleod Moore says in *The Sunday Times* of 26th August 1928:

"It is an ancient grey house, forming with its great wall, a square. A green lawn lies at the foot of the high stone wall, and in the centre of the square is a formal garden, ablaze with gay flowers, guarded by ancient clipped bushes. Above, an old clock reminds one of the passage of sunny days, and below a sun-dial tells that the bird of time is on the wing. An old gateway in one corner of the square was there when the Tudors reigned ... Hundreds of years ago this place ... was a farmhouse. Then the Lord of the Manor lived therein. Next it was an abbey, monks worked and read in the sunny quadrangle. For two hundred years a school was housed there, and the ... schoolroom ... has been in use for centuries."

The house seems to have been called St Chloe's or Sinkley's in the days of the Rev. William Bond, and it is mentioned as St Chloe's in a scrapbook which belonged to Mr Bond's great-great-niece, who knew Nailsworth and Minchinhampton well, and had constantly visited the Westleys' delightful old house at Springhill, Nailsworth, where the last of the family, Edward Pinfold Westley lived to about ninety-six years of age. The late Rev. Francis William Fowler, great-great-nephew of the Rev. W. Bond, thought once of taking over St Chloe's school (then also, so his niece says, called Sinkley's), but the house was then dilapidated and the project came to nothing.

II

The House of Hanover

Cheltenham Spa before the Visit of George III, 1755–1788—1715–1743;
The Discovery of the Mineral Waters and the early days of the Spa—
1744–1772; John Wesley, Handel, and Dr Johnson and Shenstone—
1773–1774; Mrs Siddons, the Kemble family and John Boles Watson.

In about 1715 or 1716 a member of the Society of Friends, Mr Mason, had bought from Mr Higgs of Charlton Kings some land in Cheltenham upon which was a spring. It is said that several people in the neighbourhood were aware of the healing properties of the water of this spring, but the accepted legend is that either some pigeons or a decrepit old horse came to eat the deposits of salt which collected round the spring, and that thus Mr Mason, the owner of adjoining property, discovered that Mr Higgs had a valuable saline spring in his grounds, which the Quaker promptly acquired. At first the spring was left open, and anyone who wished to do so could drink the waters, but later on it was railed in, and in 1720 the famous purging mineral waters of Cheltenham were advertised with the further attraction of a good bowling-green, while in 1721 the spring was leased to a Mr Spencer at a rental of £61 per annum.

On Mr Mason's death his son-in-law, Captain Skillicorne, a Manxman, became proprietor of the Old Well, and made many improvements. In the summer of 1738, he not only built the old room on the west side for the drinkers, but secured the spring from all extraneous matter, erected a square brick building on four arches, as a dome over it, with a pump on the east side, rising in the form of an obelisk. He then leased the Spa to Thomas Hughes, who sent the water in large quantities to various parts of the country where he had agents, amongst others to Mr Thomas Davies of St Albans Street, the mineral-water manufacturer.

In 1739 Captain Skillicorne made the upper walk, planted thirty-seven elm and lime trees and made a new orchard adjoining. There were several contributors of money towards the formation of the grand walk; amongst them the Rev. Mr Meyrick, the Rector; the Rev. Mr Prinn; Madam Dormer; J. Trevanion,

Gent.; Mr Benfield's clerk; Jesus College, Cambridge; Edward Timbrel and Mr Jones, churchwardens; Mr Pruen; the Hon. Sir John Dutton, Bt, and the Rev. Francis Welles.

In the winter of 1740 Captain Skillicorne made the Lower Walk, and planted 96 elms at the expense of £66. He writes: "Had that summer 414 subscribers at the Wells at 12d per piece. Built a yard round it and 18 little houses ... The summer of 1741 proving very dry, 30 trees died, and a great part of quick set hedge, planted by the wall and several other sorts set, as elms, ash, sally and crabsticks, sets and withy and pollards, set about Ashmead and other parts of the estate died, which I planted again."

In 1742 he built another room, two stories high.

In spite of these improvements, visitors came slowly to Cheltenham at first. One good reason for this was the difficulty of communications. The famous Mrs Delany on 9th August 1733, writes to Mr Granville: "Cheltenham, 9th August 1733—We arrived here last night, I thank God, safe, after a very tedious journey, occasioned by the restiveness of two out of our six horses, four of which were hired at Warwick. We breakfasted on our way at Mickleton, and Mrs Chapone and Sally came with us in a Post Chaise to guide us. The road to Mickleton was most terrible, and bad enough to foil the best horses in England, but all that is over. We have got a charming lodging, and a room at your service, if you will make us a visit at Mrs Hughes's near the Well. I begin with one glass to-morrow morning."

In 1736 Sir Edward Seymour arrived in Cheltenham, and could not get a lodging. There was no post-chaise in the town to take him to Gloucester, so he had to send over for one from Gloucester to take him there.

In 1738 the first coach or "flying machine" from Cheltenham to London was advertised, the journey to be accomplished, "if God permitted," in "the short space of three days." People sometimes made their wills before they started out on this perilous journey.

One or two quaint echoes of the political controversies of the day have come down to us. The diary of Mr Welles of Prestbury (a clergyman and magistrate) records for 1716: "Mary Careless committed to quarter sessions for saying twice King George was a Papist Dog. Mary Hill likewise committed for saying, No, he was a Presbyterian." In 1743, on the Duke of Cumberland's birthday in April, the Pretender was burnt in effigy in Cheltenham. "The morning was ushered in with ringing of bells and other demonstrations of joy; at noon a considerable number of our young men arrived, assembled at the Town Hall with the Pretender in effigy. The figure was dressed in a coat of paper, a Scotch bonnet and a hay wig, and had a cross on his breast and a halter about his neck and was fixed on a wooden horse. The effigy was taken round the town and afterwards burnt. A speech was made, followed by a general discharge of small arms and loud huzzas from the populace. The evening concluded with the drinking of loyal healths."

On 11th August 1743, the Duke and Duchess of Argyll and Lady Mary Campbell were in Cheltenham, also the Earl of Chesterfield, Lady Suffolk, Lady Caroline Lennox, Lord and Lady Tracy and their three daughters, Lord A. Hamilton, Lord Chedworth, Sir Francis Dashwood, Judge Fortescue and his lady, Sir Henry Slingsby, Lord Gage, Lord and Lady Somerville and their daughters; the two Priors of Brecon and Thetford and many other well-known people. William Shenstone the poet had been in Cheltenham in 1734, and he came again in 1743. Probably the prim pretty town, with its romantically wild and beautiful surroundings, and with its own avenues of trees and ordered gardens, appealed to the man who was both a poet and a landscape gardener. Amongst Shenstone's friends were William Seward, whom Fanny Burney met here in 1788, and Hull of the Covent Garden Opera House, who had made his name first at Bath Theatre, and almost certainly knew Cheltenham well. Seward wrote a little book about Shenstone, and Hull's *Select Letters* include some written by the poet.

In 1743 Shenstone got lost on the Cotswold Hills on his way to Cheltenham. He embodied that night's experience in the seventh Elegy.

> "On distant heaths beneath autumnal skies,
> Pensive I saw the circling shade descend,
> Weary and faint I heard the storm arise,
> While the sun vanish'd like a faithless friend.
>
> No kind companion led my steps aright,
> No friendly planet lent its shimmering ray;
> E'en the lone cot refused its wonted light
> When toil in peaceful slumber dosed the day.
>
> Then the dull bell had given a pleasing sound;
> The village cur 'twere transport then to hear.
> In dreadful silence all was hush'd around,
> While the rude storm above distress'd my ear."

Before Shenstone came to Cheltenham in 1743 he is said to have sketched out his Pastoral Ballad, after parting from his friend, Miss Graves. At Cheltenham he fell romantically in love with Miss C _____ whom he thought to be out of his reach because her sister had married a baronet of considerable means. Dr Johnson, with his good horse-sense, often threw cold water on the transports of his friends, and he remarked that Shenstone could easily have married Miss C _____ if he had so wished.

In "Hope," one of the four poems in the Pastoral Ballad finally dedicated to Miss C _____ Shenstone perhaps reached his high-water-mark as a poet:

"My banks they are furnished with bees,
Whose murmur invites one to sleep.
My grottos are shaded with trees
And my hills are white over with sheep;
I seldom have met with a loss,
Such health do my fountains bestow;
My fountains all bordered with moss,
Where the harebells and violets grow.
Not a pine in my groves is there seen,
But with tendrils of woodbine is bound,

Not a beech's more beautiful green,
But a sweet briar entwines it around.
Not my friends in the prime of the year,
More charms than my cattle enfold;
Not a brook that is limpid and clear,
But it glitters with fishes of gold.

I have found out a gift for my fair,
I have found where the wood-pigeons breed;
But let me that plunder forbear;
She will say 'twere a barbarous deed.'"

The Wesleyan connection in Cheltenham, which has always been strong, was established at this time, and by John Wesley himself. Wesley says in his journal that he first came to town on 4th August 1744. The place was then in a transition state between a village and a town and the only dissenting places of worship were the Baptist Chapel, the Friends' Meeting-House and the Unitarian Chapel. As they were all of them very small and old and ramshackle, Wesley went to the old stone-pillared Market Place which was situated where the front of the present Plough Hotel now stands. "Here," says Mr Wesley, "it being the season for drinking the waters, I addressed one of the largest audiences ever assembled there. The footmen in livery created a disturbance but upon my speaking to them they were attentive." Mr Wesley collected the congregation as it cane from the Parish Church and preached them a second sermon. He was not very well received and, perhaps for that reason, he returned to the charge on 25th October of the same year, when he preached from the text, "By grace are ye saved." Wesley was evidently not much impressed by the Cheltenham folk for, said he, "the company seemed just as much to understand what I said as if I had been talking Greek or Latin." The same day he went out to the village of Gotherington, where he found a more intelligent audience, and a very attentive one into the bargain. The seed sown there took root so that the obscure and remote little place became a stronghold of Wesleyanism.

Handel (one of whose biographers, John Bishop, was a Cheltenham man) came to Cheltenham in 1744, according to the *Gentleman's Magazine*. Perhaps it was on this occasion that he went to Tewkesbury Abbey and played on the organ there.

On the 21st of September 1751, he was apparently again drinking the Cheltenham waters, for we read in a letter from Miss Viney to Mrs Dewes: "I hope Mr Handel will not stay all the winter at the Spa, at least hope that he will not neglect Jeptha's Vow."

The *Gentleman's Magazine* says that Dr Samuel Johnson visited Cheltenham in 1749. The *Rambler*, published in the following years, makes allusion to some of the beautiful scenery of the locality. On 19th February 1751, a comparison is drawn between the fashionable parties of Cheltenham, Scarborough and other places, which give the impression to the reader that the great man must have several times visited the Spa. On 8th July 1758 the visitors to the Spa included Lord Chedworth, Lord and Lady Tracy, the Hon. Captain Tracy, Sir Leicester Holt, Lady Holt and family, and Mrs Matthew and family; and on 8th August the arrivals included the Earl of Massereene, Mr Fazackerley, MP, Mr Gore, MP, Mr Kynaston, MP, the Hon. and Rev. Mr Noel, the Rev. Dr Bourchier, etc. The *Gloucester Journal* for July 1758 says: "There is a great appearance of gaiety at Cheltenham at the balls and the card Assemblies. Mr George's Concert (same as year before at the Great House) will be about the middle of next month."

In 1762 Shenstone had returned to the Spa, and writes to Mrs A _____:

"CHELTENHAM, 1762.

I am but just arrived home, though I left Cheltenham the day after you. I stayed indeed to hear Mr B _____ preach a morning sermon, for which I find Mrs C _____ has allotted him the hat preferable to Mr C _____ Perhaps you do not remember, nor did I hear until very lately that there is a hat given annually at Cheltenham for the use of the best preacher, of which the disposal is assigned to Mrs C _____ to her and her heirs for ever. I remember I used to be a little misdeemful that all who preached there had some such premium in their eye. The hat, it is true, is not quite as valuable as a Cardinal's, but while it is made a retribution for excellence, is so (if properly considered), it is an object for a preacher in any degree. I am sorry at the same time, to say that as a common hat, merely for its uses, it would be an object to too many country curates whose situations and slender incomes too often excite our blushes as well as our compassion.

SHENSTONE."

Very likely Mrs C _____ was the mother of the lady with whom Shenstone had been in love when he came to Cheltenham in 1743. He went this time over to Gloucester where, by the tomb of Richard Pates in the Cathedral, he wrote the following lines:

"Pure charity, that comes not in a shower,
Sudden and loud, oppressing what it feeds;
But, like the dew, with gradual silent power,
Felt in the bloom it leaves along the meads.

The happy grateful spirit that improves
And brightens every gift by fortune given;
That wander where it will, with those it loves,
Makes every place a home, and home a heaven.

All these were his—oh! thou who read'st this stone,
When for thyself thy children to the sky,
Thou humbly prayest, ask this boon alone,
That ye like him may live, like him may die."

Wesley returned to the Spa on 17th March 1766, nearly twenty-two years after the first visit. This time he was lent a dwelling-house to preach in. "At ten," he says, "I preached in Cheltenham. Here I was in a strait. The house would not hold half the people and the wind was keen enough. I preached in the open air and I did not observe any, rich or poor, go away until I had completed." By the next time he visited Cheltenham, the Wesleyans had grown into a community, and Wesley says: "I visited the little society and found them quite free from bigotry or prejudice." On 16th January 1768, he is there yet again, and says: "About ten I preached at Cheltenham, a quiet and comfortable place, though it would not have been so if either the Rector or the Anabaptist preacher had prevented." So Wesley watched the town and his little band of disciples growing together.

The dramatic history of Cheltenham is extraordinarily interesting, as our later chapters, we hope, will show. The earlier records are rather scanty; but as early as 1612 the following advertisement appears in the Manor Roll: "Presentment—that Dobbins sounded his drum up and down the town of Cheltenham, in the market, accompanied by R. Clerke and divers young fellows; Clerke following Dobbins with a truncheon, like a lyvtenant or marshallman, and proclaiming what whosoever would hear a play should come to the sign of the Crown."

There is a paragraph on 6th August 1744 in the *Cirencester Flying Post*: "We hear from Cheltenham Spa that the Warwick Company of Comedians, who are now entertaining the quality and gentry there, intend going from thence to Stratford-upon-Avon, with ten plays selected from Beaumont and Fletcher, Shakespeare, Ben Jonson, Dryden, Congreve, etc., never performed there before being provided with clothes, scenes and decorations for performing the plays of those celebrated authors."

In July 1758, the *Gloucester Journal* says "that Mr Williams's Company of Comedians is arrived in Cheltenham, and will act three times this season." The trade of

Cheltenham, such as it was, up to the close of the eighteenth century was chiefly in knitted stockings and in malt, and it was in the local malt houses, or else in barns and booths, that plays were often presented in early days.

In Pittville Street, Cheltenham, there is to-day a china shop called Fletcher's, and on its site in the eighteenth century, and probably before that time, was, in Coffee House Lane, an old malt-house, attached to a sort of boarding-house, known as Newcastle House.

This malt-house had been fitted up as a theatre when Cheltenham first began to acquire some fame as a spa. The proprietor, Mr Pope, also owned the coffee-house which gave its name to Coffee House Lane, and a boarding-house known as The Great House. This building, which was later called The Clarence, was finally pulled down to make room for the temporary church. Mr Pope's malt-house was bought in or about 1773 by John Boles Watson, son of a Quaker gentleman of Clonmel. John Watson, although destined by his father for a merchant, was devoted to the theatre, and probably acted for several years. He appears to have been a man of some means, for, as we shall see later on, he ended by becoming a theatrical manager and proprietor on a considerable scale; but at first his arrangements were primitive.

Weller says that "the tiring room at the Cheltenham Theatre was a hayloft, and the arena a stable, fitted up for the nonce. The heroine of a tragedy, in her sable garb of woe, came always in her Sedan chair, dressed for the character she had to perform and was conducted by a miserable flight of steps to the general green room." From the boards of this humble theatre, however, Sarah Siddons was destined to step to fame and fortune at Drury Lane; and it is said also that her brother, John Philip Kemble, made in Cheltenham his first appearance on any stage.

Of all the great actresses who have adorned the English stage, Sarah Siddons was the greatest. This assertion can be made without qualification, despite the difficulty, nay the impossibility, of comparing the giants of one generation with those of another. For while every contemporary was willing to recognise in Sarah the supreme living genius of the stage, not one of her British predecessors or successors has ever received anything like the same appreciation and homage. Only one woman—a French Sarah—the great Bernhardt has ever been similarly acclaimed.

Mrs Siddons was by birth a Kemble, and was thus a member of a family which ranks among the aristocracy of the stage. Her brother, John Philip Kemble, has a place among the immortals, though he was not so superbly great as Sarah Siddons. A Mr Ward, apparently an extraordinarily clever actor, though little is known of him nowadays, had a strolling theatrical company which gave performances in the midlands and in the western counties. He must have been well known in Cheltenham, as was doubtless also his brilliant daughter, Sarah. In 1753, Sarah Ward married Roger Kemble, a Roman Catholic, who claimed descent (presumably collateral) from another Roger Kemble, a martyred priest. When Mr Kemble and

Miss Ward were married in 1753 it was arranged that if they had children the sons should be brought up in their father's faith and the daughters should be members, like Sarah Kemble, of the Church of England.

Mr Ward appears to have retired or died before his daughter's marriage, for we are told that Sarah had brought as her dowry a strolling company, so that Roger Kemble started forth upon a varied career as a theatrical manager, with the goodwill of a circuit of the midlands and the western counties, though his principal asset was his clever wife. From the fact that Kemble married Sarah Ward in Cirencester, sixteen miles from Cheltenham, it seems possible that her home was there, or at least her father's headquarters, for he must have been often moving about from place to place. It may have however been only by chance that the Kembles were married at Cirencester. Of their children, Sarah Kemble (Mrs Siddons) was born on 5th July 1755, and John Philip Kemble was born 1st February 1757 at Prescott, in Lancashire. They had ten brothers and sisters. Though Roger Kemble spent a great deal of time on tour, his headquarters appear to have been Brecknock, where he ruled his theatre and his children sternly but well. He and his wife were not at all anxious that their talented sons and daughters should follow their own profession. John was destined for a priest, and with that object in view was sent to a Roman Catholic seminary at Sedgeley Park, Staffordshire, and later to the College at Douay, while it was made plain to Sarah and to all the children that, though they were almost born on the stage and had acted nearly all their lives, their parents wanted them to find fresh careers for themselves.

It seems that the Kemble children, to a great extent, inherited their extraordinary talents from their mother and maternal grandfather, for Roger Kemble, albeit apparently a good actor, was not a remarkable one. The Wards had forbidden their daughter to marry an actor, and when the girl begged for her father's forgiveness, the harassed parent, who had decided to make the best of a bad job, found an ingenious way of avoiding eating his own words of the past, while at the same time having a hit at his son-in-law's professional attainments. He forgave Mrs Kemble, remarking that he had indeed forbidden her to marry *an actor*, but that *that* she had certainly not done. Kemble was a man of respectable family, and though his claims to a distinguished ancestry could never be proved, there is no reason to doubt them. He himself possessed some small hereditary property in Herefordshire, but when the twelve children were young Roger Kemble and his wife seem at times to have been short of money. When John Philip Kemble ran away from Douay, as he was determined to be an actor and not a priest, Roger Kemble may not have known of his son's plight, but at any rate he did not send John any money. The theatrical company at Brecknock, however, heard that the boy had walked from Bristol to Wales, and thence to Gloucester and Cheltenham, and was almost destitute. They got up a subscription for him, but even when he secured work, his pay was absurdly small, and he was still at times in the most fearful straits.

One night when Kemble was to appear at Cheltenham as Ventidius in "All for Love" he was much embarrassed because his landlady had kept back his only shirt, which he had given to her to wash, until he should pay fifteen pence which was due to her—a sum which John was unable to raise. The rest of the company were in equal distress. They could not raise a shirt between them and only one ruffle could be found. In order to elude the observation (and observations) of the audience, poor Ventidius was therefore obliged to manoeuvre and he pinned the single ruffle on his right-hand sleeve, and went through the first act with his left hand wrapped in his cloak; but as he thought that the onlookers would wonder why he only used his right hand, he occasionally shifted the ruffle from one hand to the other.

In John Kemble's early days he and young John Boles Watson were in the same company. They were great allies and lived, or sometimes starved, together. In Watson's later days in Cheltenham he used to tell Michael Kelly, the actor, stories of his young days and of those of other actors and actresses, especially the Kembles. At one time when he and John Philip Kemble were on tour in 1773 with a strolling company, acting on alternate nights at Oldbury, Tewkesbury and at the Coffee House Yard Theatre, they were left penniless. "After continued vicissitudes," says Kelly, "Watson assured me such was their distress that they were glad to get into a turnip field and make a meal of its produce uncooked, and," he adds, "it was while regaling on the raw vegetable, that they hit upon a scheme to recruit their finances. And a lucky turnip it turned out. It was neither more nor less than that Kemble should turn Methodist preacher, and Watson perform the part of clerk. The scheme was organised, and Tewkesbury was the first scene of action. They drew together, in a field, a numerous congregation; and Kemble preached with such piety, and so much effect, that a large collection rewarded his labours." Two members of the Kemble family were driven to perform the same act during their journeys along the foot-road between the towns. The money on these occasions was collected by Watson, or by Watson and others, in a large old-fashioned nutmeg grater, with a hinged cover. This relic was preserved at Cheltenham Theatre with scrupulous care by Mr Adamson the box-office keeper, who finally presented it to Earl Fitzhardinge.

When Michael Kelly visited Cheltenham in 1796, Watson told him about his own first appearance in the Garden Town, and how John Kemble met with the second of his Cheltenham adventures. Cheltenham was certainly an exciting place for Roger Kemble's children, and John Kemble probably smiled to himself in 1788 when the newspapers said he had promised to come there and act for Watson, *his old companion in the field*. Kelly tells us that in after years he questioned John Kemble as to whether or not he had really preached in the fields, and John replied that it was a true bill.

Having failed in his efforts to make a priest of John, Roger Kemble forbade his daughter Sally to marry an actor and said that he would never forgive her if she should do so.

Sally, however, while still almost a child, fell deeply in love with William Siddons, a member of Kemble's company, who returned her love. Roger Kemble was greatly troubled by Sarah's infatuation, and got her a post as a sort of companion to a lady, but failed to cure her of her attachment to the handsome, fair-haired Siddons. In 1773 the lovers were secretly married, Sarah being little more than eighteen, and thus Roger Kemble's plans for another child's future were frustrated.

Thomas Campbell, the poet, writes:

"In the course of the year 1774, Mr and Mrs Siddons were both engaged to act at Cheltenham. That place, though now an opulent and considerable town, consisted in those days of only one tolerable street, through the middle of which ran a clear stream of water, with stepping-stones that served as a bridge. At that time the Honourable Miss Boyle, the only daughter of Lord Dungarvan ... happened to be at Cheltenham. She had come accompanied by her mother and her mother's second husband, the Earl of Ailesbury. One morning she and some other fashionables went to the box-keeper's office, they were told that the tragedy to be performed that evening was 'Venice Preserved.' They all laughed heartily and promised themselves a treat of the ludicrous in the misrepresentation of the piece. Someone who overheard their mirth kindly reported it to Mrs Siddons. She had the part of Belvidera allotted to her, and prepared for the performance of it with no very enviable feelings. It may be doubted, indeed, whether Otway had imagined in Belvidera a personage more to be pitied than her representative now thought herself. The rabble in 'Venice Preserved' showed compassion for the heroine, and when they saw her feather-bed put up to auction 'governed their roaring throats and grumbled pity.' But our actress anticipated refined scorners, more pitiless than the rabble, and the prospect was certainly calculated to prepare her more for the madness than the dignity of her part. In spite of much agitation, however, she got through it. In about the middle of the piece she heard some unusual and apparently suppressed noises, and therefore concluded that the fashionables were in the full enjoyment of their anticipated amusement, tittering and laughing, as she thought, with unmerciful derision. She went home after the play, grievously mortified. Next day, however, Mr Siddons met in the street with Lord Ailesbury, who inquired after Mrs Siddons's health, and expressed not only his own admiration of her exquisite acting, but described its effects on the ladies of his party. They had wept, he said, so copiously that they were unpresentable in the morning, and were confined to their rooms with headaches. Mr Siddons hastened home to gratify his fair spouse with this intelligence. Miss Boyle soon afterwards visited Mrs Siddons at her lodgings, took the deepest interest in her fortunes, and continued her ardent friend till her death. She married Lord O'Neil of Shane's Castle, in Ireland. Lady O'Neil is described as a beauty of the first order. Though Mrs Siddons's powers were, by her own confession, still crude, yet her noble young friend consoled and cheered her and with the prophetic eye of taste, foresaw her glory. Miss Boyle took upon herself the direction of her wardrobe, enriched it from her own, and made many of her dresses with her own hands."

According to Mrs Siddons: "Mr King, by order of Mr Garrick, who had heard some account of me from the Ailesbury family, came to Cheltenham to see me in 'The Fair Penitent.' I knew neither Mr King nor his purpose, but I shortly afterwards received an offer from Garrick himself, upon very low terms. Happy to be placed where I presumptuously argued that I should do all that I have since achieved, if I could but once gain the opportunity, I instantly paid my respects to the great man. I was at that time good-looking; and certainly, all things considered, an actress well worthy my poor five pounds per week."

Another chronicler says that the Rev. Henry Bate was sent by Garrick to see how Mrs Siddons shaped as an actress. Possibly both King and Bate came on the same errand.

After Mrs Siddons's first appearance, the theatre was enlarged and improved. *The Cheltenham Guide* of 1780 contains the following entry: "The Old Play House, which has lately been fitted up and beautified, is neat, but not sufficiently spacious to seat a large audience, so that on particular nights, many are obliged to forego the amusement of the theatre. Plays are here acted thrice a week, Tuesday, Thursday and Saturday, during the season by a Company of Comedians, chiefly from Worcester; who, without aiming at elegance of scenery and decorations, exert their best endeavours to deserve approbation, and accordingly meet with encouragement. The subscription is a guinea for eighteen nights, or two shillings the Pit, and one shilling, Gallery, each evening. It has been proposed to form a Committee of Gentlemen, and erect a new and commodious theatre by subscriptions ; each subscriber to receive a proportionable share of the net rent according to his deposit."

In 1782, Watson had built a new theatre near the site of the York Tavern of later days, and here in the same year Mrs Siddons performed for five nights after the theatre was opened, in the characters of Portia, Calista, Mrs Sullen, Belvidera and Indiana. About 1785, on account of Mr Watson's health, he was obliged to "decline exertion and hand the management over to Messrs Ray and Gibbons." The charms of Watson's Cambray Theatre, which he built later on, are praised in the highly-coloured language of the day by the proprietor of *The Regent Gardens in a Guide,* published in 1803, Ruff's *Beauties of Cheltenham*:

"Of the theatre itself, it may be said, without flattery or falsehood, that it vies with any throughout the kingdom, except those of the metropolis. The band is led by Mr Buckingham, a veteran in the Service of Euterpe … Every season the visitors are regaled with the most popular performances, in which the rich notes of Incledon, the naiveté of De Camp or Mellon, or the broad farce of Munden or Bannister, are displayed with the happiest effect. We cannot omit to notice the achievements of Mr Richer on the tight-rope. Fortune can do little in befriending such a man, since he is without a rival. Mr Richer (Mr Watson's son-in-law) was," says Goding, in about 1863, "we believe the most eminent tight-rope dancer on record, and was highly esteemed and admitted into the first circles of society. This individual … died recently at the adjacent village of Swindon in affluent circumstances."

Mr Watson and his son at one time and another had control of the Gloucester, Bristol, Circencester, Tewkesbury, and Stroud Theatres, and for whole seasons of the Birmingham and Coventry ones, Cheltenham always, however, remaining the headquarters of Watson *père*. Among his multifarious theatrical enterprises Mr Watson revived at the beginning of the nineteenth century, the performances of the "Messiah" in the midland and western counties. In 1809, he paid Madame Catalani 1000 guineas for six nights' performance at Birmingham, which is described in the *Cheltenham Chronicle*, and in 1811 the same newspaper advertises the production of the "Messiah" at Cheltenham Parish Church by 100 performers, of whom Madame Catalani was one.

The Cheltenham theatre languished considerably after Watson's death in 1813, and his son seems to have lost all or most of his money, and given up the management.

III

1775–1788

The A'Court Murder—The Duchess of Devonshire and Maude's Elm—
Miss Wells's Romance—The Rev. H. B. Fowler.

In September 1776 the town was staggered by a dreadful occurrence, of which a monument in the Parish Church briefly states the main facts:

> "In Memory of Katherine,
> The wife of William P. A'Court, of Heytesbury in the
> County of Wilts., Esq.
> Who departed this life on the 23rd day of September 1776,
> In the 32nd year of her age.
> The strictest Honour and Virtue, Elegance of Manners,
> Integrity of Heart and Delicacy of Sentiment,
> Endeared her to a select circle of Friends and Acquaintances.
> She was cherished as an only child by an indulgent Father,
> Beloved from infancy by a tender husband,
> In whose arms she died an unnatural death effected by poison
> Administered by the hands of a cruelly wicked Livery Servant
> Whose resentment at being detected in theft
> Prompted him to perpetrate this horrid and execrable crime."

Thus in the manner of the time, with capital letters strewn at random, a grief-stricken family recorded on a monument in Cheltenham Parish Church, the story of a crime which was a nine days' wonder in the fashionable watering-place.

Captain William Ashe A'Court was Member of Parliament for Heytesbury from 1781 to 1806, being created baronet in 1795. In the summer of 1776 he and his wife came to Cheltenham, and brought with them their three little girls and their four servants. Neither the selectness of Mrs A'Court's walk in life, nor the love of an indulgent father and a tender husband who "had cherished her from infancy," not her elegance of manners, nor her delicacy of sentiment, availed to save her from an early grave. The chief interest in the crime at the date of its committal was derived from the fact that the victim was related by marriage to an old and distinguished county family. More interesting to us latter-day Georgians in the gruesome sequel, the windswept gibbet, with its dreadful burden pointing a public moral to all the passers-by, and the harrowing ghost-stories that were the inevitable sequence to the tragedy.

Captain and Mrs A'Court took a house on the site afterwards occupied by the York Tavern, and settled down to the usual business of life at the Spa. They drank the waters and revolved as stars of some magnitude in their "select circle of friends and acquaintances." One of their menservants was Joseph Armstrong, who is said to have been a gentleman by birth. His family "of respectable origin" had but lately come from Dublin and settled near Cheltenham when Joseph came to the town with his new master and mistress, from their home in Wiltshire. This man was the villain of the tragedy which now occurred. The contemporary accounts of the dreadful affair differ very greatly. Coding says that, "Amongst the number of the domestics was a footman, thirty years of age, of the name of Joseph Armstrong. At different periods, sums of money and articles of value had been missed from the dwelling-house, and the robber was in vain searched for. One morning Mrs A'Court accidentally passed by the dressing-room of her husband at an early hour and detected Joseph Armstrong in the act of taking jewellery from a chest. Crime too often begets crime. Armstrong, stung with terror at the thought of being discovered, resolved upon destroying the only being who could give evidence in a court of law against him. The serving up of breakfast offered an opportunity of carrying his crime into effect, and which proved to be, unfortunately, successful. Armstrong infused a large portion of arsenic into the teacup of his innocent mistress, which produced its deleterious effects almost immediately; she only lingered until the following morning 23rd September 1776, when she expired in the thirty-second year of her age."

The *London Gazetteer* and *New Daily Advertiser* of Wednesday, 2nd October 1776, publishes the following account by a Gloucester correspondent: "This lady had been ill ten days, but no suspicion of poison was started till the morning after her decease, when information was given by an apothecary of that place, that the servant had bought some arsenic at his shop the day preceding her first attack of illness, and again in the course of the following week."

The *Morning Chronicle* and *Morning Advertiser* for 19th March 1777, ascribes Armstrong's conduct to revenge, Mrs A'Court having taken a dislike to him, and begged her husband, on frequent occasions, to discharge him.

The *London Gazetteer*, published on Wednesday, 2nd October 1776, says that: "On Friday a man was committed to our jail by George Nayler, Gent., one of the Coroners for this County, on suspicion of having poisoned the lady of Captain A'Court with whom he had lived a servant, and who was then at Cheltenham."

On the 27th of September, then, four days after Mrs A'Court's death, Armstrong was in Gloucester Gaol, charged with murder.

The report of the *Morning Chronicle* on the trial (19th March 1777) again simply asserts that Mrs A'Court had begged her husband to discharge Armstrong, because she disliked him.

Apparently, then, the statement that Mrs A'Court had seen Armstrong in her husband's dressing-room was only a surmise on the part of Mrs A'Court's relatives and friends. One would have thought also that a thief would have at least shut the door of the dressing-room before he began to rummage amongst his master's belongings.

Yet the marble tablet in the church says that Mrs A'Court was murdered on account of Armstrong's resentment at being detected in theft, and Goding says that the lady actually *saw* the theft of the jewellery. He also tells us, however, that, although at different periods sums of money and articles of value had been missed from the dwelling-house, yet "*the robber was in vain searched for.*"

Why, if Mrs A'Court had repeatedly expressed her dislike for Armstrong's conduct, was he not suspected of stealing the jewellery and money, and searched, or simply dismissed if nothing could be proved, without being accused of anything? The contradictions in the different reports are really irreconcilable. From Goding's description one would think that Armstrong had the arsenic ready and put some into his mistress's teacup almost directly after she detected his theft of the jewellery, so that she should not have time to accuse him of larceny, which in itself was enough in those days to bring a man to the gallows.

The local writer continues: "The husband of the victim had strong suspicions of the causes which led Armstrong to perpetrate the execrable crime, and upon search being made, a paper containing arsenic and many of the articles stolen were found in his private chest, and he was handed over to the officers of justice, charged with the twofold crime of robbery and murder. The murderer escaped from the house immediately after the funeral of his mistress, which increased the opinion of his guilt. With him went a spaniel dog, a favourite one of the master. This animal led to the discovery of Armstrong's hiding-place. The officers had been in search for three days, and on the evening of the third day, they observed the dog on the London Road, near to Frogmill. Considering that this was a good clue, they watched the animal into a wood adjoining and, following him, they found the murderer secreted in a tree."

Here again, Goding's account differs from that of the Gloucester correspondent of the *London Gazetteer* and other London papers of and October 1776 which, after the statement made on 24th September, the day after the lady's death, that the apothecary had sold poison to Armstrong, remark: "On receiving this intelligence, the man, who had that morning got leave from his master to set out for London in consequence of a letter the had received from his friends there, was pursued to Frogmill by Colonel Bradford, the lady's father, and after some time was apprehended in a neighbouring wood whither he had fled on seeing the Colonel drive up in a chariot and four. Upon being interrogated for what purpose he bought the poison, he prevaricated very much, and since his confinement has been in several different stories. Upon an examination by several gentlemen of the faculty, it said the lady's bowels were found mortified."

In their description of the murderer's death Goding and the London papers are still at issue. The local historian says he "was conveyed to Gloucester Gaol, and took his trial at the Spring Assizes, 1777. He was convicted, ordered to be executed at Gloucester, and his body afterwards to be hung in chains on a gibbet, as near the spot where he committed the foul crime as the Parish authorities would allow. Between the day of his condemnation and that fixed for his execution, Armstrong made several determined attempts at self-destruction, but they were all thwarted by the vigilance of the gaoler ... Armstrong was duly executed amidst the execrations of a numerous multitude, and died the death of ignominy; and the remaining portion of the sentence was carried out." But the London newspapers, *i.e.* the *Daily Advertiser* of 22nd March 1777, the *Gazetteer* and the *New Daily Advertiser* of the same date, provide fresh thrills for their readers. On 22nd March, the *Daily Advertiser* provided a new sensation. "On Monday morning last between seven and eight Joseph Armstrong, who was to be executed that morning at Gloucester, hung himself with a leather girth in his apartment. He requested to be left a few minutes by himself, and on the return of his friends he was dead!"

Most likely the London papers were right in this instance and Armstrong at least cheated the gallows to the extent that only his dead body was hung in chains.

By this time people, at least in Cheltenham, were losing their taste for public executions and for the exhibition of the remains of those who had paid the last penalty of the law. The pleasantest drive in the immediate neighbourhood of Cheltenham was completely spoilt, not only by the public exhibition of Armstrong's corpse, but by a succession of horrible events relating thereto. Mr Moreau, the first Master of the Ceremonies in his Guide to Cheltenham thus describes what, in his time, was one of the most attractive parts of Cheltenham. "The most common ride has generally been in The Marsh at the back of the town, a mile round, with a pleasant view of the neighbouring hills. It was situated a little below North Lodge, once Lord Dunalley's Cheltenham residence, and was both a public road and waste land." The swift-footed and heavy-handed justice of those days chose The Marsh, the haunt of the Cheltenham Belles and Exquisites, as a suitable place for the exposure of Armstrong's dead body. Whether he was hanged in public by the executioner or in private by himself, it is certain that his remains were brought from Gloucester to The Marsh in public procession on a low open-four-wheel-truck, drawn by a horse. Goding says: "The relatives of the murderer, who resided near this town, were of respectable origin, and had but recently settled here from Dublin. They were, of course, annoyed" (a nice euphemism) "at the public exhibition that was being made of the corpse. One morning, about twelve months after the erection of the gibbet, the body and the ponderous chains were missing. It was believed at the time that the friends of the deceased had removed it, the ground was broken up by the hoofs of horses, so that it appeared to have been forced down by horse power, but all search for the body proved fruitless."

When the posts of the gallows were being removed for the purpose of planting hedges and enclosing the ground, the chain and the bones of the murderer were found, a few feet below the surface, directly beneath the cross-bar from whence they had been suspended. The man, a very young one, who made the discovery, was so terror-stricken that he died in a few days afterwards

The skull of the murderer was purchased by Dr Minster, and the remainder of the skeleton by Dr Newell. The spot was a very solitary one, and some idea may be formed of its desolate character, when it is stated that it formed a marsh, without a single habitation. The main posts were removed to near the present Clonbrock House, and were used as gate-posts, where they formed the entrance to a boarding-school which then existed, and not only their removal but their final destruction was resolved upon for fear they should again conjure up some more "midnight spectres." This was ultimately accomplished by committing them to a bonfire, and thus ends the last link in the history of the tragical murder committed at Cheltenham.

Many years later another murder was committed almost on the spot whereon the fatal gibbet of Armstrong had stood.

In 1780 Cheltenham began to emerge from its villagedom. Visitors were coming to the Spa in considerable numbers, though there was but little accommodation for them. Half the charm of the place had been its pleasant rusticity, when life in the tiny Spa was a kind of continuous picnic. In that year one Simeon Moreau arrived upon the scene and either took the title of Master of the Ceremonies, or induced a few of the visitors and residents to create such an office and elect him as its first occupant. He was not popular at first, as many thought that he was without a regular claim to the title which he had assumed. In the following year the author of *The Cheltenham Guide: or Memoirs of the Barnard Family Continued,* wrote:

"Lately an ape in the shape of a *beau,*
By the outlandish name of Monsieur M_____u,
Has officiously come at the balls to preside,
To preserve etiquette and pay homage to pride."

The company, however, soon became used to Moreau's government, though Cheltenham cannot boast of such distinguished Masters of the Ceremonies as its great rival, Bath, the gentlemen who were elected to the post of MC were of considerable local importance and filled a big place in the general scheme of things in Georgian Cheltenham.

The beautiful Georgiana, Duchess of Devonshire, was in Cheltenham in about the year 1780. Born in 1757, the daughter of John Spencer, second Earl Spencer, she had married William Cavendish, fifth Duke of Devonshire. On one occasion, and probably at this time, the Duchess stayed at The Great House, which had in 1757 been known as "Mr Pope's Great House."

At the time of the Duchess of Devonshire's visit and, indeed, until not so very many years ago, a magnificent tree, called Maude's Elm, stood at a short distance from the centre of the town of Cheltenham, about a quarter of a mile from the road which forms the parish boundary at Swindon. Part still remains of the trunk of this tree which was once so lofty in stature that it could be seen from miles around.

The fascinating Duchess was exceedingly fond of this tree, and during her residence at Cheltenham Spa would go every day with a book and sit for a time under the spreading branches of Maude's Elm. One day a poorly-clad little boy of nine years old came along, leading a horse, and the Duchess was struck by his intelligent expression, spoke to him, and gave him some money. The child, whose name was Miles Watkins, was grateful for this kindness, and when the beautiful lady questioned him he was glad to tell her what he knew of the story of Maude's Elm. His story greatly interested the Duchess and she afterwards undertook to educate and provide for the child, who grew up into an eccentric man, and though the Duchess on several occasions gave him capital in order to set him up in business, Miles never seemed to be able to keep money long, even when he managed to make it. One week he would be rolling in money and in the next he would be destitute. In after years the became a sort of secretary to a man as eccentric as himself, Mr Webb, the philanthropist, who went about the country, giving away money in a most reckless manner. The lovely Duchess Georgiana died at Devonshire House in 1806. Long years afterwards her only son, George Spencer Cavendish, sixth Duke of Devonshire, Paxton's patron and friend, and the President of the Royal Horticultural Society, arrived in Cheltenham. The Duke, as kind-hearted and as fond of trees as his mother, from whom he had probably inherited his taste for landscape gardening, had a drawing made of Maude's Elm, the tree of which the Duchess had been so fond. Finding that Miles Watkins was still alive, he provided enough money for the old man to spend his two or three remaining years in comfort.

Maude's Elm took its name from a tragedy enacted at the bridge which led from the Cheltenham road into Swindon, which was in the Duchess of Devonshire's time a very pretty little village with a unique Norman church tower still in existence. The Swindon villagers were alarmed one night by the agonised shrieks of a frantic mother, who declared that her only child was lost. The girl, Maude Bowen, by name, a beautiful young creature of twenty-one, whose loveliness was the pride of the whole village, had been sent in to Cheltenham with some wool, spun by herself and her mother. Throughout the rest of the night the Swindon people searched in vain for Maude, but at daybreak they found her lifeless body lying in the brook. She appeared to have been there for some time. On the bridge close by was found another corpse; that of Godfrey Bowen, Maude's uncle. An arrow had pierced his heart; he grasped with his left hand the handrail of the

The High Street, Cheltenham. From a drawing by John Claude Nattes, 1804

bridge, and in his right hand were some rent fragments of Maude's dress. Every-one hated Godfrey Bowen, but the Lord of the Manor summoned his Coroner who brought in a verdict of *felo-de-se* against Maude, and buried Godfrey in the ordinary way. Maude, according to the cruel custom of the time, was buried at the cross-roads on a spot which was probably then the centre from which four roads branched off, to Tewkesbury, Cheltenham, Cleeve and Gloucester respectively. Here, with a stake driven through her body, the once fair and beautiful village maid was buried at dead of night, uncoffined and without Christian rites. The stake grew into the most wonderful tree in all the country round.

The Lord of the Manor said that, in consequence of his Coroner's verdict, old Margaret Bowen's freehold cottage was an escheat to him. Margaret nearly died of grief, and became a permanent melancholic. She wandered from house to house in the village; but though she often disappeared, she could generally be found by her daughter's grave.

One morning, as she was sitting there, a procession came by. Sir Robert de Vere (at least that is the name by which he is mentioned in the various writings about Maude's Elm), the Lord of the Manor, with his followers, was on his way to Cleeve Church, for the christening of his son and heir. He told his attendants to move Margaret from under the tree while the cavalcade passed by, but neither threats nor persuasions could induce her to go. At last a servant was told to remove her forcibly, but as his arm was raised to drag the old woman away, an arrow struck him through the heart, and he fell dead. The arrow came from a thick wood which then grew on the side of the old Gloucester Road, but no traces of the archer could be found. By the orders of the Lord of the Manor, the poor old woman was seized and bound, and thrown into Gloucester Gaol, charged with the twofold crime of murder and witchcraft.

A fortnight afterwards, by the influence of Sir Robert de Vere, a verdict of guilty was brought in against Margaret Bowen, and she was sentenced to be burnt to death on her daughter's grave, the scene of her alleged crime. Margaret was brought in a rude cart from Gloucester guarded by officers, and seated on the bundle of straw which was to kindle the flames that were to burn her alive. A heap of faggots had been piled up in a circle, and as Margaret was being led to the stake to be tied up, a groan came from her assembled neighbours, when they saw the wan and shrunken form of one who had ever, in happier days, been kind and charitable to all. The fire was only just kindled when the Lord of the Manor came forward through the crowd, and jeered at the doomed woman as a witch. He had not spoken many words when an arrow, sped by some invisible hand, shot him down, and he fell and, after a few convulsive shudders and groans, lay dead at the feet of the burning Margaret. In a few moments the fire reached its height, the stake fell, and nothing was to be seen but a heap of smouldering ashes.

The wife and son of the Lord of the Manor had predeceased him, and shortly afterwards the property passed into the hands of strangers.

Nearly fifty years after the last tragedy a stranger, an old man of nearly eighty years of age, came to the village. He spent his days sitting beneath Maude's Elm and slept at night in the dilapidated dwelling of the alleged witch. Subsequently this old man cleared up the mystery of Maude's death and the succeeding tragedies.

His name was (so the poets say) Walter Gray, and he was a Swindon man who, from his youth up had loved Maude Bowen and had been tenderly loved by her. Godfrey Bowen, Maude's uncle, wanting to get possession of Margaret's freehold cottage, had offered to marry his niece, and had been indignantly refused. Directly afterwards the Lord of the Manor, struck by the girl's great beauty, desired to get possession of her for himself and Godfrey, smarting at his own rejection, undertook to help him.

On the night of Maude's disappearance, Gray, whose skill with the arrow had gained him the name of Walter the Archer, took his bow and arrows and was searching the thickets, when he heard a sudden shriek, and saw Maude struggling with her uncle Godfrey, while the Lord of the Manor stood by. He drew his bow and shot Godfrey dead on the end of the bridge. Maude fled, and Walter hoped that she had reached her home in safety. But her foot must have slipped, and she was drowned in the brook.

Walter, fearing prosecution for murder, fled and no traces of him were found until he came once more to live in Swindon. In reality he had been living not far away, on the main road to Gloucester, which then passed not far from the present one, where, under an assumed name, he had kept an inn, not far from the House in the Tree. There Margaret Bowen had spent the intervals of her absence from Swindon, while from the thicket Walter had watched and guarded her when she was seated by her daughter's grave. He it was, of course, who had shot both the Lord of the Manor and his servant.

Another curious story which exercised the minds of the Cheltenham gossips of the year 1781 was the romance of Miss Wells, who was nearly sixty years old and possessed of a good deal of property. She lived in one of her own houses in Cheltenham, at No 172 High Street (nearly opposite to the High Street entrance to the Presbyterian Church). A great deal of the site of the present St George's Street belonged to this lady, as did also St George's Square. The house was elegantly furnished throughout and its ground in the rear was so extensive as to reach to Regent Place; it formed, in fact, the site on which the east side of St George's Street and the Wesleyan Chapel were subsequently erected. It was delightfully laid out as an ornamental garden. A summer-house, covered with honeysuckle, and a "moss house" stood on a mound at the extreme end, on either side of which were statues of Cupid and Psyche.

Two lovers were often seen walking about in this garden: Miss Wells and a gay and fashionable young man of twenty-one. A wedding was arranged, and many guests were invited; but on the day before the marriage was to take place, the young man backed out. The poor lady brought a breach of promise suit against her former fiancé; the case was heard at Gloucester Assizes on 30th August 1782, and Miss Wells was awarded £170 damages, the interest of which she gave as a charity to the Parish Church and to Bethel Chapel, Cheltenham. Miss Wells consoled herself by marrying the Rev. H. H. Williams, formerly minister of Bethel Baptist Chapel. She died in 1815, aged eighty-seven.

Christopher Bailey, MA, an inscription to whose memory is in the south aisle of the Parish Church, had died in 1654, and had bequeathed the money with which to build a corn and wool market in the centre of the road, between the original Plough Inn and the equally ancient Crown. It was taken down in 1787, and at the same time the part of the Chelt that flowed by it was diverted into its main course. Mr Bailey had been head master of Pates's Grammar School for thirty-two years.

Prinn's MS mentions Robert Rogers, MA (Oxon), who died in 1701, head master of the Grammar School, and Mr W. John Palmer, editor of the *Patesian*, has discovered that Francis Owen of Norledge (perhaps Northleach), said to have been a master of Pates's school, died in 1702.

The head master of the Grammar School from 1781 or before, until some time subsequent to 1803, was the before-mentioned Rev. Henry Bond Fowler, MA, who was educated at St Paul's School and at Trinity College, Cambridge, and who "took young gentlemen to lodge and board, besides the day scholars."

Mr Fowler was Vicar of Elmstone Hardwick from 1789 to 1829, Vicar of Uttoxeter from 1515 to 1829, and Perpetual Curate of Tredington from some unknown date up to 1829, when he died, aged seventy-six, and was buried, with his wife and daughters, at Elmstone Hardwick, while his mother, Hester Fowler lies buried near the main entrance to the Parish Church, though her tombstone was taken away some years ago, when the churchyard was being improved.

The Rev. H. B. Fowler had two sons, of whom Charles was one of the best-known surgeons in the West of England in his day, and was, like his elder brother

Henry, a general practitioner in Cheltenham, as well as some daughters, two of whom were Charlotte and Elizabeth. Henry Fowler once took his little daughter out to Elmstone Hardwick Vicarage to stay, and bought her a new writing-desk in order to console her for her separation from her parents. When Dr Fowler was leaving the Vicarage his poor little daughter cried because she did not like to be left. That grim old clergyman, the Rev. H. B. Fowler, took away little Mary Anne's new writing-desk from her as a punishment for her unauthorised tears. Charlotte Fowler in later years taught Mary Anne's children. Backboards and other horrors were part of the regime under which the poor children suffered and groaned. Charlotte had apparently in her old age one soft spot in her heart and that was for her father's successor at Elmstone Hardwick, Mr Byron, a relative of Lord Byron's. Some old villager said that the Vicar and Miss Charlotte used to walk about the village arm-in-arm; the only lady he ever saw Mr Byron arm-in-arm with. Probably Charlotte's antiquity made the Vicar feel safe with her. Mr Fowler had died in 1829, aged seventy-six. Of the other Grammar School masters mentioned above, Christopher Bailey or Bayley was educated at Corpus Christi College, Oxford, and the Rev. R. Rogers, son of W. Rogers of Dowdeswell, at Pembroke College, Oxford.

William Vick, junior, of Minchinhampton, a wealthy Bristol merchant, died in 1753 and left his money to his sister Rebecca and to his partner, Roger Watt, with £20 each to his cousins Mary Day and Anne and Frances Vick, of whom the two last mentioned were probably Mrs Samuel Remmington and her sister. He bequeathed a sum of money to the Merchant Venturers' Society of Bristol, which was to accumulate until it became £10,000 and was then to be used to build a stone bridge over the Avon from Clifton to Leigh Downs. Failing this the money was to go to cloth-workers of Minchinhampton, young burgesses of Bristol, or to found a hospital for illegitimate children. In 1829, when Vick's bequest amounted to £8000, the bridge was begun, but it was not finished until 1864, and was an expensive suspension bridge, which cost a very great deal more than the sum bequeathed by the Bristol merchant.

Mary Day, youngest daughter of Jeremiah and Fanny Day and sister of Mrs Henry Fowler, married John Pinfold Westley of Nailsworth, and she left to one of her sister Anne's granddaughters, a ring on which was engraved: "W. Vick died April 5th, 1753. *Suspensa vix via fit.*"

Other records say that Mr Vick died in January 1753. William Vick and his sister Rebecca left charities to Minchinhampton, and both were married there.

Mr Vick's £300 was to provide bread for the poor which was to be distributed annually on 15th November when a sermon was to be preached; and also a peal was to be rung by the Church bell-ringers who were to be entertained at the Talbot Inn. Vick's Charity was given "in commemoration of our late King William III, and our happy deliverance and the security of our country and religion caused by the Revolution."

IV

1788

The First Part of the Visit of King George III, 14th July to 23rd July 1788

Watson, the theatre manager, was in his element, for a pleasant pageant was to be staged in the village Spa of Cheltenham, in which he himself, son of the Quaker gentleman of Clonmel, would doubtless play a leading part. If some of the county people on the hills held aloof, and a few of the townspeople, including perhaps the young parson at the Grammar School with his Jacobite wife, the little town, as a whole, was literally seething and boiling with excitement, and Mr Moreau, the Master of the Ceremonies, was here, there and everywhere—like a flea on a gridiron, as Tom Oliver would have said. Most of the fashionables had already arrived in the town and others were coming in, fast and fain to see and hear all that was to be seen and heard. From the country round poured in the Cotswold yeomen with their wives and children and labourers, ruddy of countenance, kindly, slow of speech and thought and action, but not easily taken in, and good fighting-men as Crécy and countless battles before and since have proved. Their hearts warmed to the simple-hearted Sovereign who, before he left Windsor, had said to his bailiff: "I may pick up some hints from the farmers in Gloucestershire."

This year of 1788, when Cheltenham was all agog and on the tiptoe of expectation, was the red-letter year in its history, for on 12th July of that year the Court was temporarily removed to the little Cotswold Spa, and George III, his Consort, and their three elder daughters became, for the time being, residents in the quiet watering-place. A prolonged stay of the royal family at any place so far from the metropolis was quite a novelty and attracted to the Spa a very large number of fashionable visitors. The "Cheltenham Cap," the "Cheltenham Bonnet," the "Cheltenham Buttons" and the "Cheltenham Buckles" were *de rigueur*, and, in the words of a London newspaper, all the fashions were completely Cheltenhamised.

The King was then fifty years old and throughout his life had hardly known a day's illness. On 11th June, while in residence at Windsor, he began to show symptoms that were possibly premonitory of the great affliction to which he afterwards fell a victim. These symptoms included violent spasms in the stomach, which lasted some days. On his recovery, Sir George Baker, the King's physician, prescribed a course of Cheltenham waters. Lord Courtown, Controller of the Household, and Colonel The Honourable Stephen Digby, the Queen's Chamberlain, were sent down to the Spa to make all the necessary arrangements. Their choice of a residence fell upon Bayshill Lodge (also called Fauconberg House) which, though small from a royal point of view, was the largest house in the town and was readily placed at His Majesty's disposal by Lord Fauconberg. This nobleman had come to Cheltenham for the cure of "a violent scorbutic humour in his face," and had been so much pleased with the effects of the Cheltenham waters that he had a house built for himself there in 1781 by Mr Skillicorne.

From the windows of Lord Fauconberg's house—which was surrounded by a pretty little natural park—the little straggling town and the graceful spire of its old Parish Church could be seen in the hollow. To the right, on rising ground, was the primitive well where the waters were dispensed, while on three sides the Cotswolds overhung the village. Westward lay the rich valley of the Severn, and in the distance, twenty miles away, the Malverns bounded the plain.

Close to Fauconberg House, on the right upon the hill, a well was dug at the King's expense, in order to supply His Majesty's household with drinking-water. It tapped, however, a new spring of drinking-water similar in quality to that at the original well, and was thus a disappointment to those who were making arrangements for the royal visit. It subsequently, however, proved to be of great benefit to the town as the supply of mineral water at the original well was not always equal to the demands made upon it. At a depth of forty feet the workmen found a variety of marine shells, cockles, mussels and small oysters, etc., in the clay. This clay was twenty miles away from any part of the sea and was at least forty feet above the level of the Severn, though it was at the same time twenty feet below the surface of the earth.

During the royal visit no soldiers were to be stationed at or near Cheltenham, and no state was to be kept up. The officials of the royal household were cut down to the smallest number deemed possible, consisting only of Lord Courtown, Colonel Digby, and Colonel Gwyn, an equerry. As no room could be found for any of these at Bayshill Lodge, quarters were secured for them in the town. It is said that some members of the royal household stayed at what is now known as Birdlip House in the Bath Road.

Lord Courtown, during the visit, was often mistaken for the King, owing to his star, and the cheers with which he was greeted caused him much embarrassment.

The ladies in attendance on the Queen and Princesses were Lady Courtown, the Queen's lady-in-waiting in the country, Lady Weymouth, as lady of the bedchamber, Miss Fanny Burney, the famous author, dresser to the Queen, and Miss Planta. After the first fortnight Lady Harcourt took Lady Weymouth's place as lady of the bedchamber. The absence of all state on a visit of this kind was then

Gipsy tent, near Brockworth, looking towards Cheltenham. From a watercolour by W. J. Hardy

far more remarkable than it would be in these less formal days, and the King was well pleased to appear in his favourite roles of Citizen George and Farmer George. No doubt the free and unguarded manner in which he mingled with his subjects in Cheltenham brought him some much-needed popularity; for during recent years the course of events in America and his interference in political affairs at home had robbed him of much of the affectionate regard which had been his when he first ascended the throne.

Those who would read the story of the visit in full must turn to Fanny Burney's famous diary, where an intimate description of the royal doings from day to day will be found. Fanny, who was born on the 13th June 1752, was the second daughter of Dr Charles Burney, the author of the *History of Music*. Hers had been an exceedingly desultory education but she had had the advantage of meeting in her father's house some of the most brilliant people of the time, including Johnson, Burke and Reynolds. She had scribbled much in secret; her brother took a novel to a publisher who accepted it, and *Evelina; or A Young Lady's Entrance into the World*, brought to its author immediate fame and led to her appointment as a dresser to Queen Charlotte—a sort of glorified lady's maid. Fanny had a terribly dull time at Court, which must have seemed all the more tedious by contrast with her old life amongst the wits and intellectuals of her day. Still, she received many kindnesses from the King and Queen, by whom she was greatly esteemed.

No one else could have described the Cheltenham of her day as this woman did, who is the diarist of all time and was the novelist of her own. A creature with a man's mind in a frail and feminine body, she hit off the foibles of her contemporaries much as Bunbury did their features. She is a charming little being, with her sincere and straightforward soul, thickly plastered over with the affectations of her time. How splendidly she stuck it out in after years with that uninteresting husband of hers, the French refugee, M. D'Arblay, whom she married in 1793, and followed into an exile which to her must have been worse than death. She loved M. D'Arblay sincerely and very well, and yet one thinks that when Colonel The Honourable Stephen Digby ("Mr Fairly" of the *Diary*) rode out of Cheltenham one fine day up Charlton way and out on to the Oxford Road towards Northleach, he had Fanny's heart of gold in his possession. That sublime egoist flung the treasure away and married Miss Gunning (Fanny's "Miss Fuzilier"), and now Time has his revenge. For nobody nowadays would ever have a thought to cast into oblivion after the Honourable Stephen Digby if Fanny Burney hadn't taken a fancy to him years and years ago.

No one need try to describe Fanny; that she has done for herself. She has laid her very soul bare for our inspection, except as regards "Mr Fairly," and even then it is only a sort of thin white lie. Her pretence that she doesn't want him one bit is only a sop to her pride, a rag thrown over her shivering soul, a concession to her sex and time. But the great novelist and student of human nature is all the time ruthlessly dissecting herself before the admiring eyes of posterity, which is so far off that it does not get her out of focus and can look upon that dazzling and dauntless spirit with pitying yet reverent eyes. And so she tells her Daddy Crisp and the girls at home that "Miss Fuzilier" is welcome to her "Mr Fairly," when all the time she would give her eyes to get him, and we know it, and she knows that we know it.

Another valuable source of information as to the royalties in Cheltenham is the Harcourt Papers, in which Lady Harcourt gives her impressions of the latter part of the visit. Fanny Burney says of Lady Harcourt that she was "very courteous, indeed, but the native stiffness of her character and deportment never wears away and the effect upon me was, I am afraid, unsympathetic." This stiffness is, indeed, apparent even in Lady Harcourt's journal, which is very far removed from Fanny's sprightly narrative.

An amusing but unkind description of the King's sojourn in Cheltenham is given to us by "Peter Pindar" (Dr Wolcot), in the scathing satire entitled *Royal Recollections of a Tour in Cheltenham*. This pamphlet contains the King's imaginary reflections in a supposititious diary, which achieved its purpose in holding the King up to ridicule. Dr Wolcot must either have been present at the Spa or have been kept very well posted up in the royal doings, for he describes minutely and fairly accurately each day's occurrences, and displays an intimate knowledge of the town. From these diaries, real and imaginary, and from the London and local papers, we can imagine the excitement caused in the little town by the advent of a real king and queen and three princesses. When the King and Queen and Princesses arrived about five o'clock, on 12th July, immense holiday crowds thronged the street to greet their Sovereign, and a further crowd surrounded the approach to Fauconberg House. Musicians were playing at every corner and the church bells rang joyful peals. "When we arrived in Cheltenham," wrote the little diarist,

> "which is almost all one street, extremely long, clean and well-paved, we had to turn out of the public way about a quarter of a mile, to proceed to Fauconberg Hall, which my Lord Fauconberg has lent for the King's use during his stay at this place. When we had mounted the gradual ascent on which the house stands, the crowd all around it was as one head. We stopped within twenty yards of the door, uncertain how to proceed. All the Royals were at the windows; and to pass this multitude—to wade through it rather—was a most disagreeable operation. However, we had no choice; we therefore got out, and leaving the wardrobe women to make their way to the back door, Miss Planta and I glided to the front one, where we saw the two gentlemen, and where, as soon as we got up the steps, we encountered the King. He inquired most graciously concerning our journey; and Lady Weymouth came downstairs to summon me to the Queen."

The King later managed to issue from the front door and strolled through the Well Walk. A local historian says: "About half-past six a tall, portly man, with florid complexion and in the prime of life, dressed in a blue coat with scarlet cape and cuffs, slightly decorated with gold lace and wearing high military boots, was seen descending the steps of Fauconberg House, followed in his descent by two others, for whom he waited a moment when he reached the first step, and then with a quick, firm pace, resting his hand as he walked upon a gold-headed cane, he crossed the meadow and entered the Mall—as we termed what we now designate as the Royal Well Walk, with the footway leading through the church meadow—passed the churchyard and entered the residence of Lord Courtown." The evening was fine and the town was beautifully illuminated. We are told that the musicians from the orchestra of the theatre left the performance unfinished, and followed by the audience, formed a triumphant procession which increased like a snowball as it passed along the one long street; playing and singing all the national and popular airs and catches and glees. Every pause in the music was the signal for long reiterated cheers, and squibs and crackers "added their rattling detonations to the sound of the twanking instruments," and their sparkling and sprinkling glare to the brilliant light of the illumined houses, amongst which the George Inn blazed conspicuously, almost outshining the rival establishments of the worthy Byrch, who was at that time mine host of The Plough and of The Swan, which were then *vis-à-vis* inns. "The premises now" (in the writer's time) "known as the York Hotel, behind which the theatre then stood, also sent forth a stream of light, for when was the elder, the popular Watson, that best and most assiduous of ex-metropolitan managers, behindhand in such demonstrations of public feeling as tended to enhance the welfare of the town, or, secure a 'patronage' for his well-conducted theatre?"

The manager was already in treaty with Mrs Crouch and Kelly; Mrs Goodall was to perform on her way to Drury Lane. "The Chapter of Accidents" and "The Agreeable Surprise" had been given out for the next night, with Mrs Welles as Bridget and as Cowslip. At the last moment, however, Mrs Welles sprained her ankle, and the play had to be changed to "The Jealous Wife," with Mrs Hunter in the name part. Mrs Hunter rose to the occasion and showed sterling acting, while Miss Williams from Bath, with a beautiful face, "delighted in a pretty song." When the change from Mrs Welles's Isabella to Mrs Hunter in "The Jealous Wife" was made known, "not a change was made in the boxes, which showed that merit would be countenanced."

This great day in Cheltenham's Calendar concluded with "plentiful, though not blameable or licentious libations to the health of George III, the Queen, and the Royal Family."

The following morning was Sunday, and the King was at the Spa a little after six o'clock, accompanied only by the Princess Royal. They were served with the waters by Mrs Forty, the well-known pumper, who, thereafter, during their visit, always attended on the royalties at the Wells. This indefatigable lady had at that time been pumper for upwards of thirty years. She pumped the Cheltenham waters for two Kings of England, *ie* George III and George IV, besides many other celebrities. George III took a great interest in her and her family, and one of his recorded jokes at the Spa was that he said to Hannah, "Mrs Forty, you and your husband together make eighty." Hannah Forty's portrait was painted by His Majesty's command.

After taking the waters, their Majesties attended service in the Parish Church, which had never been so crowded nor so honoured before. The King was dressed, just as usual, in plain blue, with the same brown bob. The dresses of the Queen and Princesses were very plain, their bonnets only commanding attention. Her Majesty's and the Princess Royal's were very elegantly trimmed with light green and white ribbons—an improvement on the Turc bonnets—and the Princesses Augusta and Elizabeth wore bonnets of straw, trimmed in the same taste with light blue. All seemed to be exceedingly happy. The Bishop of Gloucester gave one of the best sermons ever preached, whilst the service was read by the Rev. W. Hughes, the Incumbent. The members of the rustic choir were so nervous that they lost their voices. The King, walking down the aisle, bowed gracefully to the crowded congregation. The Bishop and Incumbent walked before their Majesties to the end of the churchyard; then bowed, and took their leave.

The royal visitors then walked into the High Street, attended by a great number of persons, particularly young ashen and maidens from the country. When they came to Coffee House Yard they turned up the passage and paid a visit to Lady Mary Boulby. The King later explored the town, attended by Lord Courtown and Colonel Digby. In the evening His Majesty walked up the town alone, and when he came to the farther end he saw Mr Cooke, a farmer, and crossed over the street to ask him if there was a path through the meadows to the Hall. After being bade to keep on his hat, the farmer conducted his royal master across the fields and continued in conversation until they came to the walk which leads to His Majesty's residence, where Mr Cooke took his leave, and His Majesty thanked him very politely.

The fashions of the Court now pervaded all classes, and early rising and water-drinking were the business of the morning. The general dinner-hour took the note of time from Fauconberg House, and the evening promenade was regulated by the first and last notes of "God Save the King." King George took the waters, like everything else, extremely seriously. He would arrive at the Well a little after six, drink his first glass, walk for half an hour with the Queen, and other members of the family, take a second glass, and at half-past seven return to Bayshill Lodge. At about eleven in the morning the King on horseback and the royal ladies in a carriage went about the country and visited the beauty-spots and the places of historic interest.

Many of the ladies who visited Cheltenham in the summer of 1788 went about in riding-habits, made as much like the King's usual attire as possible with red collars, etc. These habits were called The Uniform or the Windsor Uniform. In such a garb did Lady Hope drive about an elegant equipage, and her skill as a charioteer was much admired. As riding-habits were the fashion, the fair visitors wore theirs until they appeared old and threadbare. "One morning a gallant water-drinker observed to the eccentric Whitefoord, who shone conspicuously amongst our men of wit, that the ladies had a good habit of coming early to the Spa. 'Yes, sir,' replied Whitefoord, 'they have good *habits* in coming here, but they come in damned bad ones!'" The Well was more than once drunk dry, but the infatuated water-drinkers had not wasted it, for some of them drank the very dregs, straining the muddy water through their handkerchiefs. Whitefoord once arrived at the Well too late and pettishly exclaimed: "This is a pretty joke indeed!" Lord Mountmorres asked him what kind of a joke it was, and the humorist replied: "Why, a very dry joke, indeed, my Lord!"

The King met George Selwyn on The Walks one day and accosted him with "Ha, ha! Selwyn, glad to see you. What wind blew you here?" "In the words of the merry Master Heywood," said Selwyn, "do I reply. Two winds, especially the one to see your Majesty and the other that your Majesty might see me!" "Good, very good, excellent good," said the King, "good, very good, Selwyn, only better, much better if original, Selwyn."

On Monday, the 14th July, their Majesties were at the Spa at six o'clock, attended by their ladies-in-waiting. They remained in The Walk for an hour and a half. Not above half a dozen ladies and gentlemen were present. The band of wind instruments was "infinitely better than could have been expected." At ten o'clock they took an airing to Dowdeswell.

As they passed up the High Street they met a subaltern walking along. The King stopped his horse and asked: "What corps?" The boy replied: "The Third Dragoons," whereupon his Majesty put a piece of gold into his hand, and said:

"When you are asked that question again, say that you belong to the King's Own Regiment of Dragoons."

On this day the King wrote to Lord Harcourt:

"CHELTENHAM, 14*th July* 1788.

It may not be improper as time is necessary to prepare a wardrobe for any water-drinking place, that Lord Harcourt should be apprised that on coming on Saturday to Cheltenham no one appeared with a cocked hat except the modest Lieutenant-General Borough. This has obliged round hats alone to be worn, and the plain coat, the other is kept for more public occurrences. On communicating this hint, the writer is desired to add that: 'Lady Harcourt is desired, when she comes to bring linen gowns for the morning as silk ones are immediately destroyed.' This night is the Ball given by the Master of the Ceremonies to the Company. He thinks it will be very brilliant. Lord Oxford is arrived and he means to beg his Lordship to open the Ball; but if he cannot succeed there is no doubt that Lieutenant-Colonel Borough who dances every night, will make that conspicuous figure to which the fame of having been an admirer of the Divine Cecilia gives him a just claim."

In the end, however, His Majesty was not present at this function, as he got wet, and in the afternoon had a slight cold. There were two hundred and six ladies and gentlemen present but many more would have attended the ball had the royal visitants been there.

At midday their Majesties and the Princesses walked in the town and despite the care of the constables the pressure of the crowd became inconvenient and even annoying to the Queen. The King said to her: "Well, Charlotte, we must walk about for a day or two to please these good people, and then we will walk about to please ourselves." A shower of rain came on soon afterwards, and forced the royal family to take refuge in the Assembly Room, of which Henry Rooke was then proprietor. There they waited until their carriages could be brought. The royal visitors spent the evening with Lady Mary Boulby who lived in Coffee House Yard.

On the 15th His Majesty and the Princess Royal were at the Spa very early, and the King, after handing his daughter into her carriage, walked across the meadows attended only by two little dogs. Later the royalties went privately to the rooms and walks and came back with numerous toys and trifles which they had bought as presents for their suites, and for various friends.

All the papers which required the King's signature had, of course, to be sent down to Fauconberg House, and on about 15th July the Secretary of State sent a full pardon to Mr Wilkins the printer, then in Newgate, which document His Majesty had signed in Cheltenham. Lord George Gordon, the author of the publications in favour of the prisoners, was not so fortunate as Mr Wilkins, and "continued in Newgate."

On the 16th His Majesty and the Princess Royal were early at the Spring, and at seven o'clock they returned home.

On the 17th, notwithstanding the rain, the royal family went early to the Spa, and later on in the morning the King and Lord Courtown rode out and the Queen and Princesses accompanied them in coaches. They appear to have gone up the Bath Road to the Sandiland Hills (wherever that may have been), described as being "one of the prettiest spots in England." Thence they went to Mr Baghot's of Hewletts, and to the hills behind it, to see the view from Cleeve Hill. They returned to Fauconberg House at about five o'clock.

On 19th July the King, Queen and Princesses went to visit Lord Bathurst at Cirencester. Owing to their absence, Cheltenham was thinly populated, and Mrs Welles played to indifferent houses.

One day at the theatre, after "The Agreeable Surprise," the pantomime of "Don Juan" was presented, and that, we are told, "in a style of excellence not to be equalled out of London." "The scenery and machinery were prepared at the Royalty Theatre. Mr Penn's *Don Juan* deserved the encomiums of the whole house, and Mr Kelly, brother to the gentleman of the same name at Drury Lane, pleased much in a soft song. Mr Kelly copies his brother with great exactness. Signor Rossignol is here, and at Mr Watson's dinner yesterday performed a solo on the poker with great wit and humour. Mr Watson gave the Toast of the Nobility and Gentry of Cheltenham; an attractive introduction to the favourite air of 'The Roast Beef of Old England.' The theatre is a very elegant and commodious structure, erected by Mr Watson, the proprietor and manager. There are two rows of boxes, one in the form of a gallery, behind which in a most ingenious manner is erected another gallery for the servants, etc. The whole of the theatre, scenery, etc., is above mediocrity and the performers are equal to the task of doing their parts justice. His Majesty having given his sanction to the performance, the bills now mount up to 'Theatre Royal,' 'By Their Majesties' Servants,' etc., etc. Lord and Lady Maitland, Sir John and Lady D'Oyley, Captain and Mrs Bertie, Mr and Mrs Milbanke, Mr and Mrs Auriol and Lady Hildyard were among the audience last night, which was very genteel, and testified the greatest approbation. The scenery was last year at the Royalty Theatre, and retouched by the vivifying hand of Mr Dixon, gave great satisfaction. Mrs Welles appears to-night as Cowslip, and the boxes are all bespoke. Last night their Majesties and the Princesses were at the Spa very early. His Majesty, reading a playbill, observed the name of Mr Shuter, said he must be a droll dog from his name. Mrs Welles appeared in Cowslip only, as she was advised not to fatigue herself. She performed the part of Cowslip with her usual simplicity."

On the 10th of July their Majesties and the Princesses walked from the Lodge to St Mary's Church, attended by an immense concourse, and were received at the Church door by the Bishop of Worcester and by the Incumbent, the Rev. Mr Freeman, who conducted them to the large pew in the gallery, fronting the pulpit. The choir by this time had mustered up courage to sing before royalty and, with the help of a bassoon, they got on extremely well. One of the specially chosen psalms was "How pleasant is Thy Dwelling-place." After Church the royal party went to call upon Lady Mary Boulby, stayed for an hour, and then returned through the fields to dinner, after which they walked in the fields again.

A large crowd had assembled outside Fauconberg House in the hope of seeing the King who would sometimes sit and read or write near the window for the benefit of his subjects outside.

On Monday, the King went to call upon Lord Harcourt, who was lodging in Mr Watson's house "No 21"—probably No 21 Cambray. It was contrived that His Majesty should see Watson and the result was a command performance.

A local scribe says: "'The Mogul Tale' and Mrs Welles's 'Young Kelly's Imitations' were given at Mrs Welles's Benefit at the Theatre, which produced upwards of £40 besides presents. Last night the 'Chapter of Accidents' at the Theatre, Mrs Welles as Bridget; Gawky by Mr Shuter and, without flattery an excellent Gawky he is. Mrs Boon is to bespeak a play. Such a name at the top of the bills will be well for the manager; a lady so much beloved and respected will be followed by those who have a sense of merit. The Prince of Wales and the Duke of York are hourly expected."

Part of the band of the 29th Regiment played at Cheltenham for the first time on the 21st July.

A newspaper says: "On the 22nd, their Majesties and the Princesses were as usual at the Spa, but no water drunk. The Prince of Wales will be at Cheltenham this day. Two nights only, near Lord Fauconberg's."

The Royal Family appears to have visited Tewkesbury on the 23rd. On that day among the topics of conversation were the arrival of Lord Coventry with his wife at the Spa, where her ladyship was once the bright particular star; the order given by the King for bats and balls, in order that his servants might play cricket; and the King's preparations for the arrival of his second and favourite son, the Duke of York. There was no room to accommodate the Prince at Bayshill Lodge, and as the devoted father was determined to have his son near at hand, the idea had struck him of moving a neatly built timber house from the other end of the town. An ingenious surveyor and mechanic, named Ashton, was found ready to gratify the royal whim, and effected the removal with the aid of some twenty or thirty strong pairs of arms, between the 22nd and 28th July, though there was a bridge to pass and an incline of fifty feet to surmount.

23rd July. "Last night Mrs Welles finished here with her Imitations. Her best she has performed. Her presents considerable. This evening Mrs Jordan makes her appearance here. The manager of our theatre cannot too much be praised for his exertions to please. Already he has had Mr Ryder, Mrs Welles, Mrs Belfield, and Mrs Hunter. In addition to these he will have Mrs Jordan, who has finally closed with the Manager of the Theatre Royal for four nights, Mrs Goodall, Mrs Crouch, and Mr Kelly, Mr Bloomfield from Bath and Mr Kemble. Nay, report says he is in treaty with Mrs Siddons! What manager out of London ever presented such a variety in one season!" Thus the local chronicler, whose comments on the visitors and events at the Spa are quaint: "Mrs Dillon is here to give joy to those most amiable in the place; the beautiful Miss O'Moore, her sister. The Countess de Civerac comes here for the most commendable of purposes; to see a good father. Her Ladyship's chief residence is in Paris, where her consort, the Count, has his regiment of horse. Mrs Bertie for equestrian graces is more noticed than any lady here. Mr Dew has taken lodgings at Mr Watson's. Cavendish Square must for a time part with some of its genteelest inhabitants. The Prince of Wales and the Duke of York are daily expected."

The King one morning met a farmer on The Walk, in a great heat. "So, friend," said the King, "you seem very warm." "Yes, sir," replied the man, "I came a long way for I want to see the King." "Well, my friend," said His Majesty, "here is something to refresh you after your walk," giving him half a guinea. "But where, sir," said the man, "can I see the King?" "Friend," said the Monarch, "you see him now before you."

"Major Crosbie has arrived as have Colonel and Mrs Ironsides who, regular visitors here, are not frightened away from the place because the King is here. Sensible of former and good treatment they came and found the inhabitants as kind as ever. There are three blacksmiths here, whose names are Pain, Care, and Bliss. The Miss Boons, lately arrived in The Walks, evening and morning, are not unnoticed."

The journalist comments favourably on Lady Maitland's complexion and also remarks on Mr De la Bere's town house (the present Lamb Hotel) which, he says, is the most elegant in Cheltenham, and he continues: "Mrs Auriol is amongst the first of our beauties; of this her husband is very sensible. Lord Berwick is a constant attendant at the Spa." Of one of Lady Milltown's daughters he says: "With Lady Leeson in particular His Majesty is delighted, and who more capable of delighting than one where every grace has set his seal to give the world assurance of a beauty."

"Report says that a number of London hairdressers are here, but this is like the report of the dearness of lodging. There are not above three, and one of them yesterday got his hair dressed exceedingly well, and on purpose to obtain business, stood in the doorway of the Swan Inn, crying: 'Twas I did this!'"

The scribe meanders on: "The Recorder of London and Lady (Mr and Mrs Adair) are here. Miss Clayton will not remain here longer than her company is desired. General Gabbot has followed the rest of the military men. With military men this town is well planted. As a proof of His Majesty's complacency a nobleman desirous of knowing what were the Levée days in Cheltenham received the answer, 'Every morning in the Well Walk.'"

Miss Wiley was in Cheltenham, a girl who had lied from London to avoid a marriage with a man of whom she did not approve. Though she had a handsome fortune she had become a servant at Evesham. Some other well-known visitors were Lord Bathurst, the Duke of Norfolk, Lady Milltown with the Ladies Leeson, Sir James Fraser and party from Evesham village, Gen. Baugh, Colonels Keppel and Cosmo Gordon, Major Cameron, Captains West, Bertie and McMahon. Lady Ann Bellasayse, the daughter of Lord Fauconberg went on little excursions with the Princesses. The Countess of Hopetoun and her daughter were expected.

V

1788

The Visit of George III to Cheltenham, 23rd July to 16th August 1788—
The First Appearance of Mrs Jordan at the Spa, 23rd August 1788.

The first visit of Mrs Jordan to Cheltenham took place in the midst of the royal sojourn at the Spa, and aroused enormous interest amongst London and local journalists as well as amongst the residents and visitors assembled in the town. Dorothy Jordan is said to have been the daughter of a Mr Bland and of Grace Phillips, an actress, whose father was a Welsh clergyman. The future Queen of Comedy was brought out, when fifteen years of age, at Cork, in Daly's Theatre. Dorothy was born almost on the stage and history really encounters her first (for the rest is somewhat mythical) in 1778, fleeing away from before the face of Daly, of the Smock Alley Theatre in Dublin, and afterwards of many other enterprises, who, having lent the Blands money, exacted payment in kind from the bewitching Dorothy. Ruined and in debt, but accompanied by her mother, father and brother, she fled like Hagar into the wilderness. Somehow it seemed at first as if the Angel of the Lord was with them in the way, for the terrified creatures fled to Leeds and made their way to the manager of the local theatre, for them the sun round which all things revolved.

In the faded but still attractive mother, Tate Wilkinson recognised his old Rosalind, who begged for a chance for her persecuted girl. Wilkinson asked the footsore, tear-stained child if she could play tragedy, comedy, opera; and she replied simply "All." Her two chief parts up to this time had been Lopez, a male character, in "The Governess," and Phoebe in "As You Like It," with Daly in Dublin. For old times' sake, Wilkinson engaged the girl, and promised to pay her fifteen shillings a week. He and her mother decided that Dorothy had better play under the name of Mrs Jordan, although so far as is known, Mr Jordan never existed. Wilkinson's benevolence was immediately rewarded, for in the role of Calista, in "The Fair Penitent," the Irish girl sang "The Greenwood Laddie" in such dulcet tones as to win her way into all hearts. Mrs Jordan now played regularly on the York Circuit, but "indolent, capricious, impudent, and at times refractory," she made less headway on the stage than might have been expected. Indeed, Yates, a future manager of the Cheltenham Theatre, described her as a mere piece of theatrical mechanism. When, on the recommendation of "Gentleman Smith," Dorothy was engaged for Drury Lane Theatre, Mrs Siddons doubted the wisdom of the step.

Mrs Jordan bade farewell to Wakefield in September 1785, and appeared on the 18th of October as Peggy in "The Country Girl." She got on very well, but no conspicuous success attended on her London debut. Still, as the season wore on, she established herself in the hearts of the theatre-goers in the metropolis, and *The English Magazine* of December 1785 said that, as Miss Tomboy, she excelled any person then on the English stage, and almost equalled the celebrated Mrs Clive.

Mrs Jordan was at Drury Lane from this time onwards until 1811, except for one or two prolonged absences. Almost any character came easily to her, but she was of unparalleled excellence in comedy. Two of her great parts were Lydia Languish and Nell, in "The Devil to Pay." The retirement of Elizabeth Farren on her marriage with Lord Derby gave both Miss Mellon and Mrs Jordan fresh opportunities, and the latter successfully essayed parts hitherto thought to be out of her range. Hazlitt called her "the Child of Nature, whose voice was a cordial to the heart, to hear whose laugh was to drink nectar, who talked far above singing, and whose singing was like the winging of Cupid's bow." He added that "her form was large, soft and generous; like her soul, all opulence and grace." Byron remarked briefly that she was superb; while Leigh Hunt extolled her artless vivacity and said that she seemed to speak with all her soul, and that her voice delighted the ear with exquisite tones and perfect emphasis. He admitted, however, that she was not sufficiently ladylike, but for all that, he judged her as "not only the first actress of the day, but, from what I read, the first that has adorned our stage." Lamb praised her in equally high terms, and Hayden said that her acting was touching beyond description, and the elder Mathews called her an extraordinary and exquisite being, as distinguished from any other being in the world, as she was superior to all her contemporaries in her own special line of acting. Campbell, who was teased by his own wife about his infatuation for Mrs Siddons's acting, allows that Mrs Jordan beat the great Sarah out of the field in her character of Rosalind, while that great authority on charm and beauty, Sir Joshua Reynolds, delighted in "a being who ran upon the stage as a playground, and laughed from sheer wildness of delight," and he thought her beyond all actresses of her time. Boaden, who wrote Mrs Jordan's life, is wildly enthusiastic. Despite her numerous love-affairs, and her many faults and follies, there was an infinite charm about the wayward and capricious Dorothy. She was exceedingly charitable, and once, when visiting an invalid *protegée* she met a Wesleyan minister, who thanked her for her kindness to a member of his flock. "If you knew who I was," said Dorothy, "you would not speak to me," but the clergyman blessed her for her goodness, and made an appointment to meet her in Heaven.

Mrs Jordan seems to have made her first appearance at Cheltenham on 23rd July 1788, in "Roxalana," and also as Lucy in "The Virgin Unmask'd." "The King was not at the theatre," regrets the insatiable news collector of Cheltenham, but plucks up heart and continues; "Yet some of the best of his subjects amongst these were Lords Kenmare and Maitland, the Countess de Civerac, Lady Maitland, Sir John D'Oyley, General Baugh, Colonel Gordon, Captain Bertie, Mr De la Bere, Lord Salisbury in the Balcony, with Mr and Mrs Milbanke.

On 24th July, Cheltenham chronicler records: "Nothing new. The Duke of Beaufort and Earl Bathurst have left the town this morning. Mr and Mrs Milbanke will remain while the Monarch does; when he is gone they remove to the North; their attraction is for the sports of the field. The lady can leap a five-bar gate with the greatest ease."

On the 24th, their Majesties, attended by Lady Weymouth, Lady Courtown, Colonel Gwyn and Major Price went for a visit to Gloucester, where, in the Cathedral the King stood for a long time mournfully contemplating the tomb of Edward II. They next visited the famous pin factory.

On 25th July their Majesties and the Duke of Queensberry walked near an hour near the Wells, in close conversation. Old Q had driven down to the Spa in so splendid a chariot that many people thought that he must be the long-expected Prince of Wales. The Prestbury bells rang out a merry peal and the Cheltenham people prepared illuminations. On his return from the Wells the King sat with the windows of the parlour at Fauconberg House open, reading the dispatches which he had just received by the Mail. "A great concourse of people took the opportunity of gratifying their curiosity, which, His Majesty observing, was pleased graciously to countenance by showing himself to their full view."

Mrs Jordan played the part of Rosalind in the evening to "the most elegant and numerous audience ever known in Cheltenham. About two hundred and eighty were turned back from the boxes only. The scenes were crowded … and the applause was great. Rosalind was given with much arch playfulness and the serious passages were delivered in a manner that astonished all present. Her dress in the first part of "As You Like It" was such as good taste only could fancy. The slave cap which she wore was particularly admired. It had been very attractive in London. Several handsome presents had been sent to Mrs Jordan."

On Saturday, the 26th, their Majesties journeyed to Croome Court, the residence of Lord Coventry. On their way they stopped at Tewkesbury, and alighted at a field on the Mythe Hill, from which there was a lovely view of the Severn and Avon and the grand old Abbey. We are told that Sabrina glittered with joy at their presence and that the loyalty of Walter Wakeman, the owner of the field, broke out into a bonfire and an illuminated house.

It was on the 26th of July that Lord and Lady Harcourt went to Cheltenham. "I found," says Lady Harcourt, "an apartment prepared for me in Fauconberg House. My Lord had apartments in the town, but dwelt every day and passed the evening with their Majesties."

On Sunday morning, 27th July, the royal family attended service in Gloucester Cathedral and on account of their presence later, The Walks at Cheltenham were more honoured with nobility than ever. The Duke of Queensberry, Lords Salisbury, Coventry, Courtown, Harcourt, Maitland and Kenmare were there.

On Monday, 28th July, the King, Queen and Princesses were early at the Wells. There was in Cheltenham at this time an old veteran, a sergeant of dragoons, who had been dreadfully wounded at the Battle of Warburg in Germany, notwithstanding which, he had killed his man and brought a prisoner off the field. This old man had been superannuated and to add to his small pittance, he cut cyphers for watch-papers in a most elegant manner. Mr Millar, the proprietor of the Wells, allowed him to sit at a table in the Pump Room. His Majesty on Monday, the 28th, inquired who he was and went to the table and examined his performances, which he declared to be the most ingenious he had ever beheld. The royal party were near a quarter of an hour looking over him at his work, and the King and the Princess Royal gave him orders to execute a cypher for each of their watches. The King afterwards came down to the Wells again, in company with Lord Harcourt and the Duke of Queensberry. His Majesty asked Lord Harcourt what sort of a place the theatre was, upon which his lordship informed him that it was a very neat and convenient building, well worthy of His Majesty's attention. Mr Watson subsequently received a message that their Majesties would visit the theatre the next evening, when Mrs Jordan was to appear as Hypolita and in "The Romp."

At eleven on the same Monday morning His Majesty, attended by the Duke of Queensberry, took a drive round Hewlett's Hill, and paid a short visit to Mr Baghot, returning at three o'clock. In the evening the King took his usual walk and the programme for the following day included a visit to Mr Darke's Grotto, about two miles from the town at the village of Prestbury, directly under Cleeve Hill.

On Monday forenoon their Majesties and the Princesses "took an airing to Shrewdly Castle, and returned by two o'clock. On their way they visited The Grotto, at Prestbury, which is more praised than it deserves." Either on this occasion or a day or two afterwards the King visited Southam de la Bere. His Majesty was evidently gratified with the delightful situation and the curious reliques which that ancient edifice then contained; he was not less charmed by the unaffected simplicity of character, the unsophisticated excellence of understanding and the benevolence of heart which his host, Mr De la Bere displayed. He was, as the King justly observed, "a noble specimen of the fine old English gentleman." George III was very observant, both of people and things, and Lady Harcourt remarked that on his visit to Stroud she was amazed at his understanding of machinery and of the mysteries of the weaving and cloth-making trade and that on many other occasions his quickness of comprehension astonished her, when he saw and discussed things quite out of his usual walk in life. Very possibly the King's intellect would have been far more highly valued nowadays than it was in his own time, when every sort of trade and almost every profession was looked upon with scorn.

Mr Ashton, the surveyor, had about the 28th, comfortably fixed his wooden house alongside Fauconberg House. His Majesty went into it, lamenting, but not wondering, that it should have taken a week to accomplish. The King would not allow the Wooden House to stand on the bowling-green as it would have spoiled his servants' play.

There is a queer old rhyme which shows that bowls were from early times played at the Spa:

"Cheltenham is a pretty town.
It stands all in the valley,
Beside the pretty ring o' bells
And the bowling alley.
And the bowling alley.

The soldiers go in red and blue
And pretty girls a-plenty.
What can the rogues desire more?
The finest town in twenty.

There's Prestbury; there's Tom Ruck the newsman,
There's Squire Johnny Darke.
And Stumping John of Prestbury,
And Welles of the Park."

A curious circumstance took place at Cheltenham. A hairdresser whom upon emergency a certain great Character called in, instead of the person whose peculiar office it was to attend upon the royal peruke, ordered a painter to blazon over his door: "Hairdresser to the King." The person to whom this honour really belonged, felt his dignity hurt and sent to the usurper of his title a challenge. It was accepted and might have had serious consequences had not His Majesty been obliged to interpose his royal authority and declare that if they must fight, they should not, upon pain of his displeasure, use any other powder than Marechale or any other weapon than the puff.

Sir William Altham's fondness for good fruits was remarked by the cormorant-like journalists who scoured the Spa for spicy snips of news, and they also noticed that a little fruit shop—which had had the honour of selling some fruit to their Majesties—had now got a board inscribed: "Long live the King! Fruiterer to His Majesty."

A paragraph in the papers was evidently inspired by Watson.

"A mistaken idea had got into the heads of some people here. They imagined the theatre would hurt most the rooms, when the fact is the contrary. Nothing is more common than to sit an act or two of a play, and then go and have a rubber at whist. To the rooms admission is free, as every genteel person subscribes; but to the theatre every one must pay for admission. All is now found pleasant and amicably adjusted—there is no play on the two ball nights; and the rest of the week, theatre and rooms open to all parties."

But later on we hear that Mrs Jordan has drawn the company from the walks and rooms and that it was highly to be regretted that the house was not as large again and that the actress had received several very handsome presents which were considerable, but more considerable ones were expected. The house was all taken and could have been taken twice over for her benefit on the following Wednesday.

Fanny Burney says of Wednesday, 30th July:

"In the afternoon I went again to the play … It was Sir Harry Wildair, and Mrs Jordan performed it extremely well, but very little to my satisfaction. It is a very disagreeable play and wholly abounding in all that can do violence to innocence and morality. It was for the benefit of Mrs Jordan. In Sir Harry Wildair she displayed the eccentric rake so well that even vice appeared agreeable." It is evident from above quotations that Mrs Jordan did not, as a comparatively recent biographer has stated, refrain from acting men's parts in Cheltenham out of deference to Queen Charlotte's ideas of propriety.

In the evening Mrs Jordan's benefit took place. "A considerable sum was taken at the door, more than the preceding evening; two such audiences, immediately following, were never before heard of in this country. The presents would have been a great benefit in themselves—Notes from several persons. From the King something per Colonel Digby, which, no doubt, well worth the carrying. But all, all, and much more, she deserves."

The whole theatre was more crowded than ever and exceeded the receipts of Rosalind by ten pounds. The balcony box, which had become "quite the ton," contained Lords Harcourt and Faulkland, who were observed in regimentals. Mrs Jordan performed most charmingly as Hypolita and in The Romp, and "in her second dress in the play she looked beautifully picturesque. She introduced the favourite song: 'When I began, Sir, to ogle the Ladies,' which was a treat that the audience did not expect; as such it was doubly good. Mr Lewes in Don Manuel, Mr Shuter in Barnacle, and Mr Hervey in Watty were not allowed to pass without commendation. Their merits merited the situation—in a Theatre Royal. During the performance of the comedy of 'The Constant Couple,' a bloody tragedy took place between the Cheltenham and Bath chairmen. The contest lasted for three-quarters of an hour, and, when several bloody noses had been given on both sides, the combatants desisted, neither side being victorious. So far from the street is the theatre situated that no riot could alarm the audience, none of whom heard of the affray until it was over."

It was at one time apprehended that Mrs Jordan's wonderful success might injure the benefits of the other performers, but this appears not to have been the case.

On 31st July, a chronicler says:

"A general benefit night for all the actors at the theatre is fixed for Friday. Above 20 guineas are already subscribed, and more presents will be given. For this idea let Captain Bertie be thanked, and Mrs Jordan, who on the first intimation kindly offered her services, though her engagement expires this evening. Mrs Jordan, sensible of polite treatment, and willing to make a return, will perform on Saturday for the Manager likewise."

It was probably on the 31st that, as it was generally believed to be Mrs Jordan's last night, "many country people came from miles around, such was the fame of her merits. In Roxalana she shone in a new light, and shone brightly. The Sultan (who seems to have been nervous on a previous occasion) recovered all that he had lost before. The part he spoke and deported with exactness."

One of the reporters says of 31st July:

"This morning their Majesties and the Princesses took an airing for a few hours along the Hewlett's Road. The ladies here dress very badly, and many go on to the balls without caps. Three ladies have but one cap between them, which they wear by turns. I would whisper to them that dress has as great attraction in Cheltenham as in London.

"This morning, His Majesty and the Princess Royal, attended by Lord Courtown, Lady Harcourt, Mrs Milbanke, Colonel Digby, etc, went to see Carey's Mechanical representation of the different stages of the woollen manufactory, which stands in the meadow leading to the Spa. They were much pleased with its ingenuity and bestowed on the proprietor 15 very weighty tokens of approbation. "This show was brought to Cheltenham by Edmund Kean's two uncles, and it was owned then or previously by his grandfather, whilst he himself, together with his mother, used to go on tour with the Careys who had all sorts of performances and shows. Kean's reputed father, who was, like his brother, a lecturer and entertainer, was also at the Spa during the King's visit.

On 1st August 1788 (Friday), *The Public Advertiser* says:

"A gentleman who arrived yesterday from Cheltenham says that, on His Majesty's hearing on the bloodthirsty conduct of the Coalition at Westminster, the Monarch remarked: 'That it was no matter of surprise to him; he knew they were so abandoned, that they would *sacrifice* one-half of his subjects with pleasure, to become the *tyrants* of the other half; but,' added he, 'while I have breath, I'll hazard all, as it is for me and my people's good, rather than admit a set of men into my service, whose sole object is to fetter myself, that they may the more securely plunder my subjects.' Afterwards, turning upon his heel, and spying Mr Selwyn, he said with much good humour: 'Fox may take up his residence in Switzerland as soon as he pleases;—and—ha! ha! ha! and all his Swiss may follow him—would you, would you, Selwyn, have such *serpents* sting you *twice?*' This electioneering remark of His Majesty is the general topic!

The King was walking up the High Street when the common Crier of Cheltenham concluded her harangue with "God save the King." His Majesty turned round and said: "God save the crier and the people."

On Friday morning, 1st August, to the King's intense joy, the Duke of York arrived so unexpectedly that he drove his superb new curricle with its long-tailed black horses through the High Street and up to Bayshill Lodge without being recognised. He waited on his royal parents immediately after his arrival and a chorus of newspapers began: "The Duke took an airing with His Majesty although he seemed much fatigued with his journey. His countenance seemed to bespeak great satisfaction. The bell-ringers set to work immediately and continued all the morning, and a vast concourse of people assembled together at Lord Fauconberg's house to see His Royal Highness. The Wooden House is elegantly fitted up for him. In the evening their Majesties and the rest of the Royal Family walked in the Mall for an hour."

With the Duke of York came as his equerry, Harry Bunbury (husband of Little Comedy and brother-in-law, of Colonel Gwyn's wife, the Jessamy Bride), the famous caricaturist, and one of Mrs Jordan's most fervent admirers. Of her, he had somewhat prophetically written the lines:

"How strange! methinks I hear a critic say,
'What, *she* the serious heroine of a play,'
The manager his want of sense evinces
To pitch on *Hoydens* for the love of Princes!
To trick out *Chambermaids* in awkward pomp—
Horrid! to make a Princess of a *Romp*."

Bunbury raved to Fanny Burney about his divinity and managed to drag off the whole Royal Family that evening to the theatre. The news being spread in the town, the boxes were immediately taken, and the house in every part overflowed. The play was "She wou'd and She wou'd not." Mrs Jordan in the part of Hypolita.

The entertainment, by desire of their Majesties, was "The, Sultan," the part of Roxalana by Mrs Jordan.

The notice being so short, His Majesty made it late before he came into the house. He was accompanied by the Queen, the Princesses and the Duke of York. Mrs Jordan appeared as Hypolita and Roxalana. A passage (somewhat allusive) in Mrs Jordan's part was highly relished. A reply of hers to the Sultan: "I am a native of that country where liberty smiles on every brow, from the King to the Peasant, where every Citizen is a King, and the King is a Citizen," was very much applauded by the royal visitors and by the rest of the audience. There was immense applause also at the passage, "Just such a Queen as she that reigns in the country I came

George III and the Fair Maid of Cheltenham (the Lady is said to have lived at Shurdington).

"Did you know the lad that courts you?   Prince of Songs, of Dance, of Sports.
He not long need sue in vain: You scarce will meet his like again.—Midas"

from." Their Majesties at the theatre were upon their legs at least five minutes, paying their respects to the Company. Lord Harcourt, Lord Courtown and their ladies were in waiting, Colonel Digby, Colonel Gwyn and Captain Bunbury were the attendants. At eleven their Majesties withdrew, and were followed by the multitude with a band of music. There were illuminations in honour of the Duke of York. Altogether the royal party had met with a wonderful reception and Harry Bunbury's impromptu theatre party had been an unqualified success.

After all King George's preparations his son did not stay long. The Prince declared that he must be back in London on Sunday for his military duties, but that he would travel all night on Saturday in order to be as long as possible with his parents. One of the King's imaginary reflections in Peter Pindar's book is: "My face will not bear caricature and this Frederick must tell Bunbury." On the following day, Saturday, and August, the Duke of York agreed to attend his royal parents to Hartlebury, where a call was to be made upon Dr Hurd, the Bishop of Worcester. They started off thither at seven in the morning, attended by Colonel Digby and Captain Bunbury. At five o'clock they returned to Cheltenham and in the evening walked in the Mall. That night Mrs Jordan was to have played for the last time during that season in Cheltenham (though she eventually stayed a week longer) and the infatuated Harry Bunbury paid another visit to the theatre, but had to leave in the middle of the performance, in order to attend the Duke of York back to London.

We are told by the newspaper men that Lord Faulkland, for a nobleman, stood much in favour with the ladies. Lords were often old and ugly, but with him it was the reverse. Councillor Sheldon was at Cheltenham, mingling Blackstone and Coke with the waters of the Spa Royal. Lord Oxford also, had arrived. Mrs Clements attended the theatre constantly and "a pretty face, with great vivacity of manner, were with pleasure observed in the front row of boxes." Mrs Stuart and family were to depart on the following Friday. Mrs Meynell had taken Cheltenham on her way from Bath to Hill Street. "Her stay was wished. Her presence in Cheltenham was required. The chief part of the marriage vow was to obey."

Fanny Burney says that on Sunday morning, 3rd August, she was "oppressed by a cold," which turned out to be influenza. The Princess Royal had had similar symptoms for some days and was attended to by Mr Clerke (Clarke), the apothecary. The presence of the Royal Family so much embarrassed the good doctor that he could only stammer out: "You are not well, Ma'am?" "No, sir, not quite," replied Fanny. On the King confidently saying, "Mr Clerke will cure you," the latter ventured, "Are you feverish, Ma'am?" "Yes, sir, a little." "I—I will send you a saline draught, Ma'am," was all that he could prescribe. Dr Thomas Clarke was the leading physician in Cheltenham for many years. He died in 1816, sincerely regretted by all who knew him. He was then sixty-six years of age, and is described as "the eminent surgeon, who, until 1793, when he retired," possessed the thief practice in Cheltenham. He was perhaps the Thomas Clarke of Tooley Street, who was granted a diploma on 6th November 1783, and became a member of the Company of Surgeons. Moreau says that in 1783 Mr Clarke, Mr Hinde and Mr Hooper were the leading doctors or apothecaries in Cheltenham, and that Dr Smith (Professor of Geometry at Oxford) practised there in Summer.

On this Sunday, the King, Queen and the two youngest Princesses sat down for a considerable time on the benches in the Upper Walk. His Majesty conversed the whole time with the Marquess of Carmarthen.

Cheltenham had apparently not given up hope of a visit from the Prince of Wales, and there were constant reports of his intended appearance in the town during the King's residence. Some authorities say that he did come, but if so it must have been unofficially.

Lord Maitland's fall from his horse at the Queen's feet in the High Street; Mr Duncan's interest in the works of his friseur, Lady Hopetown's departure, when she left her four beautiful grey ponies with her daughter, the Cox family, who kept the pump going, Mrs Meynell, "amongst the few in Cheltenham whose dress attracted attention," were themes for the energetic journalist, who prophesied that when the girls in Cheltenham had the patronage of the Church, Mr Egerton would soon be a bishop. Mr Hollingsworth had danced himself into great fame. Stiles's fruit shop was much indebted to General Baugh for custom and company.

Lord Mountmorres had come to behold the rays of royalty; Mr and Mrs Bertie were leaving in a few days. Mrs O'Neal had for some time been ill at Tewkesbury; Sir John and Lady Lade were expected to arrive as soon as Lewes Races should be over: "Ye Pha'tons beware of an eclipse."

Sir John it was who stood in with Leader, the great coachbuilder, who drove his coach and horses on the frozen Thames, and, was always making extravagant bets of all sorts. General Trepaud had left the fatigues of the field for the pleasure of lolling out of the Well Room. Mrs Goodall had gone to Worcester, and she was engaged to play with Mr Millar. Her terms are said to have been—as her merits deserved—liberal, and it was added that all who had seen her in Bath would concur. The Earl of Salisbury had returned from Hatfield. Now, however, the royalties were leaving for the Three Choirs Festival. The invalid Fanny Burney was sufficiently recovered to accompany the royal party to Worcester, but no sooner had they reached it than Lady Harcourt and Miss Planta fell victims to influenza and there was no Mr Clarke to prescribe for them!

On Monday, 4th August 1788, the Cheltenham chronicler laments: "This day their Majesties and the Princesses set off for Worcester, where they will remain till Friday. The difference between yesterday and to-day is like the difference between the Ballrooms of St James's and the Cock and Hen Club of St Giles … To-day beating up recruits, pigs squealing, horses neighing, cows bellowing, the streets covered with booths, crockery-ware, toys, gingerbread, and hundreds of country bumpkins who came to see His Majesty, as well as to be present at the fair, which is held this day. His Majesty on purpose to please them rode through the thickest part of the fair about two o'clock. Mrs Jordan's engagement expired on Saturday, but she has been prevailed upon to stay this week. The Command is fixed for Saturday. A wish being made known for that purpose Mrs Jordan is to perform Lady Bab Lardoon and The Poor Soldier, Clapham" (a local cook or confectioner) "who has made many a lord lick his lips, should now fasten up his own. His custards are a prey to the wasps; his tarts he must eat himself; his charcoal fire is cold; and, his patty pans begin to rust. The Grotto is as forlorn as an hermitage. One cheery star continues: we can go and laugh at the Jordan, whose pleasantry, seconded by Mrs Hunter, will send us cheery to bed. The Welles is coming again when Mrs Jordan departs. Happy for the manager that he has persuaded Mrs Jordan to perform this week. Rosalind last night. Mrs Hunter came forward as Mrs Brittle. The Theatre holds but £40, but the presents for the performers make it a hundred. Kean has been here. His powers of pleasantry are well-known, both in London and Cheltenham." It was probably Mr Kean of whom we are told that in August 1788, "a well-known lecturer, who for six weeks was violently ill of a fever, was liberally relieved before his departure."

Rosenberg, the silhouette artist, like the greater Eduart, spent much time in Cheltenham, and before the Royal Family left for Worcester he had got orders to take the countenances of the Queen and Princesses, and they sat by him before they left, and had left him employment until their return.

On Friday, the 9th of August, the King, Queen and Princesses arrived in Cheltenham from Worcester at five o'clock, and went immediately to Fauconberg House to dinner. At six they walked in the Mall as usual. "The Merry Wives of Windsor" was to be given at the theatre by Command on this evening, but some of the royal household were ill. Miss Planta had influenza, and Fanny Burney sat with her most of the evening when they had a visit from Lady Harcourt, who was herself not convalescent enough to go to the play. At a little past seven their Majesties walked across the meadows, and through Millar's Rooms as before, to the theatre. Mr Watson had had a week's notice, and had prepared the Royal Box most elegantly. The front projected, and it had a canopy, with crimson curtains, trimmed with silver.

Lords Harcourt, Pembroke and Courtown sat on the right of His Majesty, and Lady Maitland and Mrs Keppel on his left. There were many disputes over seats, and two-thirds of the theatre was laid out in boxes. "Mrs Jordan was very successful as Bab Lardoon, and was, as she always was, genteel in the Lady; the Mawkin, awkward. Her first dress was elegant in the extreme. In 'The Poor Soldier' she delighted as much as ever with her 'Row de dow dow,' while Miss Williams introduced 'The Tuneful Lark' into 'The Maid of the Oaks,' and sang it and other tuneful interludes with great taste. Mr Bloomfield gave 'Sir Harry Groveley' with much animation." Tea was served in the royal box and when their Majesties were done, the lords-in-waiting came out into the lobby and partook of what the Manager had provided. As some of the performers had influenza, Mrs Watson came forward and although she has not been on the stage for years the audience was much satisfied. The *Champêtre* was represented with great taste and grandeur, and the scenes were decorated with artificial flowers, the production of Coe, who has been honoured by the patronage of royalty. The theatre was so full that several people fainted away through the heat.

Mrs Jordan's last appearance during the royal visit was in the farce, and between twelve and one on the 9th August, the Queen of Mirth set out for Worcester. Dorothy carried away with her many handsome presents including "an elegant medallion locket," richly set on one side with fine pearls, in the centre of which was a painting of the Comic Muse, after a picture of Sir Joshua Reynolds. This was a tribute from the gentlemen and noblemen resident in Cheltenham.

On 9th or 10th August came a letter to Miss Burney from Mr "Fairly" (Colonel Digby) who had just left Cheltenham. It ran as follows:

"MISS BURNEY, Fauconberg Hall.

NORTHLEACH, 10*th August* 1788.

Her Majesty may not have heard that Mr Edmund Waller died on Thursday night. He was Master of St Catherine's which is in Her Majesty's gift. It may be useful to her to have this early intelligence of this circumstance, and you will have the goodness to mention it to her. Mr W. was in a house upon his own estate, within a mile and a half of this place.—Very truly and sincerely yours, s. FAIRLY."

The Queen gave Colonel Digby the post, which was the richest sinecure in Her Majesty's gift.

On 11th August, "their Majesties and the three Princesses attended divine service yesterday morning for the last time during their residence at that place this season, and Lord Harcourt's chaplain preached.

"On 11th August, le Comte de Meudon dined with Mrs Boon, he was presented to their Majesties before he left for Birmingham. The Walks were crowded. His Majesty conversed very familiarly with many ladies and gentlemen, particularly Mrs Milbanke."

In the evening of this day, "His Majesty and the Princesses were on The Walks for a considerable time. We were sorry to miss Her Majesty for the first time. She was confined to her room by indisposition. His Majesty has honoured Rosenberg highly. On Monday they sat alone while the King's portrait was taking, and so much pleased was His Majesty that he has desired him to come to Windsor, to take likenesses of all the rest of the family, but not till the hurry at Cheltenham shall be over."

"This day, 12th August, about twelve o'clock His Majesty, attended by Lords Rivers and Spencer and Colonel Gwyn, took shelter in Tewkesbury from heavy rain and called on Lord Harrington at the Swan Inn. The King returned through Tenterden between one and two o'clock, after visiting Overbury, the seat of Mr Martin. Their Majesties have commanded a play for next Friday. Mrs Welles is engaged and Mr Watson has this day taken chaise to Worcester and Birmingham to bring back a Cowslip for his dramatic nosegay, that he shall not be again disappointed."

On the evening of the 12th, His Majesty and the three Princesses were on The Walks for a considerable time. His Majesty was "very jocular with the Earls of Coventry and Rivers and with Lord Spencer Hamilton. The Princesses were in pink gowns, black gauze and white bonnets, spotted with silver. The gowns we thought rather unseasonable. It rained. Lady Harcourt remains and seems to be much in favour. Mrs Welles was expected last night, but has not arrived, Mrs Watson gave Cowslip with much natural simplicity. Lord and Lady Carlisle will be here on the 25th. The lodgings which were lately possessed by Mr Milbanke are engaged by them. Mr and Mrs Milbanke go this afternoon. The Miss Keppels are very fond of riding. Such equestrians compensate for the loss of Mrs Bertie and Mrs Milbanke. The Royal Family would have been at the theatre but for the indisposition of the King. Mrs Welles returns from Worcester to Mr Watson, and performs for a few nights.

"13th August. A messenger was yesterday sent to Lord Dude and to Sir G. Paul, near "Rodbury," to say that the visit this day was postponed, but that the Royal Family would go on Thursday if the Queen's health permitted."

It is said that during his Cheltenham visit, the King one day rode out to Burley, and, the weather being rainy, wore his greatcoat. On his return he overtook a farmer, with his drove of sheep. His Majesty rode with him for a quarter of an hour, conversing upon the value and properties of the land, and the properties of sheep and cattle. After satisfactorily answering His Majesty's inquiries, the farmer, grown familiar, asked the gentleman if he had seen the King, and being answered in the affirmative, he, no doubt supposing that His Majesty always appeared in his Coronation robes, said: "Our neighbours say he is a good-natured sort of man, but dresses very plain." "Aye," said the King, "as plain as I do," and rode on.

"A Cheltenham anecdote: Two clowns, lately hearing of the visit to Cheltenham, were anxious to be present at the conversation of His Majesty, which they concluded would abound with maxims and proverbs equal to the maxims of King Solomon. One of them got into the ring of personages round the King, while the other waited to hear the news when the talk should be over. Upon the conclusion, therefore, when they met, he who had been in the ring was asked by the other what he thought of it. To which the other fellow with a look of great disappointment, scratched his head and replied: 'Why, I can't say I saw anything in it.'"

It is said that one morning King George saw a little granddaughter of Captain Skillicorne's standing on the banks of the Chelt. He picked the child up and put her on the opposite side. When he saw by her indignant expression that he had done the wrong thing, he picked her up again and put her back where he had found her.

On Thursday, 14th August, their Majesties and the Princesses and attendants set off in carriages "to Lord Ducie Morton and Sir George Paul's at 'Rodbury.' They will breakfast with Sir George and dine with Lord Ducie. They mean to visit the manufactory for scarlet cloth at Stroud, which is the best in the world. Her Majesty is quite recovered from her cold which for a few days confined her to her rooms.

"At Hill House, Radbrooke (Rodborough) their Majesties visited Sir George Paul, Bt, and at Woodchester Park they visited Lord Ducie." Lady Harcourt tells us how the process of manufacturing cloth was shown by Sir G. Paul to the royal visitors. "A sort of temporary building, open in front, and formed of white cloth, was erected upon the side of a beautiful hill. This was where a different part of the business was carried on, from the first taking the wool off the sheep's back, to the making up the bales of cloth for sale.

"The men who were employed were dressed in white shirts tied with ribbons, the women as neat as possible, and the instant their Majesties entered the enclosure all was set in motion. The questions the King asked and the observations he made showed such intelligence as surprised and delighted the manufacturers, many of whom said they had never seen a person have such just and dear ideas of the business who had not been actually bred to it. I have often heard the same remark made when I have attended their Majesties to other manufactories, and have myself been astonished how the King with the many important affairs he has had to occupy him, should have been able to make himself master of so many subjects which naturally fall so little in his way."

Some sheep given by George III to Mr Macarthur were crossed with others of the Spanish merino breed and were the ancestors of most of the present-day Australian sheep; as it is said that Cotswold sheep had previously been the ancestors of the Spanish ones. On 13th August, at about 10 am, the King and Queen went up the town and paid a visit to Lady Mary Boulby. His Majesty was this day "very jocular with the Earl of Coventry." Of the visits paid by the King during his last few days at Cheltenham, Peter Pindar gives the following detailed account: "13th, 14th and 15th I passed in visits to the Bishop of Salisbury, Sir George Paul, and Martin Starling near Tewkesbury. Rendcombe, the Bishop's residence—descended to him on the death of Sir William Guise. The aspect forms a beautiful combination of wood, lawn and water. Sir William was one of the respectable beings A Country Gentleman. There is not a farmer who had the happiness of being one of his tenants but what shed tears on mention of his name. Such is the end of a good man. Should death call Salisbury away there would be few mourners. Sir George is an ostentatious mechanic, and Martin is vain of his apparent honesty." Peter Pindar makes very merry over His Majesty's predilection for the company of Doddington Hunt, whom he visited at Charlton Park. They were always walking together and according to the irreverent Dr Wolcot, were a pair of as arrant old gossips as ever stepped.

There is a curious old print in the Cheltenham Municipal Art Gallery of King George and the Fair Quaker of Cheltenham. This represents the King in earnest conversation with a Quakeress, while Queen Charlotte watches them from behind a tree. There is a representation of Brighton Pavilion in the background. Evidently some echoes of the tales about George III and Hannah Lightfoot were in the memory of the caricaturist responsible for this production. It has been said that "The Fair Quaker of Cheltenham" lived at Shurdington, but really the whole thing is most likely a complete invention.

On the 15th of August, the evening before their departure, the Royal Family patronised the Theatre, and as this was the last occasion on which their Majesties designed to appear in public in Cheltenham great preparations had been made by Watson. An address was especially written by Mr Stuart and was spoken by Mr Charlton, at that time a very favourite actor, who was later for many years the manager of the Bath Theatre.

On this occasion the pit was laid into the boxes, and the two front rows of the gallery. The remaining part of the gallery was at the pit prices. The King and Queen came early. Amongst the audience were Earls Bathurst, Harrington and Ducie, Ladies Pembroke, Harcourt, Courtown and Maitland. The upper boxes were crowded with all the fashion that Gloucester, Worcester, and the county could send. Mrs Welles, who had been sent for by order, appeared both in the play and the farce. Julia in "The Midnight Hour" and Cowslip. "The best applause was the express admiration of their Majesties, signified through the manager, Mr Watson. The playbills of the evening were printed upon satin. Mrs Watson attended their Majesties with tea." A procession accompanied their Majesties back to Fauconberg House.

In the morning when he took his leave of the Wells "the King went immediately to the old fellow who cuts watch-papers and spoke to him for a short time, during which he promised him the King's letter. Old Lewis, the actor, likewise attracted his attention and he has signified his intention to make some provision for him during the remainder of his days."

On the 16th of August the royal visitors took their departure, and as his Majesty was driving off he espied the theatre manager in the High Street and said: "Good-bye, Watson."

"All Cheltenham," wrote Fanny Burney, "was drawn out into the High Street, the gentles on one side and the Commons on the other, and a band and 'God Save The King' playing and singing. My dear Miss P_____ with all her friends was there for a last look, and a sorrowful one, we interchanged: Mr Seward also, whom I am not likely to meet for another two years at least. The journey was quite without accident or adventure. And thus ends the Cheltenham episode."

George III thoroughly enjoyed Cheltenham, mineral waters and all. A courtier once complained that he had been troubled with some complaint since he had a cure at the Spa. "The Cheltenham Waters," remarked the King, "*do good by bringing out the humours of the constitution.*" So that was that.

Some years later, when walking on Weymouth Esplanade one evening, His Majesty thought that he recognised one of the other promenaders, and he sent one of his suite to ask if the gentleman was not from Cheltenham. The latter at once came to the King who seemed delighted at an opportunity of making many paternal inquiries with respect to the town, its prosperity and general condition, saying with peculiar emphasis: "Ah, you have come from one of the finest counties of England, and good as Dorsetshire may be, it can bear no comparison with Cheltenham and the Vale of Gloucester, the finest part of my kingdom that I have beheld."

VI

1789–1804

Dr Jenner—Mr King—Mrs Siddons—Charles James Fox—Mr Watson and Colonel Riddell.

After the visit of George III the history of Cheltenham was for some years comparatively uneventful, though the Spa prospered and attracted a number of well-to-do, residents and visitors. Among them was one whose connection with Cheltenham was of far greater real importance, if of less spectacular interest, than the royalties and peers of a few years before.

Dr Jenner, who had probably for some time been connected with the town, and greatly admired its beauties, had in 1795 become at least a part-time resident in Cheltenham, where he hoped to enlist the help of the residents and visitors in his new crusade against smallpox.

Born on the 7th of May 1749, Edward Jenner was the third son of the Rev. Stephen Jenner, who was Vicar of Berkeley, as his father-in-law, the Rev. Henry Head, had also been. Stephen Jenner came of a distinguished Gloucestershire family, had considerable landed property, and had acted as tutor to two Earls of Berkeley. He died when the future discoverer of vaccination was an infant. Edward was brought up by an elder brother, and was eventually apprenticed to Dr Ludlow, an eminent surgeon at Sodbury, near Bristol. One day a young countrywoman came into the surgery, and remarked casually when smallpox was mentioned: "I cannot take that disease, for I have had cowpox." Thus Jenner first heard what had been for many months a tradition amongst the peasantry in the dairying districts of Gloucestershire and other counties. The girl's speech made a deep impression upon him and when subsequently he studied under the great John Hunter, he confided to his tutor his theories about cowpox. The famous surgeon did not scoff at Jenner's ideas, but on the contrary mentioned them in his lectures.

Jenner married in 1780 Catherine Kingscote, an almost chronic invalid, who was a member of an ancient Gloucestershire family. In the following year their son Edmund was born, and was soon inoculated by his father against smallpox. Later, Jenner persuaded Lady Ducie to have her only child also inoculated.

In 1800 Lord Berkeley presented Jenner to the King, and the Prince of Wales also received him, while Queen Charlotte showed him the greatest kindness, and the Duke of York ordered every man of the 85th Regiment to be vaccinated.

In 1801 the Countess of Berkeley, Mr Henry Hicks, the Rev. Mr Pruen, and a few other friends presented Dr Jenner with a service of plate, but the county as a whole showed little enthusiasm for the great discovery and its beneficent results. In Cheltenham, however, he was a prominent figure. He was a Justice of the Peace and one of the original Commissioners named in the Cheltenham Improvement Act. He was also founder (in 1814) of a Literary and Philosophical Society.

Jenner has left a vivid account of some of his Cheltenham experiences: "I permitted," he says, "persons of all descriptions, not only those of the town but from the districts round, to come to me weekly. The smallpox was at their heels, and this drove them to my house in immense numbers. I was literally mobbed, driven into a corner and made a prisoner, necessitated to bow to their will. '*The man shall do me next.*' '*No, he shan't—he shall do me*' was the language I was often obliged to hear and submit to. For many successive inoculating days the numbers that assembled were on the average about 300 … It would be absurd to suppose that out of this vast body all could go through the disease with that correctness which protects them from smallpox infection; in numerous instances indeed, they did not afford me an opportunity of judging of their security by ever returning to show me their arms, and this teasing occurrence not infrequently happened among the common people of Cheltenham whom I vaccinated on a reduced scale." Dr Jenner is here showing that he cannot absolutely guarantee that every person he ever vaccinated is immune from smallpox infection. He goes on to state that there are some persons whom an attack of smallpox itself does not render germ-proof. One instance, indeed, is so very remarkable. I allude to the lady of Mr Gwinnett, who had had smallpox five times."

Once when the smallpox appeared in Cheltenham, in one of the lanes that led out of the High Street, no children who had been vaccinated took the disease. It is said that the inhabitants of one village close to Cheltenham showed the greatest hostility to vaccination; suddenly they began coming in crowds to be vaccinated, and Dr Jenner was greatly delighted to think that they had come to their senses. He found later that the Guardians had stopped all outdoor relief until the people were vaccinated, as the expense of *coffins* was so great!

There was a summer-house in Jenner's time in the midst of a wood on Cleeve Hill, perhaps Queen's Wood, where the primroses are so heavenly. Hither the great man came to get vaccine from cows belonging to one of the farmers in the neighbourhood.

Jenner was greatly beloved by children, and once Sir Ralph Woodford, the former Minister-Plenipotentiary to Denmark, whose monument is in the Parish

Church, gave a children's party in the town, and the little guests danced in a ring round the doctor and crowned him with flowers.

Dr Jenner was by this time sending vaccine all over the world. In Ceylon the inhabitants were beguiled into the hands of vaccinators by Dr Thomas Christie, the Medical Superintendent-General, who later settled down in Cheltenham, and became an intimate friend of Jenner's.

Another local convert to vaccination was Dr Baron, who was devoted to Jenner, and afterwards wrote his life. Jenner used to vaccinate his free patients at what is now called Alpha House, but was known at the time to the ungrateful townspeople as "The Pest House." Henry and Charles Fowler, the sons of the old Vicar of Elmstone Hardwick, used to help him.

In 1796 Michael Kelly, the actor, says:

"I then accompanied Mrs Crouch to Cheltenham, where she had been ordered to drink the waters. Our excellent friend, the Colonel (North) promised to meet us there; and, punctually to his word, was there before us. We agreed during our stay at this delightful place to take a house together, and we were fortunate enough to get a beautiful cottage in the midst of cornfields, then called Wyatt's Cottage; there, indeed, I enjoyed his delightful society; for in repartee and ready wit, who was his equal?

The Colonel was ordered by his medical adviser, while drinking the Cheltenham waters, not to exceed one pint of wine a day; he promised not to exceed his pint, nor did he; but it was a Scotch pint, six of claret or port, which was the daily portion; white wine, at dinner, he said, went for nothing, though he flirted with the best part of a bottle of old Madeira every day.

Here I had the pleasure of meeting my eccentric countryman, the Earl of Howth, whose skill in horsemanship was so celebrated. The very apex of his ambition—the pride of his heart—was, not only to be thought a coachman-like lord, but actually a coachman —his wig—his coat, every part of his dress—was a coachman's; and in his conversation he imitated the slang of the fraternity; but his actions, and manner of thinking, were those of a perfect gentleman; he was upright, good-natured and honourable. He rarely visited his beautiful place near Dublin. He resided in the winter chiefly at Bath; and in the summer at Cheltenham, with his daughters, the Ladies St Lawrence, and a particular friend of theirs, a Miss Georges, a lady of polished manners and education, respected by all who had the good fortune to be acquainted with her.

The theatre at Cheltenham was, at that time, under the management of its proprietor, the eccentric Watson, who was a fellow of infinite jest and humour; full of Thespian anecdotes, and perfect master of the art of driving away wreathed melancholy.

Many a hearty laugh I had with him: he was an Irishman, and had, although I say it, who should not say it, all the natural wit of his country about him …

Watson had brought together, at Cheltenham, a respectable corps; he wished Mrs Crouch and myself to perform for a limited number of nights, and offered us a clear half of the receipts of the house, every night, and each of us a clear benefit; but as we were there for the benefit of our health, I refused his liberal terms.

Lord Howth, however, called on me one day, and said: 'My dear Kelly, everybody is wishing you would perform here for a few nights; you will get a good deal of money; and in the name of fortune, why not pick up your crumbs; sure, it will be only just an amusement to you; the house will always be full, and I will let the boxes for you myself.'

Such a good-natured offer was too tempting to be refused, and we agreed with Watson for six nights. We played to overflowing houses, and the noble box-keeper performed his share of the contract; for on the morning of the first performance, while the company were assembled in the Spa-room, after paying their devoirs to Mrs Farley, there was his lordship with the box-book in his hand, saying to one: 'Now, my lady, remember you have got a stage-box; as for the countess, she can only have a second and third row.' And so on. Nothing could exceed the warmth of his lordship's heart, although he was so eccentric; he even left his coach-box to let boxes for me.

I went one morning into a poulterer's shop, and found the noble earl buying some poultry. I ordered the poulterer to send me home a fine goose, wished his lordship 'good morning,' and was walking homeward at a quick pace, when I heard my name hallooed out; and turning round to see who was calling me, I saw his lordship in the middle of the High Street; his lordship shouting out, with a determined Irish accent: 'Kelly, Kelly! I say, Kelly! Corn your goose! Corn your goose! I tell you, now do, Kelly, corn him! Keep him in salt four days, and then boil him with a wisp of white cabbage; and by the powers he'll be mighty fine eating.' I took his lordship's advice and I found it a delicious dish.

One day I was saying to him, that I had a very bad sore throat; he told me he had a never-failing recipe for a sore throat; his directions were—just before going to bed, to get scalding water, and the finest double-refined sugar, with two juicy lemons, and above all, some old Jamaica ruin; and when in bed, to take a good jorum of it, as hot as bearable.

'Why, my Lord,' said I, 'your prescription seems to be nothing more than punch.'

'And what is better for a sore throat than good punch?' said his lordship. 'Good punch at night, and copious gargles of old port by day, would cure any mortal disease in life.'

I passed some pleasant weeks at Cheltenham; and among other reflections ... I also had the pleasure of originating a friendship with that great and worthy man, and friend to the human race, Dr Jenner, who often did me the honour to take his dinner with me: he wrote a very excellent Bacchanalian song, for which I composed the music."

Mr Kelly met Mr Coutts, who, for many years afterwards favoured him with his notice. Michael then went to London to meet Mr Taylor of the Opera House, but Mrs Crouch remained in Cheltenham, whither Kelly returned, after going on an errand for Mr Taylor to the Prince Regent at Brighton.

Mr Crouch, as William Hickey tells us, ran away with Miss Rider, but "the exquisitely beautiful" Mrs Crouch had a faithful substitute for her husband in the devoted Kelly.

Simeon Moreau, the first Master of the Ceremonies, died in December 1801, and was buried in a vault in the middle aisle of the church. He was the author of the *Tour to Cheltenham Spa*, which was founded on Butler's *Cheltenham Guide*, and went into several editions. For some years, owing to ill-health, Moreau had become rather slack, and had allowed rules and regulations to be disregarded, so that his successor, James King, found that indecorum had sometimes stepped in, and he had a hard task to pull the social life of the town together, and to secure a willing recognition of his authority.

His conciliatory manners, however, and the authority which he possessed as MC of the Upper Rooms at Bath, enabled him by degrees to restore order and regularity. At length, with the consent of the Company who attended the Spa, he laid down certain rules and orders which were adopted *en bloc* by subsequent masters of the Ceremonies, with a few additions, made as experience proved them to be necessary, such as "The Ladies are to be perfectly free in accepting or declining partners."

"Undress trousers or coloured pantaloons are not permitted on any account."

"No theatrical or other public performers by profession are to be admitted."

Mr King was able to combine the two posts at Bath and Cheltenham, respectively, because the former was a winter resort and the latter was in those days a summer Spa. The Master of the Ceremonies used to take round a subscription book at the end of each season, and as the number of visitors increased, the office became quite a lucrative one, and Mr King apparently looked about for a good investment for his fees. Having faith in the future of the town, he chose land at Cambray, an almost undeveloped part of Cheltenham, as a likely speculation in real estate, and was particularly fortunate in his venture.

In 1801 Mrs Byron, mother of the future poet, came to Cheltenham with her son just before he went to Harrow. She went to a local fortune-teller, probably a well-known practitioner, named Mrs Williams, who appears to have prophesied, amongst other things, that young Byron would be married in his twenty-seventh year, and die in his thirty-seventh—a prognostic which made a deep impression on the boy, while part of it at least actually came true.

It was during this visit to Cheltenham, in the summer of 1801, that the strange, solitude-loving boy used to watch the sunset every evening over the Malvern Hills, which recalled to him the mountains of Scotland. Describing how mountains and hills affected him all his life, Byron wrote: "I can never forget the effect of the only thing I had long seen, even in miniature, of a mountain, in the Malvern Hills. After I returned to Cheltenham I used to watch them every evening at sunset, with a sensation which I cannot describe."

It is said that Byron had a favourite haunt in Cheltenham where Christ Church now stands at the top of the steep little Bayshill, where there was an uninterrupted view of the Malverns. The poet used to lean on a little, old gate there and look at the hills and meditate. In 1829 there was a fashion, perhaps set years before by Byron, of going to Lansdown Terrace, quite near to the place where Byron's gate used to stand, to see the sun set over the Malverns.

In 1803 Mrs Siddons, overwhelmed with grief by the death of her daughter Sally, was advised to visit Cheltenham. She stayed at Birch Farm, at the top of what is now North Street, and on the site of Camden Villa, near the present Clarence Square.

Campbell, the poet, says in his *Life of Mrs Siddons,* that her little daughter Cecilia was with her at Birch Farm and that her brother, John Kemble, and also Charles Moore, brother of Sir John Moore, came to her there. They left the farm in July to make an excursion in the Wye Valley.

Warren Hastings and his family were much connected with Gloucestershire. Some of his relatives are said to have been buried in St Mary's Churchyard. His father, Penyston Hastings, had married Hester Warren, the daughter of the proprietor of Stubhill, a small estate near Twining in Gloucestershire.

When Warren Hastings first sailed for India in the winter of 1749 he handed over to his sister some property owned by him in Cheltenham. He mentions this property in 1789 and says that he received it on the death of his uncle, Howard Hastings, who had apparently been made his trustee. It consisted of two houses, which at the time of writing, and probably long before that time, had been merged into the ancient Plough Hotel at Cheltenham. On landing in England on his return from India, on 13th June 1785, Hastings heard that his wife was at Cheltenham, whither he dispatched an express letter to her, following it two days later himself; they met on Maidenhead Bridge, and probably he came with her to the Spa.

In 1803, after Lady D'Oyley's death, Sir John D'Oyley returned to India, and asked Hastings to see to the erection of Diana D'Oyley's monument in the Parish Church, which the great proconsul did, with the most zealous care, taking endless trouble over the inscription and the stone. Two or three rough drafts of the epitaph have been preserved, for he could not at first write it to his satisfaction, and he asked various friends for their advice in the matter. These letters, together with the drafts, are now in the British Museum. Hastings eventually died at Daylesford, on 22nd August 1818, in the eighty-second year of his age.

In 1803 and, indeed, it is said, every year, Charles James Fox came to Cheltenham and stayed at Vernon House. He was curious about Dr Jenner's discoveries, and said to him one day, in Jenner's house in St George's Place: "What is this cowpox like that everybody is talking about?"

"It is," replied the enthusiast, "just exactly like a pearl in a section of a rose-leaf."

Part of the MS diary, written by a Quakeress, preserved in the Library at Cheltenham, describes its authoress's visit to the Grotto at Prestbury in 1803, when Fox, Mrs Fox and Dr Jenner came out there to tea, and the party of Quaker visitors had to hurry out of the tea-room, which Fox and Jenner had booked in advance. The Quakeress had already met and talked with Mrs Fox at a confectioner's in the town.

Fox wrote to his nephew Lord Holland from Cheltenham on 24th July 1804, as follows:

> "The Bishop of Down and his family are here. He looks thin and yellow, but I think
> him in good spirits, and am, therefore, sanguine that he will do ... There are two
> books of letters come out, Cowper's third volume, and Richardson's correspondence
> ... I have no classical book here but the *Odyssey*, which I delight in more and more."

In the *Memoirs of the Whig Party*, Lord Holland says of Fox: "A severe pain in his side which attacked him in Cheltenham in 1804, proceeded no doubt from that affection in the liver which ultimately brought him to his grave."

In 1801 Mr Henry Thompson bought for a nominal sum four hundred acres of land on which now stand the districts of Montpellier and Lansdown, and in about the previous year, Mr Watson, the theatre manager, had bought the meadow called Cambray.

There was an eccentric though benevolent officer in Cheltenham whose doings were of great interest to his neighbours. This was Colonel Riddell of Enfield, who had been for many years a "visitant" at Cheltenham before 1804, but it was not until this year that. he became an inhabitant. *The Chronicle* describes the incident which led to this change in his status at the Spa:

> "We at all times feel pleasure in announcing to the public any improvements that
> are likely to add to the celebrity of this town: and we contemplate with much
> satisfaction those now carrying on in Cambray. Mr Watson, a few years since,
> purchased the meadow so-called; and Mr King, our Master of the Ceremonies, built
> the elegant villa; in the year 1804 Colonel Riddell came on a visit, when the cottage
> he now resides in was in an unfinished state and the property of Mr Watson. The
> Colonel, from the beauty of the situation, was inclined to take such lodgings as it
> then afforded. Mr Watson determined to use all his powers of rhetoric to induce the
> Colonel to become a purchaser, as at that time there was a spirit of speculation, and
> the town flat. He considered a well he had just finished, from the unaccountable
> taste the water possessed, to be an insurmountable bar to his sanguine hopes.
>
> He ordered his servant to have plenty of the finest water, and to be careful that
> no access to the pump should be allowed, either to the Colonel or his servants.
> But as there is no guarding against the chapter of accidents, however well our plans

The Old Well Walk from the Sherborne entrance. From a lithograph by Hullmandel after a drawing by W. Leonara.

may be laid, no sooner had the Colonel taken possession, a party met at dinner, the weather uncommonly fine, the heat intense, a lady requested a glass of water. 'Water! let it be brought fresh from the pump.' The servant in a moment returned with the decanter, the water bright as crystal and steamed by the cold. The cooling draught was eyed with pleasure, but scarcely had it met the lips of the thirsty fair when it was speedily withdrawn with an exclamation: 'What an odd taste the water has.' The Colonel tasted—'Odd, indeed; where did you get it from?' 'The pump, sir.' From that moment, Mr Watson's offers were viewed by the Colonel as leading to a speculation that might prove beneficial, and terms were finally agreed upon, Mr Watson guarding the pump with increased care, lest the discovery should break off the treaty."

The Colonel's purchase was rumoured as soon as it was made; and in twenty-four hours the remaining property in Cambray rose more than double its value. All were purchasers; and Mr Watson was informed that he had sold a fine chalybeate; a piece of news he communicated to his wife, who with a faltering voice exclaimed: "Have you sold the Colonel the spring too? You know, notwithstanding the odd taste, how much benefit I have derived from it, and as for yourself, you are not the same man!" "Never mind; the Colonel has promised us we shall have the free use of the spring; and on the whole I have made a good bargain." Such was the origin of Cambray Spa. After his lucky speculation, the Colonel evidently began to fancy himself as an amateur doctor. His correspondence in the *Cheltenham Chronicle* with Dr Baron, as to the respective merits of smallpox inoculation, which the Colonel seems to have preferred, and vaccination, which Jenner's friend and biographer naturally upheld, is long, and at times, a little acrimonious.

Evidently Colonel Riddell's confidence in his own healing powers was almost unlimited. Among his medical discoveries were some powders which a few years later had reached India. *The Chronicle* is "most happy to notice the astonishing success which has attended Mr Robert Riddell (son to Colonel Riddell, lately of this town) in his medical practice at the Court of the Nizam."

In addition to the Life-restoring Powders, we read of "The Riddellian system of extraordinary cures in cases of fever performed at Cheltenham." It was also reported that Colonel Riddell was "eminently successful in relieving several persons from complaints in the eyes and other disorders." "We cannot too much regret," says the *Chronicle* scribe, "the absence of a gentleman who thus gratuitously and humanely alleviated affliction."

VII

1805–1808

Harriot Mellon and the Entwistles—The Cambray Theatre—The Duke of Gloucester—The Prince Regent—Lady Mary Lindsay.

The early years of the nineteenth century saw the beginning of Cheltenham's connection with another very famous actress: Harriot Mellon, afterwards Duchess of St Albans. This came about in a curious way.

Mrs Sarah Entwistle, Harriot's mother, had been born near Cork in 1752. Her parents were peasants, and all the girl's education consisted of the Church prayers taught orally by her mother, and the traditional songs of her native land. A company of strolling players one day came to Sarah's village, and the girl and her parents paid in eggs or potatoes for seats at the theatre—which was a barn. The play was "Romeo and Juliet" and next day, Mrs Kena (the manager's wife) gave Sarah an old copy of the play as a return for more eatables.

From this time Sarah, with the memory of the performance always in her mind, and the "book of the words in her pocket," was stage-struck to the last degree. She got people to read her the play until she knew it by heart, and was still living in a fairyland of romance when her father's sudden death brought her painfully to earth again. The widow and her daughter moved into Cork, where Sarah got employment with a cheap dressmaker and milliner. In 1776 the mother pined away, longing for the free country life she had loved; and in her twenty-fourth year Sarah was an orphan. She went to "live in" at her employer's shop, and the new bonnets were tried on the beautiful assistant. For Sarah's beauty was extraordinary and her daughter wrote in later years: "My mother had infinitely greater claims to being good-looking than myself. Any personal advantages I might have possessed were derived from her, and in addition she had a fine oval face and beautifully regular features, whereas mine are too short and the contour of my face too round for its length." In Sarah Entwistle's Cheltenham days she retained many traces of considerable personal beauty—"the full laughing dark eyes, jet-black hair and remarkably fine teeth, which her daughter inherited, with an elegantly formed mouth, and although a very large person, she had the rare advantage of a symmetrical hand and arm, on which she founded a pardonable degree of vanity. It is also said that like her daughter, she possessed in her younger days, the winning attraction of a low, sweet voice."

At the milliner's she had still dreamed of theatres and actresses, and one day she was looking out of the window, when she saw Mrs Kena and another of the actresses, strolling up the street. She dashed out and offered to join the company, which was on its way to Aberystwith. Mr Kena laughed at the idea of the peasant-girl, who thought she would make a tragic actress, but his wife suggested that Sarah would be useful in dyeing and cleaning dresses, and dressing feathers, and offered to take her on a tour through Wales. She made herself most useful to her new employers and managed their financial affairs. She also took the money at the doors and, in fact, did almost everything but act. Kena was so well off at the end of his tour, that he decided upon taking a holiday. He disbanded his company, and paid Sarah's fare back to Cork, where her former employer was glad to have her back. A hideous old member of the Wesleyan connection of which Sarah was a member, fell in love with the stage-struck beauty, and her mistress urged the girl to marry the old hypocrite, who came and prayed and expounded and tried to flirt with Sarah two or three times a week. But one day in the drawing-room window of a lodging-house facing her shop, Sarah saw her fate in the person of the new lodger, a young, handsome, dark man, who for some time spent all his spare moments at the window whence he could watch the beautiful milliner, whose acquaintance he soon made. The lover described himself as Lieutenant Matthew Mellon of the Madras Native Infantry, who had come to Europe on sick leave and was travelling through Ireland for change of air. His leave had almost expired, he said, and he had no money to support a wife in India, so he suggested that they should get married, and that when the time came for his departure for India, Sarah should go to London and there support herself with needlework until he could send for her to join him in India. So, on Twelfth Day 1777, they were married, and in March Mr Mellon sailed. Sarah never saw him again, and no letters came.

On the 11th November 1777, Harriot Mellon was born, and in the following year the Kenas, her old manager and his wife, who had resumed work, persuaded Mrs Mellon to resume her former multifarious occupations with the theatrical company.

While the Kenas were touring in Lancashire in 1782, a young musician, named Thomas Entwistle, a talented violinist, joined the company, fell in love with the handsome widow, who was considerably his senior, and married her.

Like nearly all Sarah Entwistle's connections, matrimonial or otherwise, Thomas Entwistle had a romantic family history. His mother is said to have been the daughter of Sir Fleetwood Haversham, left an orphan and married to a German musician, named Entwistle, who had come over to England in George the Second's Band.

In the first year after their marriage the Entwistles were obliged by Mr Kena's lack of business to find another engagement, and Thomas wended his way to his native Lancashire. Near Preston he encountered Bibby, an eccentric tailor who had turned itinerant theatrical manager. Bibby was glad to engage so good a violinist, and with him the Entwistles toured some of the northern counties. They were a good deal at Ulverston, where Harriot began to act in children's parts. They lodged for a time in Stafford, where Harriot made many friends, especially among the better classes: including the daughters of Mr Wright, a local banker, who interested himself much in the girl's career. Finally, he and other friends persuaded Mr Sheridan (who had seen her act) to engage her for Drury Lane, where she appeared as Lydia Languish. She played Cowslip and other roles with considerable success, receiving a good deal of help from Mrs Siddons and Mrs Jordan.

Meanwhile, however, Mr Entwistle's fortunes had declined. He had a taste for strong drink, and for the society of idlers beneath the class in which he had been brought up. He was always kind to little Harriot, and often gave music lessons in return for the child's education; but as his wife's beauty faded and her violent temper abated not a whit, she lost her previous unbounded influence over her Thomas, who took to going his own unsatisfactory way. A little before March 1804, he lost his engagement in the orchestra at Drury Lane, and as his prospects in London were not rosy, he decided to sell music in one of the watering-places. Harriot had already acted in Cheltenham in June 1802, and had very likely seen at the time that the town would be a good place for a small business, out of which the Entwistles might supplement whatever her stepfather should earn professionally. Accordingly, the Entwistles moved to Cheltenham, where Thomas opened "a musical warehouse and library on the plan of those in London," possibly on the site of Newbold and Newton's stationer's shop and district post office. The family earnings were, however, still insufficient, until Harriot found a curious means of restoring them.

In the earlier days of the Spa the postal arrangements were very primitive. The mail-coach from London, which travelled twice, or sometimes three times weekly, did not approach nearer to Cheltenham than Frog Mill, on its way to Gloucester. The Cheltenham letters were delivered in the more leisured moments of Nanny the Bellwoman, whose real name was Nancy Wells. She helped to catch criminals, and was also the Town Crier. There was then only one magistrate, and the administration of justice was quickly done between Nanny, Constable Oakey, and the kind-hearted gentleman of the Bench.

At a later period there was another feminine officer, Nanny Saunders, or "Nanny the Postmistress," who followed much the same calling as her predecessor. She devoted her evenings to the delivery of letters, and was a picturesque and well-known figure as, lanthorn and basket in hand, and attired in a red cloak and in a huge black hat, she went on her rounds.

Occasionally the London Mail managed, as it passed Frog Mill, to forward a bag of letters by the carrier to Nanny, whose husband, mounted on a donkey, delivered letters to those people who lived in the hamlets and adjacent villages.

In 1800, however, an improvement was made. In that year a Mr Smith established a post office at 127 High Street, which was taken over after his death by his next-door neighbour, also named Smith. In 1805 the first Government Post Office was established, with one postman to deliver the letters. The post office in the days of which we are about to speak is said to have been at what is now the old basket and brush shop in the High Street.

It was in this year that Harriot Mellon made her first great hit at Drury Lane as Volante in a clever comedy "The Honeymoon." The actress had made a powerful friend in Colonel MacMahon (at that time continually with the Prince of Wales), an annual visitor to Cheltenham, where he was very well known. One day Harriot told the Colonel how much she wished to secure for her mother some light salaried occupation that she might make some provision for her old age. He promised his influence when the girl should find a suitable opening. Just then the situation of postmaster of Cheltenham became vacant, and Miss Mellon thought that this would be the suitable post of which Colonel MacMahon had spoken. She therefore begged it for her stepfather, Mr Entwistle, and to her great joy her request was granted. She rushed down to Cheltenham with the splendid news. Never was a family more delighted, and no doubt kind Colonel MacMahon was equally pleased.

At the end of the Drury Lane season, late in June 1804, Harriot went to stay in Cheltenham with her parents, and in order not to waste her time she accepted the offer of the Cheltenham manager to play at the local theatre for five nights and a benefit in Mrs Jordan's and Miss Farren's parts. She played on 3rd July the parts of Letitia Hardy in "The Belle's Stratagem," and of Nell in "The Devil to Pay." On the 5th, she appeared as Miss Peggy in "The Country Girl" and Marcia in "The Citizen." On the 7th, Miss Doulton in "Wives as they Were" and Cowslip. 16th July, Amanthis in "The Child of Nature" with Roxalana. On the 12th, in her own benefit as Widow Cheerly in "The Soldier's Dream" and as Nell in "The Devil to Pay."

Harriot's engagement in Cheltenham was a very great success and the benefit produced a considerable sum. But probably in order not to make herself too cheap, she refused to engage herself for longer than the week. She then paid another visit to Liverpool, where she made a great deal more money. Though not a first-rate actress she always drew the largest benefits in the provinces. She was well-known in many country towns and very popular, from her unaffected good-nature, and never returned to London without some hundreds of pounds collected in the country. Harriot had made so much in Cheltenham that Mrs Entwistle suggested a return thither.

Harriot took her mother's advice and in September she reengaged herself at the Spa, for three nights, performing on the 6th Peggy with Mrs Kitty in "High Life," and on the 8th her favourite role of Rosalind in "As You Like It."

One of her greatest patronesses, Lady Templetown (Lady Mary Montagu, daughter of the Earl of Sandwich) was in the town at this time. She bespoke the pieces for Miss Mellon's second benefit, and advertised her *protegée* so well among the distinguished visitors at Cheltenham, that the second benefit exceeded the first. The Cheltenham people were greatly surprised at the profusion of presents sent to Mrs Entwistle from London, or brought by Harriot on her visits to her mother. While she was in Cheltenham at this time, her stepfather was ill, and nothing could exceed the affectionate care and anxiety she evinced until his recovery. These could not have been greater had she been his daughter.

Mrs Entwistle saw that Cheltenham was likely to increase rapidly; and she now schemed to advance the fortunes of her family by a building speculation.

At that time there were but few houses in Cambray, although from its (then) open situation, these were eagerly snapped up by visitors. Mrs Entwistle now suggested to Harriot that she should spend every penny of her benefit money in building a house in Cambray which would, she hoped, when let furnished, return an interest of at least fifty per cent on the sum sunk in it. Harriot agreed to the plan, and a piece of ground was bought; but the whole of the actress's savings were not enough to complete the building. However, the small gossiping town soon knew that Miss Mellon was building a house by her savings for the benefit of her mother, and the tradesmen offered to supply the required articles at once, and to be paid at the lady's convenience. Miss Mellon repaid them punctually and thanked them profusely, and the house was let at an excellent rent. Mrs Entwistle was so exhilarated by her success that she began to talk of a row of houses, and to dream of a whole street. But, as we know, there existed in Cheltenham an exalted functionary of now almost unlimited powers. This was Mr King, the Master of the Ceremonies, whose approval welcomed visitors into the gaieties of Cheltenham and found customers for tradesmen, and whose ban consigned both visitors and shopkeepers to outer darkness. They were in the place, but not of it, until Mr King had branded them as of his own flock. Therefore, when Mr King bought the block of land immediately opposite to Miss Mellon's, nothing could be said. He built a great, new, high, staring building which effectually blocked out the view which was one of the great attractions of Mrs Entwistle's speculation.

Other residents followed like a flock of sheep and soon destroyed the openness which had made Cambray Meadow most desirable. The scheming old Irish peasant in her distress appealed to Harriot to come down and have a benefit, in order to recompense her for the harm done to the property by the Master of the Ceremonies. The postmistress, from her frank, lively manner, charitable nature and love of gossip, was very popular among the middle classes, and spread wide the story of how hardly the Master of the Ceremonies had treated her dutiful child, who had relinquished every shilling of her earnings for her mother's support. There were soon few residents of Cheltenham who had not heard the tale, and they duly sympathised.

Thus Mrs Entwistle prepared the way for her daughter, and Harriot came down with the beautiful companion who always lived with her. These two charming girls, guarded by Mrs Entwistle, always a great stickler for the proprieties, went round to solicit patronage. Mrs Entwistle's sharp eyes had some time before this espied a sad-looking and exceedingly shabby, elderly, invalid gentleman, who kept much to himself and daily appeared in the Walks. His servant had, however, hinted to his landlady, a crony of Mrs Entwistle's, that his master was one of the richest men in London. The old gentleman had not given his name, but Mrs Entwistle thought that it was up to one of the richest men in London to take a box at the theatre for the benefit. The manservant had also remarked that the old gentleman's wife was going out of her mind, which worried his master so much that he had been ill and was now come to Cheltenham for a change of air.

Nevertheless, Mrs Entwistle hoped that domestic trouble would not deter the rich old man from at least paying for a box, and a respectful note inviting his patronage was given to the attendant at the Pump Room to give to the remarkable-looking old gentleman, but, as no answer was forthcoming, the three women decided that the moping, thin, old creature was too full of his own troubles to care for those of other people. However, on the next day but one after the dispatch of their missive, the two girls were in the Long Walk, when the old gentleman overtook them, and introduced himself to Miss Mellon, whom, he said, he knew by sight in the Drury Lane Green Room. He was sorry he had not sooner answered the application, but said that he would be glad to patronise her laudable filial efforts of which he had heard admirable accounts at every turn in Cheltenham. The two girls were naturally delighted and their new acquaintance said that he had had the pleasure of sending his answer to the post office. When they got home they found Mrs Entwistle wildly excited. She held in her hand a letter from Mr Coutts who had enclosed five guineas and desired that a box should be kept for him. Mr Coutts, whose name was a proverb of wealth even in country towns—Mr Coutts—*The* Mr Coutts!

Then, as her ecstasies subsided she, as usual, looked round for a safety valve for her excitement, in the person of one of her family. Her eye and her wrath fell at once upon the descendant of all the Fleetwood Havershams. Why had he not, when anyone called for letters for Mr Coutts, guessed at once that he was the thin old gentleman and told his wife so? She raved at her husband until even the girls, who were used to her ways, were indignant. The idea, they said, of anyone supposing that the great Mr Coutts, who managed the Royal Family and commanded everything he liked, could be an old, pallid, thin, sickly gentleman in a shabby scratch wig! Miss Mellon always kept this five guineas that Mr Coutts gave her "for luck." She showed them to her guests on the day of her marriage with Tom Coutts, and again twelve years afterwards when she became Duchess of St Albans.

From the time of Harriot's first acquaintance with Mr Coutts at Cheltenham, a constant and friendly intercourse was kept up between them, and Mrs Entwistle schemed her best to promote this intimacy. A lawyer declared afterwards that Mrs Entwistle left Cheltenham suddenly, and appeared in her daughter's room just after breakfast, intent on preventing her marriage with Mr "Baggy," another suitor whose real name was probably Baguet.

In May 1805 the wonderful cure at Cheltenham of Sir Francis Burdett made the reputation of the Cambray Spring. In the same year Mr Watson built a new theatre in Cambray which was continually crowded, and which was later much helped by the frequent amateur performances given by Colonel Berkeley.

In 1805 Mrs Siddons was induced to play again in Cheltenham. This was in the new theatre and in 1807 the great actress and her brother John Philip Kemble appeared at the Cambray Theatre in "Macbeth."

The Duke of Wellington, then Major-General the Hon. Sir Arthur Wellesley, KCB, came to Cheltenham in 1806. Wellesley's earliest recorded appearance in his favourite watering-place is described by Madame de Gontaut, one of the faithful ladies who followed the French Royalties into exile after the Revolution, in her *Memoirs*, which give the only detailed account available of this earlier visit, and from which we therefore quote: "After the departure of M. de Gontaut to France, my children and I joined Lady Templetown at Cheltenham ... In the evenings, sitting quietly on the terrace of our pretty house—my friends were very fond of this *astre de melancole*—Miss Upton (daughter of the Dowager Lady Templetown) charmed us with her singing. She was very warm-hearted and devoted to me, but fond as I was of her, I could not but feel grieved at the dislike she showed to certain persons who were not in her set, and *who tried* to show her kindness. This was the shadow which sometimes clouded the brightness of our friendship.

"One day at breakfast I received a letter from Lady Mornington, the sister-in-law of the Marquis of Wellesley, recommending to my kind offices her brother-in-law, Arthur Wellesley, who was coming to Cheltenham to rest on the laurels he had been gaining in India. 'He knows nobody,' wrote Lady Mornington, 'and it will be a charity if you will pay him some attention; so I trust him to your kindness and your friendship for me.'

"He was to arrive that very day; and in visiting me he would have the pleasure also of making the acquaintance of Lady Templetown and Miss Upton.

"Nothing on earth would have induced me to fail in honouring this recommendation of my friend. I announced my intention of setting off at once to find this person, who was brother or brother-in-law to all the Wellesleys, of whom, I was very fond. My companions, however, were very far from sharing my enthusiasm. Lady Templetown's indolence took alarm and Miss Upton's jealousy awoke. They were both greatly disturbed at the idea of having this man *whom nobody knew imposed upon them*. It would be a horrible bore, they said, and thereupon discord arose between us, reminding me of the fable of my childhood, *Des Poules vivaient en pais, un coq survint*, etc.

Queen Charlotte. After Sir William
Beechey, R.A.

"Without listening to their grumbling, however, I set off for the Pump Room
to look for the arrival. With great difficulty I at length persuaded Miss Upton to
accompany me. I proceeded straight to the Pump Room, where I went to look at
the list of new arrivals.

"I found the name of Wellesley and read it aloud, so that Miss Upton could
hear it, but she did not say a word. A stranger, standing beside me, was also reading
the list; he put his finger on a name, smiled, and looking at me, said: 'Madame de
Gontaut.' Nothing could be more piquant; we had never met and yet we knew
each other at once.

"Miss Upton would have been glad to slip away, but there was no escape for
her. I set Mr Wellesley at ease by proposing to introduce him to Lady Templetown
and I presented him to Miss Upton forthwith; but my disdainful companion
would not open her lips. We set off on our way home; he offered me his arm and I
accepted it, when all at once my garter dropped off and fell at Mr Wellesley's feet.

"Fancy losing one's garter in a public street in broad daylight and in England,
of all places in the world!

"I must confess that I was covered with blushes. He picked it up and with a
gracious smile and an air of perfect breeding said: 'If ever there were occasion to
say, *Honi soit qui mal y pense*, this is it.'

"Miss Upton whispered in my ear, 'How fortunate that it was a new one!'
I replied, 'I should think so indeed!'

"My introduction was made; Lady Templetown resigned herself; Miss Upton came round by degrees and as for me I did my best for the entertainment of our agreeable guest.

"After the first few minutes of awkwardness Mr Wellesley grew quite confidential and told me that the considered himself very fortunate to find at Cheltenham a lady of whom he had heard so much from all his family. Lady Templetown invited him to come and dine with us every day, Miss Upton sang and he was charmed with her voice. I found his frankness and straightforwardness delightful.

"He told us about India but he never spoke of his victories, of which all our letters were full; but he allowed us to question him and the stories we beguiled this man, who had seen so much, into telling us went straight to our hearts.

"During one of our walks he confided to me a trouble which was disturbing him greatly; but I will give it in his own words.

"'In a few days I shall leave Cheltenham on account of a very grave matter which will decide my whole future life. When I was very young I became attached to a Miss Pakenham, a very nice person, pretty and sweet, and we became engaged. We were both very young. I had an ardent desire to enter the army and I was obliged to leave her though we both cherished the hope of one day being reunited. Years passed and in the meantime Miss P. had smallpox. She wrote to me that, remembering our promise, she must warn me that she had lost her beauty. It appeared that the smallpox, while destroying her beauty, had not deprived her of her memory.'

"His manner of saying this was so peculiar and so like him that I could not help laughing: 'But she has my promise and my honour demands that I should keep it; it was rather fine of her too, to write to me with so much simplicity and truth. So I shall start for Ireland at once; I have very little time to lose. Perhaps I shall come back this way, alone or with her.'

"He went and they returned together, she in the carriage alone and he on the box.

"My *protegé* of Cheltenham became The Duke of Wellington! My father's *protegé* at the École Militaire was The Emperor Napoleon!"

William Frederick, Duke of Gloucester, a constant visitor to the Spa, was the second Duke of the Georgian creation, and was born on 15th January '77, at the Teodoli Palace at Rome. His father, the first Duke, was the third son of Frederick, Prince of Wales, and the favourite brother of George III. His mother was Maria Walpole, the illegitimate daughter of Sir Edward Walpole, widow of Earl Waldegrave, and the niece of that dear old snob and prince of diarists, Horace Walpole. She was regarded as the most beautiful woman in England after the celebrated Gunnings.

It was not until six years after the event that the Duke of Gloucester avowed his marriage with Lady Waldegrave. In 1771 the King was greatly annoyed by a marriage of another of his brothers, the Duke of Cumberland, with Anne, the daughter of Lord Irnham, afterwards Earl of Carhampton. George III cut off his brother completely, and refused to receive any persons at Court who visited him or his Duchess. The Duke of Gloucester was so horrified at the treatment meted out to his brother, that he hastened to avow his own marriage with Lady Waldegrave on the 6th September 1766. As the issue of this marriage would have come within the line of succession if His Majesty and the Duke of York died without heirs, the King, though greatly vexed at the step taken by his brother, when informed that the union had actually taken place, employed the Archbishop of Canterbury, the Lord Chancellor and the Bishop of London, to ascertain that the ceremony was valid, and to enter the proofs in the records of the Privy Council.

It was some time before the King was reconciled to the Duke of Gloucester—his other brother he never forgave—but the excellent conduct of the Duke and Duchess "caused him ultimately to admit both to all the honours of their situation and what they valued more highly, to his confidence and love."

The Duke and Duchess of Gloucester had two children, Sophia Matilda, who was born in 1773, and died unmarried in 1844, having been for many years the Ranger of Greenwich Park, and William Frederick, the devotee of Cheltenham, who succeeded his father in 1805.

On his way home from the Spa each year the Duke of Gloucester would visit Warren Hastings in his country home, for he, like most of his family, was a friend in adversity. His pretty wife was the Princess Mary, daughter of George III. She does not seem to have come to Cheltenham nearly so often as her husband.

George IV paid some flying visits to Cheltenham. Local historians have asserted that he came here in 1788, during the visit of King George III, but so far as can be ascertained this was not the case, although the *Morning Post* in 1788, according to Goding, says: "On Monday evening, 21st July, His Royal Highness the Prince of Wales arrived on a short visit to their Majesties."

There is some mention of a wonderful ball given by George IV as Prince of Wales in Cheltenham, and Goding seems to think that he had come a year or two before 1807.

On the 18th August 1807 the Prince of Wales came to Cheltenham. The royal visit was a quiet one, as his desire was for seclusion, and it was made quieter than it might otherwise have been by the death of the Duchess Dowager of Gloucester, out of respect of whose memory the Prince did not attend many social functions. The history of his doings during his retirement would, however, no doubt make interesting, if not edifying, reading, and perhaps the walls of old Fauconberg House, before the local vandal razed them to the ground, could have told some tales. What were the musical parties at which we read in the newspapers that "Mrs Billington would not perform even under great pressure from the Prince?" The elms, at least, round the Prince's Cheltenham residence are still there. One can picture the old Lord Hertford, immortalised by Thackeray as the Marquis of Steyne, and his royal patron seated beneath their shade perhaps with the lady for love of whom (according to Fox's sensation-loving nephew) Prince Florizel (the

Prince of Wales) had recently nearly bled himself to death, in order to soften the heart of the obdurate fair one by his appearance of ill-health.

We are told that (probably on the 21st): "HRH the Prince of Wales attended yesterday, and this morning between seven and eight o'clock at the Spa, and took the usual quantity of water from the hand of Mrs Forty, who had had the honour of administering it eighteen years since to his Royal Father. HRH remained in The Walks for full half an hour each time. He was accompanied by Sir R. Milbanke and Colonels MacMahon and Bloomfield.

"Messrs Chamberlain are appointed Porcelain Manufacturers to the Prince of Wales, with permission to use His Royal Highness's name, crest, etc., and they have received orders to forward China for the use of the Prince's establishment during his residence in Cheltenham.

"The Duke of Gloucester left Cheltenham on Monday morning last. Gloucester is to remain the headquarters of the Royal 18th Regiment. General Sir James Pulteney has left Gloucester with a detachment of the 18th Regiment."

On the window of the old Pump Room at Cheltenham was scratched a rhyme about the rain at Cheltenham which was so incessant that it had made the gallant Pulteney fly.

A local journalist writes: "We are exceedingly happy to report that the Prince of Wales has already derived considerable benefit from the salubrity of the air of Cheltenham and its celebrated springs. The town is full. Mr Ruff's Galas on Wednesday evening go off with *éclat*; his library is often a *fashionable squeeze*; Mr Cooke's elegant China Shop supports its well-known splendour. The balls and theatres display a blaze of beauty and elegance. The Prince has not yet partaken of the Public Amusements of Cheltenham, and has received no company except the friendly calls of a select few of the nobility, etc., but lives in complete retirement and enjoying what were the declared objects of his visit; change of scene, rest and tranquillity.

"It was very unfortunate for the interests of this town that the death of the Duchess of Gloucester happened so soon after his arrival as it made him a perfect recluse till within a few days of his departure.

"The School of Industry established by the late Mrs Williams and patronised by the Queen is in a most flourishing state. The Duke of Gloucester presented ten guineas to the fund.

"HRH the Duke of Sussex, the Earl of Leinster, Lady Rouse Boughton, and others have arrived at Cheltenham Spa. On Thursday last (3rd September) Cheltenham Theatre was honoured by the presence of the Prince of Wales and the Duke of Sussex, who were received with enthusiasm by one of the most numerous and brilliant audiences it has ever boasted. The Prince, as well as his royal brother, behaved with the utmost affability, remaining till the whole of the performances were closed, and honouring the Company with an elegant and graceful salute on their departure. The Theatre never exhibited so proud a show of dress and beauty, every one anxious to appear mindful of the Royal

Condescension, and to express their joy at the manifest benefit which HRH has derived from the visit. The performances were "The Rivals" and "The Mayor of Garratt," Russell in Acres and in Jerry the Sneak, was irresistibly entertaining, and attracted the public notice of the Prince to two comic songs he introduced; one of which happily portrayed the gaieties and absurdities of the place. All the characters were respectably filled and supported." The Duke of Beaufort, the Earl of Leicester, Sir C. Broughton, the Ladies Barrington and Myers, Sir John and Lady Callendar and Dr Jenner are all mentioned as being there too.

A newspaper says: "On Friday last the Lower Assembly Rooms were honoured with the presence of HRH the Prince of Wales and of HRH the Duke of Sussex. The expectation of seeing the Prince at the Ball attracted the Company at an earlier hour than usual, and by nine o'clock the Room was crowded. The Company amounted to 480 persons. The Prince arrived soon after ten o'clock and stayed till the conclusion of the dance at eleven. He conversed with those of rank, and others who have the honour of his acquaintance and seemed much pleased with the dancing which was highly animated. Some persons wished the ball to be continued beyond eleven; but Mr King resisted the innovation on the established hour. His spirits and gentlemanly conduct on all occasions and continued attention to the welfare of Cheltenham demands the thanks of all ranks of people."

On Saturday, the Prince of Wales and the Duke of Sussex, on their way from Cheltenham to Ragley, the seat of the Marquis of Hertford, passed through Tewkesbury, where Mr Ridler, the landlord of the Swan Inn, with whose horses the royal carriages were forwarded, presented to the Prince of Wales a copy of the *History of Tewkesbury*. The Prince of Wales sent twenty guineas to the School of Industry in Cheltenham.

Among the visitors in Cheltenham during the stay of the Prince of Wales were the Archbishop of Canterbury, the Lord Chief-Justice of Ireland, Lord and Lady Ashtown, Lords Lindsay and Cahir, Lady Mary Lindsay was also in residence at Cheltenham, probably at her home in Cambray.

"Lady Mary Lindsay gave a splendid *fête* at her elegant cottage *orné* on the 9th of August 1898. The French General Brenmer sung French and Italian songs." Colonel Riddell and Lords Kenmare, Newburgh and others were present.

Lady Mary Lindsay lived for many years in Cambray, having as her neighbours Colonel Riddell on one side, and on the other Captain Brisac, RN, an energetic resident at the Spa, who apparently filled gratuitously the office of Town Surveyor.

In 1809 a terrible quarrel arose over a boundary fence which Captain Brisac put up between his own garden and that of Lady Mary Lindsay. The accounts of the resulting warfare read rather like scenes from a farce than sober newspaper reports. Captain Brisac put forth a case addressed to Admiral Gardner, who acted as chairman to the Court of Inquiry which seems to have been held about this ridiculous squabble.

In his introduction the Captain says: "Gentlemen, self-defence is the first law of nature, and powerfully pleads my excuse for this action. Calumny has desired to malign me, and its shafts, nearly blunted by time, have been again pointed to your late decision—a decision to which I would willingly have bowed, had your justice and impartiality been as active in my case as for my opponent, etc., etc."

The Duke of Sussex and the Prince of Orange again visited Cheltenham in September 1809, the Duke of Gloucester being already there. On 3rd October these three princes honoured the theatre with their presence. The pieces played were "The Busybody" and "The Turnpike Gate," and were for the benefit of Miss Jameson. The celebrated local tight-rope dancer, Richer, Watson's son-in-law, "performed the whole of his inimitable manoeuvres with his accustomed ease and elegance, and was cheered with the warmest plaudits of their Royal Highnesses."

VIII

1808–1809

Edmund Kean—William Hickey—Macleod of Colbecks—Colonel
Berkeley and His Hounds.

Edmund Kean was much in Cheltenham, both before and after his rise to fame.
A local writer says that, at the time of the visit of George III, in addition to the
regular amusements at the Theatre "the two celebrated mimics of their time, Kean
and Carey—the one the ' reputed father,' the other the uncle, of the great modern
tragedian—displayed their powers, which were unrivalled in the zenith of their
popularity, and Carey, when his mimic attraction ceased, exhibited a mechanical
exhibition, which the King inspected with minute attention." Kean was probably
in Cheltenham as a small child, and he was certainly there during several months
of the year 1808, when he fulfilled an engagement with Mr Watson at the theatre,
became engaged to Mary Chambers, a native of Waterford, went over to Stroud
and married her on 17th July, returned and had his wedding breakfast at Mrs
Hyett's The Dog Tavern. There is an undated record of a performance at about
this time, in which Richer appeared as a baron, Mrs Watson as a female porpoise,
and Kean in green satin as Alonzo the Brave.

Tom Moore says in his diary, 2nd December 1814:

> "Dined at Kinnaird's. Present Lord Byron ... Kean. Kean told us ... that at Stroud
> in Gloucestershire he acted Shylock, danced on the tight-rope, sang a song then in
> vogue, sparred with Mendoza, and then acted Three-fingered Jack."

It was quite likely in the Careys' Company that Kean performed as above-
mentioned and probably the show visited Cheltenham as well at the time, when
the incident took place which is related by Michael Kelly in his reminiscences.
Kelly says that Kean arrived in Cheltenham with a strolling company, and in the
direst need, and he was one day driven by stern necessity to beg a meal "on tick,"
to be paid for out of the night's receipts. A butcher's daughter, whose father had

a shop near the Red Lion in Cheltenham High Street, frequented the canvas theatre, probably the Careys' glorified tent where the company performed. Kean had got acquainted with the girl and in his straits went to her and besought her to let him have a small beef-steak, for which he would pay her later. The girl complied with his request, but just at that moment her father walked into the shop. As the young actor did not want him to see the steak, he hurriedly put one hand, with the long-coveted dinner in it, behind his back. A hungry dog passed at the time and snatched the piece of meat out of Kean's hand. That night a meritorious performance of "Crooked-backed Dick" was given on an empty stomach. A few years later the great actor came back; was paid £50 in Cheltenham for a morning performance, £50 in Tewkesbury in the afternoon, and again the same sum at Gloucester in the evening, so that he earned £150 in a day—a great sum for those times.

The *Cheltenham Chronicle* of 10th March 1814, says:

"Mr Kean, whose transcendent abilities are now avowed and fostered in the metropolis, formerly resided for some time in this town, and performed at our theatre. He married his present wife at Stroud in this county."

On 2nd May 1809, the famous William Hickey set out with his sister Ann and his black servant, William Munnew for Cheltenham, and the *Cheltenham Chronicle* of 11th May 1809, announces the arrival of Mr and Miss Hickey, and again on 7th June 1810, of Miss Hickey, while the arrival of Mr Burke (almost certainly Ann's friend and the executor of her will, Thomas Haviland Burke) is mentioned on 2nd July 1810.

William Hickey, Munnew and Ann arrived in Cheltenham about noon on 3rd May 1809. Hickey did not like the Cheltenham waters, which he only tasted once; but Ann and the Turners (Hickey's former partner and his daughter) gave them a fair trial, without deriving any advantage, and, moreover, Mr Turner said that the waters brought on a headache, a pain he had never known before.

"At this celebrated watering-place," remarks Hickey, "among other Indian friends I met with Mr James Agg, a shipmate on board the *Seahorse*, Captain Arthur, in the year One thousand seven hundred and seventy-seven, he having gone out as one of Colonel Watson's assistants. Upon the failure of the Colonel's plan for establishing docks in Bengal he procured for Mr Agg a commission in the Corps of Engineers, of which he was the head, in which situation Mr Agg acquiring a handsome independence he about the year One thousand eight hundred and two resigned the Company's service and returned to England, where he settled in Cheltenham, and soon after his arrival purchased a beautiful house with a considerable quantity of land belonging to it, situate on an eminence about two miles from the town."

A coloured print, now in possession of Mr Spencer, Hickey's editor, shows Hickey, Munnew and a delightful Airedale terrier with a frilly brass collar like Dog Toby's ruff in *Punch and Judy*.

The local papers often mention Hickey's friends, Major James Agg of The Hewletts, and Arthur Wellesley.

"On the 17th August 1809, at the Bespeak of the Hon. Lady Hood at the Theatre Royal, Waring, the actor, with great *éclat* in answer to the question, 'Is there any news?' readily and happily answered, 'Great news, my boy, Sir Arthur Wellesley has given the French a good drubbing.' The effect this had on the audience with 'God Save the King,' 'Rule Britannia,' 'Britons strike home,' etc—the gallant Sir Samuel Hood being present—need not be described. The play was 'Jeremy Didler.'

There was another tale about an officer whom Wellington had ordered to lead a forlorn hope, and had told him that should he succeed his regiment would be the first in this world. "It will certainly be the first in the next," retorted the officer.

A well-known man in Cheltenham in these days was Colonel John Macleod of Colbecks, a Ramsay Macleod, of the Lewis branch of the clan. He was the son of a Jamaica planter who had made a considerable fortune in the West Indies. Colbecks is thought to have been the name of his father's plantation. It was, doubtless, the money from the Jamaica estate inherited by John that enabled him to raise the Macleod Fencibles and thus gain the favour of the Prince of Wales and of the Princess Charlotte. It also accounted for the lavish hospitality at his house, Charlotteville, Charlton Kings "Carlton House in Little." The old planter, who died in 1785, was the half-brother of that Laird of Mackinnon, who, having squandered away his lands, found himself in a state of utter destitution. The wealthy planter had frequently helped the spendthrift, but evidently the latter's appeals had become too constant and had reached the limit of what the rich brother was prepared to give.

Colonel John Macleod married a cousin, Jane Macleod, the daughter of that John Macleod who helped Prince Charlie after Culloden, and subsequently entertained Dr Johnson at Ramsay in 1773. They had a son, Barlow, and five daughters, Julia, Flora, Margaret, Charlotte and Susan. Of these only the youngest girl was married to a Mr Andrews. The only son died in 1809, a truly tragic event in the lives of poor Macleod and his wife.

Colonel Macleod was, like many of the inhabitants of Cheltenham in the dim and distant past, a crank of the first water. His particular monomania was the cult of the Princess Charlotte of Wales, and he was given permission to call the regiment of Fencibles which he raised in 1799 at Elgin, NB, "Princess Charlotte of Wales's Highlanders." "Fencibles" were corps in the nature of Militia, but raised by the ordinary mode of recruiting, instead of by ballot, and they were not available for foreign service. The Macleod Fencibles, apparently about 110 strong, marched across Scotland and there embarked for Ireland, where they remained during three critical years; difficult and important work which was well done and of great value to the Government. In 1802 this, the last of the Scottish Fencible Corps, was brought over to England and reduced at Tynemouth Barracks. Many marks of royal favour were shown to Colonel Macleod in recognition of the patriotic zeal which he had shown in raising this regiment.

The Prince of Wales in the name of his daughter had presented "superb banners" to the Macleod Fencibles, and the Princess herself had given Colonel Macleod a sword.

Every year on his idol's birthday Colonel Macleod gave a party, of which one only hears by chance before the *Cheltenham Chronicle* was established. These parties always had a splendid press, though nowadays, alas, no one seems to know where Charlotteville was. According to Mr Dobell, it might have been Charlton House. A record of an early festival runs:

> "The agreeable Mrs Trench describes an awkward scene at Cheltenham, in 1805, when Mrs Fitzherbert had been graciously invited by a gauche colonel to a fete in honour of the Princess Charlotte's birthday. He first introduced his guest as 'The Regentess,' by leading her in before all the ladies of rank; then gave toasts and discoursed on the merits of the Prince and Princess of Wales and 'The lovely Fruit of their Union.'"

Mrs Fitzherbert visited Cheltenham again in 1810, on 13th September, but by that time neither she nor the Princess of Wales had anything to do with the Prince of Wales, and Colbecks left the awkward question of the Prince's consorts alone. It would be amusing to see what the scribe of the *Chronicle* would have said about the fiasco of 1805.

On 7th January 1811, we read again:

> "In conformity with their usual observance of that glorious and propitious day which gave birth to the illustrious Princess so proudly and so justly the future hope of their virtuous grandfather's true and loyal subjects, Colonel and Mrs Macleod of Colbecks invited a select party of the Society of Cheltenham to celebrate that proud day to Englishmen."

The Princess Charlotte sent a wonderful Christmas Pie for this party. It was of exquisite size and goodness, worthy of the munificence of the illustrious donor, who, by her royal command, desired to have announced to Colonel Macleod, that the Princess Charlotte requested his acceptance of the Christmas Pie as a mere token by which Her Royal Highness wished to express her thanks to him and Mrs Macleod for so constantly and so kindly thinking of her on her birthday.

The royal fare was found excellent, and after eighty people had partaken of it, it still appeared undiminished; a truly royal pie! Finally, the sword, which was a previous present from the young Princess, was exhibited and duly admired: The healths of the Princess, of Macleod and his family, and of Captain Thomas Grey and the Cheltenham troop of Yeomanry Cavalry were drunk.

Amongst those present were the Countess Rosebery, Viscountess Strangford, Ladies Hunloke, Strong, Meredith, Mrs General Orr, The Lord and Lady of the Manor, and many other well known people.

On 21st November 1809, a great event in the sporting history of Cheltenham took place, for Colonel Berkeley then first brought over his hounds from Berkeley Castle, and hunted the Berkeley country one week and the Cotswold country the next throughout the season.

No sport had ever come amiss in Gloucestershire, from the days when the Norman Conqueror made the residents in Cheltenham pay for the upkeep of the first Cotswold pack.

In 1720 there was a good bowling-green in the town, and in 1741 and afterwards—doubtless before that time also—cudgel matches were held outside the Plough Inn, when the best man won a guinea and a new hat, while a broken head was salved with a shilling. Bull-baiting with dogs was one of the kindly sports of the early Georgians, held, like the cudgel matches, on the banks of the silvery stream that babbled down the High Street, complete with trout and kingfishers.

Sports of various kinds sometimes took place outside the old Arched Buildings in the High Street, but more often a stage was set up in front of The Bell whilst the spectators were located on The Plough side of the High Street.

A handbill, dated 26th July 1757, announced one of these exhibitions:

"A Cock Match by subscription to be fought in Cheltenham Street by the Gentlemen of Gloucestershire; to weigh on Saturday the 30th, and to fight the 1st of August.

Any person or persons that are willing to add to this match may send in their cocks as above mentioned, and depend on having particular care taken of them by Edward Sarson, Gloucester."

Printed by R. Raikes, in the Black Fryars."

Mr De la Bere had had a pack of hounds before Colonel Berkeley came to Cheltenham, but little is known of their doings, and later on Dr Townshend, the sporting Rector of Cleeve had a pack of harriers, which were sold to Mr John Bushe. It was reserved, however, for Colonel Berkeley to make Cheltenham sport famous throughout England, and to inaugurate a new era in Cheltenham.

The Colonel had been well known in the town before this time, but now he became the ruler of it. Any description of the Georgian Spa which did not include him would be Hamlet without the ghost, or rather, without the Prince himself. For fifty long and lurid years he was closely connected with the life of the Spa. Cheltenham was his hobby. He lavished his time and wealth upon the place, while his sayings and misdoings occupied the constant attention of the townsfolk and visitors. Not that he cared what anyone thought or said. He was a law unto himself, and the Cotswold Spa then lived under the shadow of Berkeley Castle, whose Norman keep raised its head full five and twenty miles away. No party was a success without Colonel Berkeley, routs and dinners were arranged to suit his convenience.

William Berkeley's father, Frederick Augustus, fifth Earl of Berkeley, had married Mary Cole, the beautiful daughter of a butcher of Gloucester or Wotton-under-Edge. Lord and Lady Berkeley had, however, lived together for a good many years *before* their marriage, and already had two daughters and four sons, of whom William, the subject of our sketch, was the eldest. After the marriage three sons and three daughters were born, and it is said that Lord and Lady Berkeley tried (to the extent of tampering with the Church register) to prove that they had been married in Berkeley Church before the birth of their eldest son, William. Out of this arose the celebrated Berkeley Peerage Case, when Dr Jenner was amongst those who gave evidence.

The story of the first marriage, as told by the old Earl of Berkeley and Mary, his Countess, was that they had been married on the 30th March 1785, in Berkeley Church, by the Rev. J. A. Hupsmann, the witnesses being William Tudor, who turned out to be William Cole, the brother of the Countess, and Richard Baines, who, being an illiterate, had merely made his mark. Richard Baines was stated to have disappeared and could never be produced. It was said that banns were read by the clergyman in an inaudible voice in November and December 1784. The page of the register was torn out by Mr Hupsmann to keep the marriage secret, and as this page was lost and the clergyman dead, it was thought necessary to go through the form of marriage a second time as a measure of caution and prudence, in case the first marriage was questioned. This second marriage took place at Lambeth on the 16th May 1796. A few years afterwards the missing page of the register was discovered and also the deceased clergyman's notes of the publication of banns.

This was the evidence on which various courts and committees were asked to declare the elder children of the fifth Earl legitimate. It is only fair to add that not only did many people believe the story at the time, but there are those to-day who implicitly accept it and strictly hold that William Berkeley and his brother Maurice should have been recognised as Earls of Berkeley.

Moreton Berkeley always believed in his parents' previous marriage and consequently thought that William ought really to be Earl of Berkeley. He himself never used the title, and William was allowed to have Berkeley Castle and the estates belonging to it, and was treated by his brothers as the head of the family.

The adverse decision of the House of Lords made little difference in Cheltenham to the position of William Berkeley, who possessed a princely fortune and was ready to spend it with a lavish hand in amusements in which others could share. As a bachelor he was desired for a son-in-law by every scheming mother. He had a great fund of conversation and most agreeable manners. He could sing a good song in a fine deep voice. If it is true, as his brother Grantley says, that his education was neglected and religion formed no part of it, Society cared little about these things. Besides, he undoubtedly had considerable mental powers, and could speak

Georgiana, Duchess of Devonshire, and Lady Georgiana Cavendish, 1784. By Sir Joshua Reynolds, R.A.

French fluently and Italian a little. It will be seen from Colonel Berkeley's remarks quoted below that his ideal sportsman and poet was Somerville. Richard Tattersall, Mr Somerville Tattersall's great-great-grandfather, married Katharine Somerville, the daughter of a clergyman, and who was related to the author of "The Chase." No one could accuse Berkeley of being a mere stable lad or gamekeeper as others of his upbringing have been contemptuously named before and since. Indeed he took a considerable interest in public affairs, could make an excellent speech, and probably would have made a name in politics, either in the Commons, had he continued his parliamentary career, or in the Lords, had his claim to the earldom been granted.

Like all the members of his family, Colonel Berkeley had always been devoted to sport of all sorts; and he had a long career as a master of hounds. At the age of sixteen he had his own pack of harriers, and at twenty-one he advanced to the dignity of a master of foxhounds, and how this came about can be told in his own words in a speech at the Plough Hotel after he had become Lord Segrave:

> "I do not know, gentlemen, how it was that I originally became imbued with the love of hunting—but I think it came about when a boy from that beautiful poem of Somerville's 'Chase' having fallen into my hands. He was a most extraordinary

person —he was not only a beautiful poet, but he was a first-rate sportsman. There has never been any work written since in any sporting review or in anything that I have since read that showed so much knowledge of hunting as is shown in Somerville's poem of 'The Chase.' Whether the perusal of this poem was the only cause of my enthusiasm I cannot say, but I was determined very early in life to become the master of a pack of foxhounds, and accordingly when I was twenty-one I commenced. I was on a very liberal allowance, but not enough to keep two whippers-in, and, therefore, I became whipper-in myself, but I had great difficulties to contend with. First of all—want of experience; so much so that when a good number of my friends used to name me after dinner, my health was generally given as: 'The Pack and the Puppy.' I had not only to contend against the country, in which there were not a great many foxes, but I also had no pack of hounds. I did not take to any original pack; and, therefore, I had to put up with what I could get, the refusal of all the other kennels, those whose sentences of capital punishment had been commuted to transportation, so that I looked upon my kennels as a sort of penal settlement, to which the reprobates of all other packs guilty of serious offences had been drafted. I had mute hounds and babblers and skirters, and hounds so slack that they would not hunt anything, and hounds so wild that they would hunt everything. But I was young and had a good constitution, and a decided love of Old English Sport, therefore, I was not easily to be daunted, or else my very first essay might have put me down."

He then related in an amusing style, his first day's sport at Newent Woods—on the 24th of September 1808, when the hounds, instead of fox-hunting, gave chase to a cur and afterwards worried a flock of sheep and after that another cur; and went on:

"The magnificent present you have given me is enough to recompense any individual for the toil and sweat of his brow for nearly fifty years—to more than amply reward him. The master of a pack of foxhounds is the servant of the public. Entirely so when there are many duties and obligations which he must faithfully discharge. In the first place, before a man takes a country, he must consider whether or not it is likely that he can take it for a term of years. He must not capriciously take it up and relinquish it, because on the faith of his undertaking, owners of coverts will preserve foxes, and many owners, too, who do not hunt themselves, and, therefore, we who do, ought to feel ourselves the more indebted for their disinterestedness. It is on the faith of this undertaking that men purchase horses, hire stablemen, that livery-stable keepers invest their capital, that lodging-house keepers and hotelkeepers provide themselves with winter-quarters for their tenants; that trades-people in general hope to participate in these benefits which necessarily arise in their neighbourhood from the establishment of a pack of foxhounds. All these considerations I have deeply felt and considered, and endeavoured to the best of my ability to discharge those duties which such an undertaking so seriously imposes."

Lord Segrave said that although his hounds were originally such an untrained band, there was some good stuff among them; they were in fact the ancestors of this present pack, which he might say, without egotism, was a good pack of hounds and did their work well. And, as a proof of this, he could only say that this hunting season (1851–2) had been admitted on all hands by huntsmen and masters of hounds, to be decidedly the worst hunting season they had ever known. They had been out from the last day of August to the 14th of April, 108 days, and they had killed 112 foxes. But the formation of a pack of foxhounds was not entirely confined to the sports of the Field; there were with it a great many other acquaintances made which were charmingly interwoven with the other relations of life. There was his old and valued friend, Charles Hanford. He knew him first in the hunting-field, and though neither of them could frolic and ride now as they could in the noontide of youth, yet those sunny days still threw a warm and agreeable tint over the evening of their lives, and as they descended into "The Vale of Tears," they looked back with grateful recollection to the occasion that produced so firm and fast a friendship. He was also tempted to believe that the formation of a pack of foxhounds in that neighbourhood had been attended with benefits to Cheltenham. He believed that his hounds had tended to the establishment of the staghounds, now under the admirable management of Mr Way, which rendered that town, by the amusements and attractions they offered during winter, more attractive than almost any other place in England.

Though Colonel Berkeley first brought the hounds to Cheltenham in 1808, it was not until the following year that he began to hunt the Cotswold country regularly. From that time till his death, in 1857, he hunted the Berkeley and the Cheltenham countries alternate months throughout every season and had kennels at both headquarters. During the months at Cheltenham he used also to hunt the Broadway country (from the North Cotswold) on Saturdays. On 1st January 1822, the Berkeley Hounds had the longest run in the Cotswold country. It is impossible to estimate the distance, but the time occupied was five and a half hours. Colonel Berkeley had one very excellent quality in a master of foxhounds—he could keep his field in order. This was very necessary for there were often a large number of wild Irish sportsmen out, who were apt to override hounds, or jump a wall at a check, when there was nothing else to do. Colonel Berkeley had a peculiar knack of applying powerful and novel epithets to such people, which had the effect of keeping them in order. On one occasion he damned a rider's "chestnut soul" in reference to the colour of the horse on which he had ridden to hounds!

The late Mr Clarence Dobell remembered Colonel Berkeley's almost royal progress into Cheltenham yearly, at the beginning of the hunting season. It was in his later years and probably when he was already Lord Segrave that Mr Dobell remembered him, but the procedure was the same each year; when a cavalcade of gentlemen from the town went out to escort Colonel Berkeley triumphantly into the Spa, and when, whether the incumbent was particularly at daggers drawn with him or not, the church bells rang out a merry peal of welcome to the master, as he rode in at the head of a procession of sportsmen.

"Lord Fitzhardinge," said Mr Dobell, "brought with him often as many as sixty hunters, splendid horses, all of them, and the members of the hunt could ride them; there was nothing to pay. There was nothing to pay for *anything.* He paid the hunt servants, he owned the hounds, he *owned* everything—and he *ordered* everything. I can see him now, sitting there swearing and giving his orders in a voice that could be heard half a mile away. He ordered which way the fox was to go, the hounds were to go, the men and horses were to go, and that way they *went.* There was none of that not knowing where to go and what to do that one so often sees nowadays. Lord Fitzhardinge arranged it all beforehand, and he arranged it *well. The thing* was a success. He was the lord of all and no mistake, *and he owned the whole lot."*

Before his father's death William Berkeley had assumed the tide of Viscount Dursley, but during most of the years in which he ruled Cheltenham Spa he was known as Colonel Berkeley. In 1831 he was created Baron Segrave, and Earl Fitzhardinge in 1854. He was the leading Liberal of the County, President of the Gloucestershire Whig Club from 1817 on, and a prominent advocate of the Reform Bill in 1831. At the time of the Russian War, he showed his patriotism by giving a bonus to every member of his militia regiment who volunteered for active service.

IX

1810–1811

*James Wood, the Miser—Lady Jersey and Lady Buckinghamshire—
Dorothy Jordan—General Lefebvre.*

James Wood, the famous miser, was one of the sheriffs of Gloucester in October
1811. He cane of a family long connected with Gloucester and Cheltenham, was
a partner in banks in both places, and owned a good deal of property and land in
Cheltenham (which was, in 1826, selling for a thousand guineas the acre), though
Gloucester was where he lived. The original well at Cheltenham was situated in
the hamlet or tithing of Alstone, which for long maintained an individuality, and
was separated from Cheltenham by the Chelt. The stream was crossed behind
Promenade Terrace by a rustic bridge, known from some legendary association
with the old miser as Jemmy Wood's Bridge. Jimmy owned the Hatherley Estate,
part of Bayshill, and the upper part of the town, known as Sandford, while the new
road by St Luke's Church was named after his principal heir, Sir Matthew Wood.

There are pictures about of Jimmy (or Jemmy) and a resident in Cheltenham
had a plaster cast of him. His profile formed an almost perfect triangle, of which
the apex was the point of his nose. "His forehead and chin sloped away from each
other at a sharp angle, while his nasal organ was well-developed, and mouth and
eyes indicated a love of pleasure."

It speaks rather well for the Gloucester people of his day that Wood's well-
known wealth did not gain for him much influence nor respect, and that he
was never elected Mayor. Indeed, he was little esteemed in his native city, and
certainly the Corporation did not toady to its millionaire alderman. Influence
of a kind no doubt he gained by his money transactions, but it would have been
almost impossible for such a man to have gained the liking or respect of his
fellow-citizens, even if any of them had truckled to his stupendous possessions.

His grandfather, also named James, had established the Old Gloucester Bank in
the year 1716, and the *History and Description of Gloucestershire* says, "that it was the
oldest private bank in the Kingdom except Child's, and that Jemmy was perhaps

the richest commoner in His Majesty's Dominions." In 1805, the Woods' Bank was licensed for the sale of tickets in the State Lottery and, indeed, the miser was a wonderful salesman of anything and everything.

Jemmy, though he never married, used to say that when he was a young man he courted a young lady at Dymock, and loved her dearly. One can hardly imagine the old miser leaving his hoards of gold in Gloucester and roaming about the gleaming and glittering golden-green and golden-daffodil fields of Dymock and Newent with a sweetheart. "And I should have married her," Jemmy would add, "but she jilted me and married another. I could not marry another woman. It was too bad of her—too bad. It can't be helped. I never could trust another."

From an entry in Mr Wood's diary he appears to have been going strong in his native city in 1795.

"July 15th, 1818: Dined at The Nag's Head. A dinner given to the Duke of Gloucester, after he had been laying the Foundation Stone at Berkeley, for the Berkeley Canal, about forty-seven dined. A large turtle given by Lord Howard to the Corporation of about 150 lbs weight. Among the Company was Lord Somers, Col. Berkeley, and his brother the Captain, Sir William Guise. The Mayor introduces J. W. to the Duke who sayd: He was happy to see me in such good health as he remembered me twenty-three years ago in Gloster and talked very friendley." The old Duke of Gloucester, therefore, was in Gloucester and very likely in Cheltenham too, in 1795, and in later days his son, the then Duke of Gloucester (who saw most objects of interest in the neighbourhood of Cheltenham), called upon James Wood. "How do you do, your Royal Highness?" inquired Jemmy, while bowing and scraping and smiling with excitement and glee: "Very well, I thank you," replied his Royal Highness. "Will you, your Royal Highness, when you go home, give my best respects to His Majesty?" The Duke laughed very heartily, and said, "I will, Mr Wood."

Mr Wood's first cousin, Anthony Ellis, lived in Westgate Street, in a house opposite to the Shire Hall, and had an ironmonger's shop. He was very rich, had large landed property in the county and was believed to have been a partner in the Old Bank. Jemmy was shorter, stouter and fatter than his cousin, who was a tall, thin, wiry man. The two were said to have made a compact that whoever died first should leave his property to the survivor.

Jemmy was very excited at the time of the bank panic, and he went about saying: "Ah! Ah! there will soon be only one bank in Gloucester." Someone repeated this remark to Robert Morris, the rival banker, and Mr Morris dashed into the Old Gloucester Bank, very angry indeed: "Do you mean to insinuate, Sir, that _____" "Stop, stop!" said Jemmy, "I meant no harm. I meant that we shall soon give up our bank, and then there will be only one bank in Gloucester, and that will be yours, Mr Morris. Ah! Ah! and that will be yours." But alas! shortly afterwards, Mr Morris's bank closed its doors. About the only known act of generosity on Mr Wood's part was that he cashed some notes of Messrs Morris and Turner's for the man who warned him to cash no more of their notes as the bank had failed. This acquaintance doubtless saved Jemmy from considerable loss by his timely warning, but, even so, he must have been surprised at the miser's unwonted liberality.

Anthony Ellis died about this time, when his immense riches passed to the miser. When Ellis was dying he had the satisfaction of a visit from his cousin, who dashed into his room in great excitement, and yelled into the ear of the dying man the delightful sentence: "Morris's Bank is broke!" It is said that Anthony's satisfaction was evident, and that "a gleam of pleasure and delight played over the surface of his lean, haggard face, like ripples gambolling over the surface of a pool." James rubbed his hands and again bawled: "There will soon be but one bank in Gloucester, and that will be ours." Anthony nodded his approval of the prophecy and then sank exhausted upon his pillow in a lethargic slumber. He was a miser too, and after his death about a ton of coppers, many of them corroded with verdigris, were got out of his cellar with a pickaxe. There were several tin boxes filled with guineas, and money was hidden about in the most unheard-of places.

It is recorded that Jemmy attended funerals in the capacity of undertaker, and that in about 1823 or 1824 he attended the funeral of Mrs Page of Honeycombe, Miserdine (either the sister or daughter of the Rev. Giles Mills), who was buried at Pitchcombe, near Stroud, upon which occasion "James Wood, Esq, was the undertaker."

James was very attentive and very obsequious, he possessed a remarkable talent for shedding tears at such times, and, indeed, the writer of a very scarce pamphlet about him says that he was too zealous a tradesman to have neglected a single detail of his profession. He would take with him a supply of gloves, scarves, hatbands, etc.

In the bank he charged an exorbitantly high rate of interest, and neglected no opportunity of getting the better of his unfortunate clients.

Jemmy Wood had been very much interested in the illuminations in Gloucester after the Peace of 1814. He says in his MS Book: "A very handsome pedistal Erected at The Cross, with the Gt. Warriors' names on, and w'ch cost upwards of £30, raised by subscription, wch was Lighted up variegated Lamps—the Tolsey and the Churchs very bright with candles … Wm. Morris, Esq., had in transparency, Bonaparte sitting on a Rock repenting his Fate, etc., and several large stars."

Cheltenham people often say that his servant Jacob once advised his master to get a new suit of clothes before he went up to London, saying that he himself would never go there in such clothes as Wood wore. But Jemmy said there was nobody in London who would know him and that his clothes would do very well. Some weeks afterwards Jacob tried again: "If I were you, Mr Wood, I would really have a new suit of clothes made; I should be ashamed to be seen in Gloucester walking about in those old shabby clothes." "Tis no odds, Jacob, these will do very well," said the miser, "tisn't as if I were going away from home, Jacob; these will do for me."

Jemmy got a thrashing once from the bailiff of one of his tenants who found the banker pulling his master's turnips early one morning in a field, and another story is that Mr Wood used to buy opium cough pills from a chemist. in Gloucester, which he re-sold at a profit. At last he went to the chemist and asked him in a coaxing manner, if he could not divide them and make two dozen pills out of one dozen. He did so, and the head of the Old Gloucester Bank doubled his former profits.

An old Gloucester man used to say: "Afore the railway kimd about, gaffer, all the coal was brought to our quay. 'Twere a bizzy pleece then, and no misteek, I duz tell 'cc; and at times thur wur a vleet of Shropshire barges thur wi' coal, and thur wuz a passul o' coal about the wharf, and thur wuz lots o' bits o'n't dropt about the pleece. You wudn't believe it, but it be sartin true, but ha' zeed old Jemmy Wood, the banker, come down in the morning and walk about, an' I ha' zeed un hundreds and hundreds o' times stoop and pick up bits o' coal and put un in his pocket." Even the Gloucester children knew of Jimmy's love of money and would sometimes heat halfpennies to an almost incandescent state, put them in the banker's path, and await results!

It is said that when a servant girl went to Jemmy's shop to buy a yard of tape for apron strings, the millionaire would use every means in his power to cajole her into buying another yard. He would fold up the tape into a kind of rosette, saying, "My nice little girl, you should have another yard; a boss would look so nice."

One day, when Jemmy was coining home from Tewkesbury a heavy shower of rain came on. The driver of a hearse offered him a lift inside, which Jemmy thankfully accepted, and lay down in the place occupied by a coffin. He told the man to set him down outside Gloucester; but the driver knew his Jemmy, drove him into the city, and set him down at his own door.

And we have seen, Mr Wood had never married, and had no relatives left so far as was known—at least he acknowledged none except his two sisters and his cousin, Anthony Ellis, all of whom had died before him. His fellow-citizens used to wonder what he would do with his great wealth. He sometimes remarked that he should do something for old Gloucester, and this would have been most acceptable to the civic authorities, for the Corporation was heavily in debt. Jemmy always remembered the injunction of his father, who said: "James, don't thee leave thy money in charity, it only makes so many rogues." When people proposed that he should build and endow almshouses, Jemmy would rub his hands and with a pleasant chuckle, reiterated the words of his parent: "Ay, ay, and make rogues." His name was never seen in subscription lists, he never gave to beggars, nor, in fact, gave anything away; but he did not starve himself, nor collect things that other people had thrown away, except coal from barges and wagons.

A Cheltenham lady remarked that some relative had told her that the miser used to have a notice up in his shop:

"Red flannel sold here: nine times dyed for rheumatism."

Alderman Sir Matthew Wood had become known to the miser's sisters, and one of them had left him some money. Sir Matthew had come down to hear her will read and to attend the funeral. Here Jimmy met him for the first time and took a great fancy to his namesake, to whom he gave a house at Hatherley, showing him other kindnesses as well, and before Mr Wood's death, which occurred on the 20th of April 1836, after a short illness, Alderman Wood was summoned by Jacob from London, and found the banker in a state of extreme drowsiness on the morning of the 20th, and this continued until the evening, when he died. There was prolonged and expensive litigation about James Wood's will. He left his property to Alderman Wood of London (who was not related to him), to John Chadborn of Gloucester and John Surman of Gloucester, and later of Cheltenham, but a half-burnt copy of a codicil was found, leaving money to other people as well, and £200,000 to the City of Gloucester. The executors in the end got all the money, though the disappointed Corporation advertised wildly in the local papers in the hope of getting the codicil to Wood's will. One of these advertisements appeared in the *Cheltenham Chronicle* of Thursday, 16th June 1836. Though the executors had won the lawsuit, the tale got about that someone put a fly in Jimmy Wood's mouth after he was dead and said that there was life in him when his dead hand was guided to sign the will, and that a codicil was destroyed.

Two of the most remarkable women of the Georgian Era spent most of the evening of their days in Cheltenham—the Countesses of Buckinghamshire and Jersey. The former continued at the Spa the series of lively and original entertainments which had made her such a social success in London. The latter appeared at all sorts of fashionable functions until she died at her residence in Cheltenham and, after her death, her ghost is said to have haunted the house in Cambray in which she died. It must be confessed that the earthly career of the famous Countess was one calculated to make any self-respecting spirit restless. Daughter of Dr Twisden, Bishop of Derry and Raphoe, she was styled "the beautiful Miss Twisden" before her marriage to the fourth Earl of Jersey, and her behaviour seems to have early shocked some of her old friends.

Mrs Delany wrote of the young lady: "She is very fine, superbly *à la mode*, and has lost much of her prettiness and will soon, I fear, lose her life. It is a pity, for she wants neither parts nor sensibility, but every good quality is lost in vanity, and the love of what is falsely called pleasure." Lady Morgan (herself, like Mrs Delany, a frequent visitor to Cheltenham) says in her *Memoirs*:

"When that most fashionable of French novels, *Les Liaisons Dangereux*, came out, it was discussed at Devonshire House whether the character of *Madame la Presidente* was not a libel on probability and female morals. The late Duke of Devonshire remarked that he thought he knew one such woman, but refused to name her.

The next moment every one present confessed that they had known one such woman also, but refused to name their fair friend. Curiosity became vehement, and Lord John Townshend proposed that each person should write their secret on a slip of paper. Each person present wrote the name of the Dowager Countess of Jersey."

To the Countess of Jersey belongs the somewhat doubtful distinction of having influenced the Prince of Wales to throw over Mrs Fitzherbert and to marry Caroline of Brunswick, who was not likely to compete with herself. At that time the Prince was completely under the influence of the adventurous Countess, although she was some years his senior. "The moment," said the Princess of Wales, "I saw my husband and Lady Jersey together, I knew how it all was."

Lady Jersey was, for many years, a frequent visitor to Cheltenham before she ultimately made her home there. Her notorious career did not make her any the less acceptable a guest in many fashionable circles in London and Cheltenham; rather the reverse. The local newspaper gives an account of one of the many entertainments graced in Cheltenham by the presence of the Countesses of Jersey and Buckinghamshire:

"On Friday last, Baron Pfeilitzer gave a *déjeuner à l'ambigu* at Ashgrove Gardens. The company arrived soon after one, and at three were seated to an elegant cold collation, consisting of every rarity of the season, with the choicest wines. The tables were laid in the grounds for 120." (Then follows a list of the Baron's distinguished guests.) "A Pandean Band played during the whole entertainment, and *fantoccini* performances were exhibited, with which the company were much amused. Dancing concluded this novel and diversified fete, which lasted till the evening closed."

Tom Moore tells in his diary how Lord Strangford came to see him, bringing for his inspection a daybook formerly belonging to George Villiers, Duke of Buckingham, which, his Lordship said, had been given to him years before, in Cheltenham, by old Lady Jersey.

The lively old lady, whose doings had once made the tongues of her many enemies wag fast, passed away at her residence in Cambray, in August 1821. Only a few days afterwards her bitter enemy, Queen Caroline, was also carried to her grave. And King George took just as little notice of one event as of the other.

If the doings of the Dowager Countess of Jersey were regarded with astonished awe by an indulgent age, Albinia, Countess of Buckinghamshire aroused the smiles and jests of her contemporaries. Despite her notoriety, it is to her credit that she was never the subject of any unpleasant scandal. In her youth, as in her old age, and, indeed, throughout her life, she was in the forefront of everything that was fashionable. Every one told tales of her, gaped at her high play, her acting and her dancing, and Society flocked to her rural breakfasts and her midnight suppers, held in insect-haunted arbours and on damp river-banks.

Albinia was born in 1736, the daughter of Lord Vere Bertie. In May 1757 she married George Hobart, son of the second Lord Buckinghamshire, and it was as Mrs Hobart that the fair Albinia shone most brightly in London Society. She got up concerts and private theatricals galore, and always had the newest lions roaring at her parties, which were constantly described in the European magazine, *Bon Ton*, and such like periodicals.

Lady Archer and Lady Mount Edgcumbe were depicted with her in Gillray's famous caricature, as Faro's Daughters, because the three of them played the game so often, so well, and for such high stakes. In her middle age the then Countess of Buckinghamshire grew very stout, and Gillray at that time made her the central figure in a series of rather cruel caricatures. She formed one of a company of amateurs who acted at Brandenburg House, Hammersmith, in the private theatre which Colonel Berkeley's aunt, the Margravine of Anspach, had built for the amusement of her "court." Despite the fact that she resembled a "spangle pudding," the Countess acted so well and danced so lightly that a wit declared that "her activity could only be accounted for on the ground that she was hollow."

Lady Buckinghamshire and Colonel Greville (a fop of the first water) founded a society of amateur, or as they styled themselves *dilettanti*, actors, under the name of The Pic Nic Club; so-called from the manner in which its members were to contribute mutually to the general entertainment. At its meeting members were called upon to perform on the flageolet, the double bass, etc, whilst the sprightly Countess herself presided at the harpsichord. At other times they performed farces and burlesques or organised other amusements then fashionable. Lady Buckinghamshire was a specialist in inventing new kinds of entertainments. Sometimes each member would draw from a bag a ticket describing the portion of the entertainment he or she was to provide. The society was in existence for some years, but in 1803 it began to sink under the attacks of the satirists. At least one of the rural breakfasts for which this sanguine-spirited lady was most famous, was attended by the Prince of Wales and the Duke of Clarence, and Horace Walpole describes another of these functions:

> "Mrs Hobart had announced a rural breakfast at Sans Souci, nothing being so pastoral as a fat grandmother in a row of houses on Ham Common. It rained early in the morning; she despatched post-boys for want of Cupids and Zephyrs to stop the nymphs and shepherds who tend their flocks in Pall Mall and St James's, but half of them missed the couriers and arrived."

Though well past three score years and ten, the lively lady continued to exercise her ingenuity in providing thrills for her friends when she settled down in Cheltenham. Thus, in September 1810, she gave an elegant fete to "all the rank and fashion." The company began to arrive soon after eight o'clock, when a Pandean Band, stationed in the grounds of her residence, St Julia's Cottage, "contributed to enliven a scene of gaiety seldom witnessed at this distance from the metropolis." Dancing was one of the amusements of the evening, though whether the active septuagenarian joined in her favourite relaxation or not is not recorded. At twelve her eighty guests were ushered into the supper-room, which had two draped recesses with painted inscriptions, "*L'ombre d'une fête dans un cabinet*," and dedicated to "Thalia," the latter out of compliment to Mrs Jordan, then playing at the theatre, who was the lioness of the evening.

On the ensuing New Year's Eve the Countess of Buckinghamshire gave a numerously and aristocratically attended *déjeuner après minuit*, to usher in the New Year. The decorations were roses in full bloom. There was a *Loterie pour les Dames* and verses had been written for the occasion by Lady Graves.

"In 1811," writes Mr Sergeant, one of her biographers, "Mrs Jordan went again to Cheltenham, and to her doom."

The Duke of Gloucester and Viscount Strangford arrived in the town, and also the Marquis of Thomond, husband of Mary Palmer, Sir Joshua Reynolds's niece and heiress, Lord Suffolk, and Lord and Lady Ormonde. The town was filled with fashionables, as it had been in the old happy days in 1788 when Dorothy Jordan had shared with George III the honours of the stage on which the Cheltenham pageant had been presented, and she herself was enormously successful, and more popular than ever.

The days of her happiness and worldly success were destined however, to end suddenly, for now a royal prince, and the future King of England had deserted the woman who had been his wife in everything but name for so many years and was the mother of all the Fitzclarences.

"In 1811," says Boaden, "Mrs Jordan was again acting in Cheltenham, when a letter from the Duke of Clarence, communicating the Duke's intention of separating from her, and desiring her to meet him if possible at Maidenhead Bridge, was received."

Despite this staggering blow, and dreadfully weakened by a succession of fainting fits, Dorothy Jordan arrived at the theatre, for it was her friend Watson's benefit, and this generous woman would not let her own supreme misery upset the manager's arrangements and injure him financially. The great actress played her part of Nell in "The Devil to Pay," and struggled on until Jobson arrived at the passage in which he had to accuse the Conjurer of making her laughing drunk. Then when Nell "here attempted to laugh, the afflicted woman burst into tears. Here Jobson, with great presence of mind, altered the text and exclaimed to her: 'Why, Nell, the Conjurer has not only made thee drunk; he has made thee crying-drunk;' thus covering her personal distress, and carrying her through the scene in character.

"After the performance she was put into a travelling chariot; still in her stage dress, to keep her appointment with the Royal Duke, in a state of anguish not easily to be described."

Harriot Mellon, as Volante
in *The Honeymoon*. After
Sir William Beechey, R.A.

Thus, at Cheltenham Spa, and on the stage of Watson's neat and commodious theatre fate did her worst with Dorothy Jordan, and the Queen of Mirth played an unrehearsed part as Queen of Tragedy, and, as Mr Sergeant has said, "her inimitable laugh died out in a wail of anguish." One can easily imagine the scene outside the theatre when the sympathetic Irishman Watson, the dramatic historian Oxberry and the ready-tongued Jobson, hustled the weeping Queen of Comedy into the "travelling chariot," which drove hurriedly off up the High Street. Mrs Siddons at the old Coffee House Yard Playhouse in Cheltenham floated off on the "tide which leads on to Fortune." To the greatest English tragic actress the Garden Town was very kind, to her less respectable but far more lovable sister, "Thalia" the Cambray Theatre turned Comedy into Tragedy once and for ever.

On Maidenhead Bridge, Warren Hastings, home from India, a broken man, had summoned his Marian from Cheltenham to meet him: Warren Hastings, perhaps the most faithful lover in history. On Maidenhead Bridge the future King of England turned the knife once more in the bleeding heart of one whose former faults and follies had been to some extent redeemed by an abiding love. What happened at Maidenhead, no one knows, nor was it ever explained why the Duke threw Mrs Jordan over. Most likely, if the truth could be revealed, the future King's financial difficulties were at the bottom of the affair, for though it was said that he made generous settlements upon her, yet these do not seem to have been paid. Not that the discarded mistress ever complained of any breach of the compact; she was too generous minded and simple of soul for that; but she found it necessary for her children's sake to return to the career on the stage which it had been agreed she should abandon. The Duke's treatment of her is as full of mysteries as were her last days, which were spent in disguise in Paris. She had fled from England, in fear of arrest for debt, having been brought into financial straits by the blackguardism of her son-in-law, Alsop. Apparently she died on the 3rd of July 1816, and was buried in the Cemetery at St Cloud, though there were those—including her daughter, Frances Alsop, an actress well-known in Cheltenham, and her biographer and confidant, Boaden—who declared that they had seen her in London after she was supposed to be dead and buried. In 1812 the affair of General Lefebvre was a nine days' wonder in Cheltenham.

At the height of the Napoleonic struggle some of the prisoners of war were quartered in Cheltenham. They consisted of three generals and several private soldiers and were located in Cambray, the Tewkesbury Road and the High Street. The three generals lived at No. 131 High Street. They were allowed a parole of three miles around the limits of the town. Among the number was General Lefebvre, who was allowed to come to Cheltenham, accompanied by his wife, at the request of Colonel Macleod of Colbecks, who was an old friend of his. Macleod had himself been detained in France and had been shown much kindness while there.

General Lefebvre Desnouettes was a great favourite with Bonaparte, who, it is said, made him a Count in one of the first creations of his own nobility; but the General did not make use of the title. He was married to the daughter of an eminent banker in Paris. The *Cheltenham Chronicle* thought that Madame Lefebvre was the daughter of Monsieur Petagaux, who was the banker of the English. General Lefebvre was taken in a skirmish between the advanced parties of the French and British cavalry at Benevale, in Spain, just at the close of the campaign of 1808, when Soult, followed by Bonaparte in person, advanced against the British army. He defended himself bravely, having his clothes much cut about by the sabres of the British dragoons. He was much distressed at the thought that he would be blamed by Bonaparte for suffering himself to be taken in so foolish a way; and Bonaparte did, indeed, blame him in the bulletin relating to the occurrence, although with some commendation of his courage.

When General Lefebvre was taken prisoner, he requested that Sir John Moore would allow him to go to Calais by land, as a passage by sea always impaired his health, saying that on his honour as an officer he would proceed to Dover and give himself up as a prisoner of war. Sir John Moore said that he might meet with some danger crossing the Channel, but he would allow him a frigate which he knew would go to any quarter of the globe without difficulty, and would soon waft him over the bay. The General and his wife arrived at the Spa in February 1811. Goding says of him that he was unquestionably one of the most remarkable and valiant men who belonged to Napoleon's armies and adds: "His life was a romance and his connection with this place necessarily links the town with the general history of the great wars. He is well remembered by many of our residents and is spoken of as a person of a very affable and mild demeanour."

In March 1811, the hospitable Lady Buckinghamshire gave "an elegant *goûter*" to Madame Lefebvre. One of the gentlemen present wrote the following lines to the Countess:

> "*Albinia, toujours nouvelle,*
> *Du temps qui fuit semble arrêter le cours,*
> *Pour 1'admirer, it s'arrête auprès d'elle,*
> *Pour plaire aux graces il prolonge les jours.*"

Verses seem to have been a necessary adjunct to entertainments in those days.

Colonel and Mrs Macleod, of course, did all in their power to lighten Lefebvre's captivity, and we are told that the General besides being allowed to come to this town and remain here on this parole, was allowed at the request of Colonel Macleod to go to London for medical advice; and on that occasion he received polite attention from several persons of distinction. The physicians whom he consulted, much to their honour, refused to take any fees from him.

On 11th June 1811 General Lefebvre's name appears in the list of fashionable arrivals at Cheltenham Spa; this is, probably, the date on which he returned from his trip to London, which he perhaps had made in the hope of getting reliable news of his beloved Emperor. The General and his wife mingled with the upper walks of Society and made themselves familiar with the residents by their attendance at all places of public resort. Albinia, Countess of Buckinghamshire, gave a party for the French *Générale*. In addition, therefore, to the indulgence shown to him by the authorities, General Lefebvre was treated with the most marked attention and politeness by the residents and visitors of distinction in the town. As an instance of the kindness shown to him on all sides, the *Chronicle* says:

> "General Lefebvre had an excellent watch when he was taken which he valued highly, and such was the attention shown to him that his watch, after three years bestowed in research and inquiry among the dragoons engaged in the skirmish, and afterwards in guarding the prisoner, was at length by the exertions of the Earl of Moira and the Prince Regent, recovered last summer, and sent down to him in this town by the hands of Major Carnac, Private Secretary to Sir H. Wellesley."

There was an idea that the General might be exchanged for the Earl of Beverley, "but no definite arrangement was come to, nor likely to be."

Lefebvre's doings in Cheltenham are told at length by the *Cheltenham Chronicle*, and one can well imagine the consternation which filled the "Fashionables" when the news of their prisoner's escape, after about a year's residence, fell like a bolt from the blue.

The *Chronicle* of 14th May 1812, says:

> "The French General, Lefebvre Desnouettes, has absconded from his parole in this town."

The Town Crier went through the streets, bell in hand, to proclaim the affair to poor Colonel Macleod and his indignant fellow-townsmen. They certainly had reason to be angry, but there is, perhaps, some excuse for Lefebvre in the fact that the fortune of war had turned against Napoleon, and it is impossible to realise the fascination this great leader exercised over his followers. The Grenadier in the poem said he should rise from his grave to guard Napoleon, and General Lefebvre, for the same reason, broke his parole and turned him again from his captivity.

The *Cheltenham Chronicle* tells us that "The Commissioners now conducting His Majesty's Transport Service have offered a reward of ten guineas for the recapture of the following prisoners to any person who shall apprehend them or deliver them at their Office, or any otherwise cause them to be securely lodged in one of the public gaols. The Secretary of State for the Home Department has received a most insolent letter from him in justification of his breach of parole. The other French Officers who are prisoners here are we understand to be removed to Abergavenny … where upwards of 120 French Officers are now on parole, and about 30 more expected. They behave remarkably well and are treated with the greatest civility by the inhabitants."

The indignant scribe of the *Chronicle* continues:

> "He was a soldier, for we will not talk of his being an officer of the Legion of Honour, and he broke his word; he was treated with particular favour and respect by the Government, and he forgot the kindness shown to him; he was at large, in a great degree upon the security of his friend and he deserted his bail. We do not think very highly of Bonaparte, but we are almost certain he will send back this fellow to be immured in a prison as his conduct demands, or at least that he will not suffer him to dishonour his presence by allowing him to appear before him, nor his service by employing him."

The journalist also commends Sir John Moore for having insisted on sending Lefebvre to England in a frigate and remarks that: "His subsequent conduct is a proof of how much his honour could have been relied upon, and it is to be hoped that if our Government demands him, Lord Cathcart will be as attentive to his conveyance as was Sir John Moore."

And again:

"It is a matter of exultation to our townsmen and genuine pleasure to ourselves to have learnt the recapture of General Lefebvre who recently broke his parole and escaped with his wife and servant from this place. He was taken by the gallant Kutusoff in the last discomfiture of the French near Wilna ... We understand Government purposes making application to the Court of St Petersburg for the above officer; but we conceive he will save the Russians the trouble of delivery by escaping to France: but should he arrive he may rely on not having the benefit of the Cheltenham Waters. (January 1813)."

And on:

"18th February 1813. General Lefebvre, in whom English hospitality engendered ingratitude, instead of being hemmed in by the frozen walls of a Russian prison (if we may believe a Parisian Declaration) is at this moment receiving the tributary cavalry horses in that capital for remounts for the proposed retaliatory campaign."

Later we are told:

"General Lefebvre Desnouettes was severely wounded in the late conflict in Brienne. He is so fully infatuated in favour of Napoleon that we anticipate he will adhere to the fragments of his ruin and eventually fall with him. He received a wound through the body with a bayonet."

From this wound Lefebvre never recovered, and he closed his chequered career as he would have chosen—dying of injuries received while fighting by the side of his beloved Emperor.

In the following March (1812) the *Cheltenham Chronicle* records the death of Albinia, Countess of Buckinghamshire. The local recording angel writes:

"Her liberality gave new life to the distressed. No tale of sorrow ever reached her ear unheeded. She was the munificent patroness of all who were distressed. The innate cheerfulness of her spotless mind endeared her to all her acquaintances."

X

1812–1813

Joseph Pitt of Pittville—Lord Byron at Berkeley Castle and at Cheltenham, 1812—Lady Oxford at Georgiana Cottage, Cambray, 1812—The Death of John Boles Watson, 1813—The French Royal Family, 1813.

One of the makers of Cheltenham was Joseph Pitt, the builder of Pittville Pump Room, and the man who developed the Pittville Estate and made the lovely Pittville Gardens. He was born in 1759, the son of Joseph and Ann Pitt of Little Widecombe, in the parish of Badgworth, near Cheltenham, and formerly of Brockenborough, in Wiltshire.

Lord Campbell, the great lawyer whom Joseph Pitt assisted in his parliamentary career, says that a solicitor had taken a fancy to his patron, Pitt, who was very poor in his youth, and had helped him on in life. Pitt moved to Cirencester, where he later became Bailiff of the Borough, and afterwards Steward, and in 1792, Clerk to the Court of Bequests. Subsequently he was a senior partner in the banking firm of Pitt, Gardner, Croome, Bowlby and Wood (afterwards the County of Gloucester Bank), which had its head office at 106 High Street, Cheltenham, and branch offices at Cirencester and Tetbury. The Wood who was one of Joseph Pitt's partners was none other than the famous Jemmy.

Lord Campbell also speaks of Mr Pitt as a brewer, and possibly he was a partner in Gardner's Brewery, as Mr John Gardner was so closely connected with him in the Bank. In 1812, Pitt started upon his parliamentary career, and sat continuously for Cricklade from that year onwards in five successive Parliaments. He was already active in Cheltenham, for the *Chronicle* of 8th October 1812, writes:

"Among the recent improvements to our town, there is none more richly deserving public approval than that which is making opposite The Crescent. The original walk from the Churchyard to the Well Bridge, which during the autumnal and winter months was generally inundated, uneven and dangerous, is now superseded by a semi-circular pathway on the left of the Crescent Road, which sweeps gradually to the termination, and although it increases the distance a few yards, compensates by affording a substantial footing and a more extended view of surrounding scenery. The space to the left of the old path is to be enclosed by palisades, and planted as a shrubbery, which will render the tout ensemble suitable in affinity with the elegant pile it fronts. The undertaking was commenced by J. Pitt, Esq, Cirencester, to whom we are indebted for several local adornments, and whose taste is only equalled by his liberality."

Pitt bought an estate at Wootton Bassett, though he never lived there, and sold it in 1818; and he had another at Southrop. His country seat was at Eastcourt, which is situated between Cirencester and Malmesbury, in the parish of Crudwell. In this house Mr Pitt, who was a great amateur of art, collected many beautiful pictures. One of these was a picture of King Charles and Henrietta Maria by Van Dyck, which he purchased with Southrop from Dr Chandler.

Mr Pitt was evidently a very keen politician, for he chose as his first London residence, 37 Great George Street, Westminster, in order that he might be near the House of Commons. One of his parliamentary successes was the Act of Enclosure for the inhabitants of Malmesbury which he succeeded in getting passed. There had been 500 acres of heath or open common land near the town. The Act of Enclosure divided this into plots of between an acre and an acre and a half for 230 freehold burgesses of the Corporation. Almost the whole of this waste land was subsequently dug over with the spade; and brought into cultivation, and the working of these small holdings enabled many poor men with large families to live without parochial relief. The cost of such relief went down from £2074 in 1819 to £1424 in 1830—30 per cent—despite a considerable increase in the population.

As Mr Pitt's fortunes rose, he invested greatly in land. Thus he had other property in Cheltenham besides Pittville, and he had a great deal to do with the "Tontine," by which the Cambray Estate was exploited.

Pitt, Henry Thompson, and other speculators had invested largely in land in Cheltenham, and had made great plans for the development of the Spa, in the hope that success would crown the labour of such an undertaking. But scarcely had these golden dreams assumed even a dreamlike consistency when the commercial panic which at this period seized the country dissolved the magic spell and the baseless fabric of prosperity melted into thin air. Such is the history of the Pittville Bubble as told ten years later by the disillusioned writer of a guide. Meantime, some one hundred of the projected six hundred houses had been built. Undaunted by the failure of the greater number of his fellow-speculators, Mr Pitt, with a magnificent courage and a splendid faith, carried out his part of the contract unfalteringly. He laid out the grounds in 1824, with many walks and drives, planted the trees and proceeded to build the imposing Pump Room. He would have made a splendid showman for he had an eye for effect, and he knew how to get a splendid advertisement for his scheme. This was nothing less than a wonderful masonic ceremony for the laying of the foundation stone which brought people from far and near.

The great day, 4th May 1825, was rung in by a peal of joy-bells by "the Painswick Youths." Later the Brethren of the Provincial Grand Lodge and many local lodges assembled at the Masonic Hall, recently erected in Portland Street; and robed in masonic costume and with full regalia they marched to a service at the Parish Church, conducted by the Rev. J. Edwards, Vicar of Prestbury. They then proceeded to the site of the new Pump Room, every window and balcony being filled with ladies anxious to witness the novel and unprecedented scene. On arrival on the scene enormous crowds had gathered to witness the solemn ceremony which was performed by Thomas Quarrington, Esquire, the Deputy Grand Master for the Province of Gloucestershire, acting by delegation from the Duke of Beaufort. Later the Masons dined together at the Victoria Hotel and the purchasers and proprietors of land in Pittville at the Imperial Hotel, Mr Pitt's partner, Mr John Gardner, presiding. The day closed by a grand display of fireworks in the vicinity of Evesham turnpike alongside the new estate, for which joyous event the principal mechanic at Vauxhall had been specially engaged. Even the elements joined in the celebrations for it is recorded that the fireworks were accompanied by a marvellous display of lightning which added very effectively to the scene.

The Pump Room took five years in building and was opened by the lessee in 1830, the opening date being postponed for a time owing to the national mourning at the death of George IV. The gala opening was a great success, twelve hundred paying the seven and sixpence for a ticket of admission to the "breakfast" held at midday. This was followed by a ball from 2.30 to 6 pm in the Pump Room for the younger people, an invisible band playing in the gallery right up the dome. Another band played by the lake for those who did not care to enter into the dancing. Subsequently other public "breakfasts" were held as well as exhibitions, panoramic views, etc, but Pittville appears to have been never really well patronised. Its distance—three quarters of a mile from the High Street and further still from the other spas—was against it. Cheltenham's days as a fashionable spa were coming to a close.

Mr Joseph Pitt therefore found the Fates against him. What might have been a most lucrative enterprise failed to attract. It was certainly due to no fault of his. The scheme was a splendid one and magnificently this man of big ideas carried it out. There was no stinting in the expenditure of money. He had built a really handsome Pump Room and thrown five stone bridges over each end of the lake. A landscape gardener with a true artist's eye had planted many a splendid tree, planned beautiful vistas through lovely flowering shrubs. The park and Pump Room remain to-day the monument of a "big" man. Yet Cheltonians know nothing of Mr Pitt and are mostly ignorant even of how Pittville got its name.

Joseph Pitt died in 1842 in the eighty-third year of his age, and was buried at Crudwell.

After Pitt's death East Court and its pictures were sold, in consequence of the heavy debts hanging over his estate, owing to the unfortunate venture at Pittville. Another bad speculation of his was £60,000 he lost in a Bristol bank. Mr Pitt must have been an extremely wealthy man at one time, but he seems to have dissipated the greater part of his property by unfortunate speculations before his death. A man of very simple tastes, he was full of culture and devoted to art. Pitt was married three times and had a numerous family. Cornelius, his son by his first wife, was vicar of Chedworth near Cheltenham, and afterwards rector of Rendcomb, being succeeded in the latter living by his son, Joe Pitt, a very celebrated sporting parson of whom many tales are told.

Sir Reginald Graham, who was master of the Cotswold Hounds in the early seventies, writes in his reminiscences: "I must not forget a quaint character who had a peculiar fascination for me and many others. This was the Reverend Joseph Pitt of Rendcomb Rectory, a fox-hunting parson of the old school. At the time I speak of he was about sixty years of age, with a grim, rugged face, shaggy eyebrows, and a twinkle in his eye which betokened the fund of comic humour concealed under his weather-beaten *visage*. Very clerical was his costume, always a tall hat, somewhat ruffled, a profusion of white neck-cloth, a long, black greatcoat and inevitable umbrella, which he carried in his hand even when mounted for the chase. In deep, sonorous tones he addressed everybody as 'Sir,' but most of his friends called him 'Joe.' He was very fond of expeditions to see other hunts, especially the Duke of Beaufort's, though the difficulty for him on these occasions was to elude the vigilance of his spouse; a lady with decided views on domestic discipline, who kept an ever-watchful eye on such proceedings, and discouraged his wanderings after what she called 'strange packs of hounds.' He sometimes asked me to organise a plan with him to meet the Duke's hounds at Trouble House or Newton Lodge, but Mrs Pitt would be sure to get wind of it, and put her foot down in opposition to the scheme.

"The Rev. Joe would say, 'But, my dear, I promised to pay my respects to the Duke. His Grace will expect me.' ... To which she would reply: 'Nonsense. Stay at home and look after your parish.' Again he pleaded: 'But, my dear, you would not have me break my word,' and sure enough the next morning would find this errant divine at Trouble House, with what I believe are called gropelows over his trousers, mounted on his old bay horse (who made a noise and rejoiced in the name of Musical) pounding on all day long, popping over the walls as they came, murmuring while in the air, 'Capital, Sir,' and on landing, 'Wonderful, Sir.' To the last moment he would stay with them, little heeding the Trouble House he would surely find that evening at the Rectory." At the end of the hunting season Sir Reginald Graham says that he himself would remark to Mr Pitt: "I wonder when we shall meet again," and that "with an air of profound mystery," the Rev.

Joseph would answer: "Perhaps, Sir, I might have to be in the neighbourhood of Epsom on some important business about the very last week in May." Sir Reginald, however, never saw him at the Derby and thought that there Mrs Pitt drew the line.

"Joseph Pitt of Pittville, the rector's grandfather," adds Sir Reginald, "had by his third wife, Ann Orlidge, of Bristol, four sons and two daughters. Of the sons the eldest, Joseph, became a barrister and afterwards stamp distributor at Lichfield; the second, William Gregson, was put in by his father to manage the County of Gloster Bank at Cheltenham. He also hunted the staghounds in Craven Berkeley's absence. He was one of the first directors of Cheltenham College and educated his five sons there. He died at the early age of forty-two. The third son, Charles, was the much-beloved and respected vicar of Malmesbury, and the youngest, George Hicks, was a Judge in India."

This sketch of Mr Pitt and his family is given at some length as the record of this very remarkable man is worth preserving, and hitherto he has been unaccountably neglected by historians of the Spa of Cheltenham.

"The visit of the great poet, Lord Byron, was the great event in 1812," says Goding. "During his visits to Cheltenham he greatly assisted to establish the drama on a popular footing. In connection with the late Earl Fitzhardinge he laboured to secure the engagement of all the most eminent characters of the day, and Mr John Kemble and Mrs Siddons performed under his patronage the respective characters of Macbeth and Lady Macbeth and Mr and Mrs Liston in the characters of Joseph and Loretta in 'The Quaker.'"

Mrs Mardyn, an attractive actress who sometimes played in Cheltenham, is said to have eventually been mainly responsible for the parting between Byron and his wife. The local papers tell us how on one of her visits to the Spa Mrs Mardyn fell from her horse in Cambray and met with some injuries.

"Lord Byron," continues Goding, "was a frequent guest at the table of the then Colonel Berkeley at Berkeley Castle, and associated with the great dramatists and literary characters of the age, who at that time daily thronged the old baronial abode.

"The interest which Byron and Colonel Berkeley took in the inimitable Joseph Grimaldi in his declining years does honour to the memory of both. 'Joe,' the Prince of Clowns, was invited to Cheltenham three times, and performed two nights on each visit, during which time he was one of the guests at the Castle and dined regularly with Byron and some of the leading nobility of the county. Some idea may be. formed of the influence of the patronage which was bestowed upon the laughter-making Joe from the fact that his proceeds of the receipts amounted on the first visit to £194, on the second to £186, and on the third to £150; and this will appear the more striking when it is mentioned that the clown's share was only half the actual sum taken, the other half going, by agreement, to Mr Watson, the proprietor of the theatre. Grimaldi's first visit was in 1812, his second in 1822, and his last in 1823, when his declining health, which was temporarily restored by drinking the Cheltenham waters, rendered him unfit for any public engagement."

Afterwards Grimaldi wrote an autobiography, which Dickens edited and published.

A member of Charles James Fox's family has a letter in which the writer says that Fox, Byron, and if memory fails not, Lord and Lady Oxford, and Lord and Lady Holland, came to see Mrs Siddons act in Cheltenham in 1812. She took her professional farewell of the stage as Lady Macbeth on the 24th of June 1812, when her powers were still undiminished. After that date she only appeared at a few charitable performances, and twice to gratify the popular young heiress to the throne, Princess Charlotte.

Lord Byron appears to have been staying for some time at Berkeley Castle in 1812 before he paid his long visit to Cheltenham. Of this period Joseph Grimaldi has left some amusing reminiscences:

> "'Grimaldi,' said Colonel Berkeley, 'after breakfast, at which meal we expect your company, and that of Mr Watson, you shall have a course with the greyhounds yonder, then you shall return and dine with us. We shall have dinner early so as to enable you to reach the theatre in time to perform.' Upon their return to the Castle Mr Watson and Grimaldi found most of the company with whom they had breakfasted assembled together, and shortly afterwards they sat down to dinner. Lord Byron sat on Grimaldi's left. Towards the end of the repast Byron invited Grimaldi to eat a little apple-tart, which he thought he could manage, as he was very fond of it, and the tart being placed before him he commenced operations. Lord Byron looked at him for a moment, and then said with seeming surprise, 'Why, Mr Grimaldi, do you not take soy with your apple-tart?'
>
> 'Soy, my Lord?'
>
> 'Yes, soy; it is very good with salmon, and, therefore, it must be nice with apple-pie.'"

Grimaldi did not see the analogy, but he bowed assent to Byron's proposal, and proceeded to pour some of the fish-sauce over his tart. After one or two attempts to swallow the vile mess, he addressed Lord Byron, remarking that however much the confession might savour of bad taste, he really did not enjoy soy with apple-tart.

Grimaldi repaired again in the month of August to Cheltenham. During his stay there he so far recovered from his illness as to be enabled to play at the theatre, then under the management of Mr Farley (probably on account of Watson's ill-health), and here he encountered Mr Bunn, who informed him that Mr Charles Kemble was then starring at Birmingham, and that, Colonel Berkeley having promised to pay for his benefit, he had come over to Cheltenham, to see what part the Colonel would wish to play.

Grimaldi strolled into the green-room, where he met Colonel Berkeley, who said that he very much wished to play Valentine to his Orson; to which Grimaldi replied it would give him great pleasure to afford him the opportunity whenever he felt disposed.

"'Very well,' said Colonel Berkeley, 'then we will consider the matter settled. You must come to Cheltenham for one night. I will make all the necessary arrangements with Farley: your son shall play the Green Knight, and I will give one hundred pounds as a remuneration. We will try what we can do together, Joe, to amuse the people of Cheltenham.'"

Lord Byron arrived in Cheltenham in August and made the Spa his headquarters for the next six months, lodging at No 430 High Street, where Haynes Bayly afterwards resided. Lord and Lady Holland, Lord and Lady Melbourne, Lord and Lady Oxford, the Milbankes and Sir Elijah Impey's family were among the numerous Fashionables who thronged the town, partly because it was the mode to come to Cheltenham and partly because Lord Byron was there.

The lion of the London season evidently occasioned tremendous interest on his arrival at the fashionable watering-place. His appearance alone would have attracted considerable attention. His figure was exceptionally well-proportioned. He was athletic looking and broad-shouldered; a veritable Greek god in appearance, and all the girls must have turned to look after him as he sauntered along Cheltenham's one long street, and many pretty ladies raved over his beautiful and regular features, his pale, interesting-looking face, his extraordinarily long eyelashes. Pictures of the poet reveal curly locks and large soulful eyes, and his voice, we are told, was soft and melodious. His only blemish was his lameness, about which we are told he was extremely sensitive. He had not actually a club-foot, as his enemies freely declared, but his left foot was about an inch and a half shorter than his right, which caused him to walk with a decided limp. Beauty was the source of his vanity, it has been said, and deformity of his bitterness, and the two laid the germs of egotism in his soul. A spoilt, unrestrained child had grown into the spoilt darling of the world. In spite of his social position and great intellectual gifts, he remained unsatisfied, cynical, and morose. It is by no means strange that he had so few friends of his own sex. Conceited, disdainful and unsociable, he never went out of his way to avert dislike or to disarm jealousy. His affectations and love of display made him an abomination in male eyes. Frightened by his sharp tongue and biting sarcasms, the bucks and Corinthians of his day were silent in his presence, but made up for their silences behind his back. Some sycophant would probably be kind enough to repeat their unkind remarks to the poet, and the repetition but added to his bitterness. But his very failings in the eyes of men seemed virtues to many women, by whom his unpopularity would often be put down to the green-eyed jealousy of disconcerted rivals.

In the autumn of 1812, two houses in the High Street of Cheltenham and another house also in the town contained persons much interested in the

The Crescent, 1813 (two of the old iron pillars for oil lamps still remain). From an aquatint by Bluch.

forthcoming opening of Drury Lane Theatre. In one of these houses Lord Byron was writing the Address which caused so many heart-burnings. In the other lived the mother of Harriot Mellon, who was to play Nell to Dowton's Jobson in the opening farce, "The Devil to Pay."

Mrs Entwistle was, for her, in a rather chastened frame of mind. For Mr Entwistle had nearly lost his job, and his affairs had formed the principal topic of conversation in the Garden Town for some time past. The carelessness with which Mr and Mrs Entwistle conducted the affairs connected with the post office had been more than once a subject of serious complaint among the residents of Cheltenham.

At last on account of a piece of unusually gross carelessness on Entwistle's part, a petition for his dismissal was signed by most of the more influential residents. This was sent to the Postmaster-General, and Mr Entwistle received a private notice that he was about to be dismissed. This was like a bomb-shell hurled into the happy-go-lucky security of the casual postmaster's daily life. Mrs Entwistle, who always rose to an emergency, left Cheltenham by the next coach for London. She rushed into her daughter's bedroom, where she had hysterics; she knew that nothing else would meet the situation. For Harriot had exerted great influence to get the post for her stepfather, and even after Mrs Entwistle's skilfully managed fainting fit, the actress suggested that matters might be left to take their course. Mrs Entwistle then left off pleading for the chief offender, and drew an artful picture of her own distress and its probable effects upon her health. Finally, Harriot consented to ask Mr Coutts, the great banker, to intervene on behalf of the Cheltenham postmaster. Mr Coutts was a good judge of character and knew that punishment would never reform the casual couple. Besides he was in love with Mrs Entwistle's daughter, and so it came about that Mr Entwistle after a severe reproof and a notice that the next offence should be decisive beyond appeal was allowed to remain as usual, enjoying his ale, and neglecting the distribution of the letters. The mercurial Irishwoman returned to her post office and was able to enjoy her daughter's theatrical triumphs with an easy mind.

Lady Melbourne, Sir Ralph Milbanke's only sister, was in Cheltenham at the time. She is known to have been the matchmaker who for her own reasons first thought of the Byron-Milbanke marriage. Byron had begun a flirtation with Lady Melbourne's daughter-in-law, the beautiful and unprincipled authoress, Lady Caroline Lamb, an affair which caused much uneasiness to the astute mother of Queen Victoria's political tutor. A brilliant idea occurred to her. She determined to secure this celebrated poet and peer of the realm for her brother's only girl. She probably thought Annabella's "pallid beauty" and cold, composed manners might attract a man who was sick to death of being run after, while the girl was not everybody's taste. At the same time Lady Melbourne hoped in this way to stop the gossip about her son's wife. So at least Mr Jeaffreson interprets Lady Melbourne's matchmaking.

Lady Caroline had thrown herself at Byron's head. A Miss Milbanke might gain his heart by her coldness. For a while, Lady Melbourne's scheme worked out admirably. It is almost certain that Byron first made an offer of marriage to his future wife, an offer then rejected—during his visit to Cheltenham. One biographer says he passed the greater part of his time there till the end of November, reading, scribbling letters, writing poetry—and bad poetry at that— and meditating on a disappointment that cannot be mentioned more particularly. This disappointment appears to have been his rejection by Miss Milbanke. As evidence of this, the following quotation from John Cordy Jeaffreson, one of the poet's biographers, who is occupied in proving that Byron did not marry for money, is pretty conclusive:

"Byron's first offer to Miss Milbanke was made at a time when Mr Claughton's offer of £140,000 for Newstead gave him a good prospect of a sure income of £1000 a year, after the payment of his debts, without selling any part of his Rochdale Estate, when things looked brighter.

Early in the autumn of 1812 Newstead was offered for sale at Garraways when it was bought in, £90,000 being the highest offer made in the auction room for the property. Soon after Mr Claughton came forward with an offer that even exceeded the vendor's hopes, 'You heard,' wrote Byron from Cheltenham to his friend William Bankes, 'that Newstead is sold: the sum £140,000.'"

These two quotations, together with one from a pamphlet written about the Cheltenham Races in 1819 make it fairly certain that Byron's first offer of marriage to Anna Isabella Milbanke was made in Cheltenham Old Assembly Rooms. The Bard of Cheltenham describes the race ball and says several things about the manners and attire, or the lack of them of some of the ladies. He continues:

"Has then a lordly poet turned your brain,
By singing sweetly of the Belles of Spain,
Was it the Grecian Maid, or dark Gazelle,
That taught the poet how to love so well?
No, 'twas the offspring of a British dame,
Whose pallid beauty fann'd the rising flame.
In Cheltenham's Rooms the accent of his tongue
Belied the warbling of the fabled song."

Miss Milbanke's refusal was possibly due to her knowledge that Byron was still enslaved by the beautiful Lady Oxford, who was living at Georgiana Cottage on the banks of the Chelt.

It seems as if Lady Oxford was the object of one of Byron's most serious love-affairs. At this time the poet wrote to Lord Holland from Cheltenham on 10th September 1812:

"My respects to Lady H. Her departure, with that of my other friends, was a sad event for me, now reduced to a state of the most cynical solitude. 'By the waters of Cheltenham I sat down and *drank,* when I remembered thee, oh, Georgiana Cottage! As for our harps, we hanged them up upon the willows that grew thereby.' Then they said: 'Sing us a song of Drury Lane,' etc, but I am dumb and dreary as the Israelites. The waters have disordered me to my heart's content. You *were* right, as you always are."

On 26th September, he writes: "I am diluted to the throat with medicine for the stone, and Boisragon wants me to try a warm climate for the winter—but I won't."

On 28th September, Byron writes to Mr William Bankes: "We had a very pleasant set here, at first the Jerseys, Melbounres, Cowpers and Hollands, but all gone; and the only persons I know are the Rawdons, Oxfords, with some later acquaintances of less brilliant descent."

It is impossible, however, to say with certainty, whether Byron went straight away from Lady Oxford to propose to Miss Milbanke, or, if he beguiled his disappointment at his rejection by the girl with a flirtation with the married woman.

Georgiana Cottage, afterwards Georgiana House, stood in that part of Cambray which is now the Bath Road, had a lovely and very long garden, and was a very pretty house with verandahs and balconies. It was at one time the residence of

Sir Felix and Lady Agar, and appears to have been let furnished to various notable visitors to the Spa.

Lady Oxford was at this time over forty years of age, but in the autumn of her beauty, the setting sun of her attractions still threw around beams which eclipsed the smaller stars—the younger women, in the meridian of their charms, or the girls in the first blush of their loveliness. Byron himself writes of his great love for Lady Oxford and says that even when he knew that she was unfaithful to him he had the greatest difficulty in tearing himself away from her. He speaks of himself elsewhere as her last lover, but on his own showing he must have been at least only the last but one. Lord Oxford's place in the scheme of things seems not to be very clearly defined, but Lady Oxford is said to have been a most good-natured and kind-hearted woman, so that probably she fitted Lord Oxford in and gave him his share of attention, unless he sought consolation elsewhere. The inconstant beauty threw over Byron for another lover and it was for this reason, and not because he was tired of her, that the poet, with dragging footsteps and a heavy heart, left her at last.

Writing to a friend at the end of September, Byron says of Cheltenham: "I do not trouble them much; and as for your rooms and your assemblies, 'they are not dreamed of in our philosophy!!' Did you hear of a sad accident in the Wye father day: A dozen drowned, and Mr Roscie, a corpulent gentleman, preserved by a boat-hook or an eel-spear, begged, when his wife was saved—no lost—to be thrown in again!! As if he could not have thrown himself in, had he wished it; but this passes for a trait of sensibility. What strange beings men are, in and out of the Wye!"

A melancholy event in February 1928 has been the demolition of Georgiana Cottage. Next to the sad site of Georgiana Cottage is Birdlip House, and beyond that formerly stood Colonel Riddell's house, Wellington Mansion, which was pulled down in 1862. Colonel Riddell's grounds extended from the present Wellington Street, along the Chelt, to the Bath Road, which road as far as Leckhampton Hill was opened for public use on 15th August 1813.

Higher up the road than Cambray House or Wellington Mansion, behind what is now Norton's Garage, was Watson's Cambray Theatre, all of which that now remains is a fire-blackened wall, which can be seen at the back of Norton's Garage. The theatre stood in what is now Bath Street, on the site of a licensed house, The Garrick's Head.

In October Byron went on a visit to Lord Oxford, but in November he was back in Cheltenham, whence he started off on an antiquarian tour with Sir Isaac Heard, the Garter King at Arms, who was so constantly at the Spa that he was almost a resident.

Lord Byron's doctor at Cheltenham, as already mentioned, was one of the fashionable physicians of the town, Doctor Boisragon. The doctor had come to settle in the town at a time when its mineral waters were rapidly rising in the public estimation, and his skill as a physician contributed in no small degree to accelerate the reputation and develop the resources of the place. "With a highly cultivated mind and an ardent attachment to the pursuit of art, literature and science he united the polished manners of the gentleman and a charity that 'thinketh no evil.'"

Dr Boisragon practised in Cheltenham for forty years, and died in 1852, but as he had left the town years before his death his very name is not remembered by many of its inhabitants. He was an extra physician to the Prince of Wales; but probably Byron was his most distinguished (if not most exalted) patient. The doctor, as has been seen, is mentioned in one of Byron's letters written from his dwelling in the High Street. Earlier in the same year the *Cheltenham Chronicle* of 4th March tells us that "A Party took place on Thursday last at Dr Boisragon's Mansion in The Crescent. Music, and at near twelve o'clock, a *récherché* supper." And the same newspaper records that "A Harmonic Society has been founded at the George Hotel, under the patronage of Dr Boisragon."

A notable figure was now to be removed from the stage of Cheltenham Theatre Royal and from the larger stage of the town generally upon which the had fretted his forty years or so.

The *Cheltenham Chronicle* of Thursday, 28th March 1813, announces the death of John Boles Watson, which had occurred on the preceding Wednesday. Watson had been the manager and proprietor of the Cheltenham Theatre during some of the most eventful years in the history of the Spa, namely from 1774 to 1813. The Cheltenham chronicler broke out into verse as if prose had been an inadequate vehicle in which to celebrate his funeral rites:

> "Faint as the breeze which scarce the vi'let moves,
> Or shakes the dewdrop from the nectar'd rose.
> Yet makes a wild note from Æolian lyre.
> Sweep slow the harp of Sorrow, that Charity
> May bend, a bright-rob'd seraph o'er the bier
> Of Watson, who, whilst on the earth oft led,
> From their dark seats, amid their pallid friends,
> Her pleading offspring."

"In unshaken loyalty to his sovereign," the *Chronicle* goes on (so moved that it forgets its verb), "in the most sincere disinterested patriotism, and in that affection for his native soil which almost invariably characterises the sons of Erin—in acts of benevolence and charity to the poor and friendless, in these and numberless other excellences, and loss for the more alluring—and with his inclinations, more profitable, business of an actor, and later a theatrical manager. His choice thus made, he, for many successive years ran his gay career, marked by all those varying scenes, all those chequered vicissitudes which seem peculiarly connected with theatrical pursuits. Though doubtless he had many equals yet could there be few if any who surpassed him. As to his religious principles, it may suffice to say that though to superficial observers it might appear otherwise, he was at heart firmly attached to the established Church. In deportment and manners he was just and considerate to his inferiors, courteous and obliging to his equals, politely respectful and attentive to his superiors."

The exiled French Royalties were very fond of Cheltenham. On 25th May 1811, Marie -Thérèse, daughter of Louis XVI, had arrived here with her husband, the Duc d'Angoulême. They lived at Sheldon's, afterwards called The York, in the High Street.

It was probably some years before 1811 that the Abbé César had arrived in the town, a most saintly man who had been one of the chaplains of Louis XVI. He earned his living by giving French lessons, and he fitted up a room in the York Hotel, or Sheldon's, where he ministered to his fellow-exiles. Earlier still, Father J. Birdsall, a wealthy and influential priest, had come to live in Cheltenham, and it was mainly by his exertions that a spacious chapel was built in Somerset Place, and was united with the Benedictine Order. Probably both Father Birdsall and the Abbé César ministered to the English Roman Catholics and to the French refugees in this chapel.

The Abbé César died in 1811. A stone was erected in the Parish Churchyard by the subscriptions of the former court chaplain's pupils, with this simple inscription:

"To the Memory of the Rev. Alexander César, French Priest, who died September 11th, 1811."

Their Royal Highnesses, the Duc and Duchesse d'Angoulême, were so pleased with Cheltenham that they came again two years later and they most likely were regular attendants at the Roman Catholic Chapel which had grown out of the Abbé César's small congregation in a room at Sheldon's Boarding-House.

The *Cheltenham Chronicle* of 22nd July 1813, says:

"Among the foreign *noblesse* which at present honour this town are la Duchesse d'Angoulême, and le Comte d'Artois. Louis XVIII is expected on Monday. The Duchess at present resides in Cambray Lodge. The Duchesse, the only daughter of Louis XVI, married the only son of his brother Comte d'Artois. The son of the Comte d'Artois is the present Duc d'Angoulême, and the Duchess is the sole surviving child of the ill-fated monarch. This interesting couple were regarded as the union which should and might perpetuate the claimants to the throne of their ancestors. They were driven from Courland, their last continental retreat, by the policy of the present Alexander, when he had formed his first alliance with Bonaparte. In England they were never received at Court by the King, but they have experienced the most delicate and marked hospitality from the Grenville family, and lately from the Prince Regent." (*Cheltenham Chronicle*, 22nd July 1813): "Louis XVIII arrived in this town on Monday, and joined the Duchesse at her residence in Cambray." (*Cheltenham Chronicle*, 5th August 1813): "During their stay they visited Boddington Manor House, and paid repeated visits to the salts manufactory. The Comte de Jarnac-Charles Rosalie de Rouen Chabot, a French refugee, died at Pine Cottage, and Mass was celebrated at the Roman Catholic Chapel in Somerset Place at which all the French Royalties then in Cheltenham were present. Afterwards the body was taken over to Gloucester, and buried in the Cathedral."

XI

1816–1818

The French Royal Family, 1816—The Duke of Wellington, 1816—
Colonel Riddell, 1816–1818.

The opening months of 1815 were eventful for Cheltenham.

At the Charlotteville party, which was held on 10th January, the guests were decorated with garter-blue ribbons bearing the motto in letters of gold, "God bless the Princess Charlotte." These ribbons were worn by the ladies as bandeaux, scarves or sashes, and by the gentlemen across their shoulders or round one arm. The guests were received by the Colonel in a full-dressed Highland uniform, the tartan sumptuously embroidered with gold lace.

The ball was opened at half-past ten by Mrs Macleod and the young Laird of Mackinnon, who were followed by about sixty couples … The company, after a squeeze *comme it faut*, sat down to six tables, covered with every luxury the season could produce with French wines, etc, sparkling briskly in unison. When the din of voices had a little subsided the Colonel arose, and, amidst a profound and respectful silence, in a voice that well bespoke his loyal feelings, gave the health of his royal patroness, the Princess Charlotte of Wales, with long life, health and prosperity. This was received as usual with God Save the King, and a song, composed especially for the occasion, was sung, of which the last verse was:

> Charlotte, our fair Princess,
> Macleod's royal patroness,
> May heav'n protect.
> > Beloved with sincerity,
> > To rule our posterity,
> > God save our Princess.

When the tumult had in some degree subsided, Colonel Macleod gave the King, HRH the Prince Regent, and the Duke of York, the Army and Navy, etc, and then Sir Charles Ross in a short but elegant speech begged leave to propose the toast in which he was sure every heart would beat in unison, health and prosperity to their worthy president, Colonel Macleod, Mrs Macleod, and their amiable family. It is unnecessary to say with what feelings this was received, or with what renewed spirit the three times three sounded ... The attractions of the table ... yielded to the reviving influences of beauty, the glass was willingly quitted at the renewed sound of the merry pipe and tabor. The early death of the beloved Princess Charlotte was a sad blow to the nation at large, and was, of course, the end of Macleod's royal birthday festivities.

On the 14th of February, Miss Mellon, in the character of Audrey in "As You Like It," bade farewell to the stage which she had adorned for nearly twenty years. She had some years previously given up some of her younger parts to Miss Kelly, as her increasing stoutness made her unsuitable for them. She had observed to the stage manager when asking to be taken out of "Blue Devils," in which she was Annette: "My dear Wroughton, what would they say to hear a large woman like me exclaim, 'I shall be eighteen next Friday fortnight!'"

On the 14th of January, Mrs Coutts had died, and Thomas Coutts had been so ill that he had despaired of his own life, and put such pressure on Miss Mellon that the *Cheltenham Chronicle* of 15th March 1815, has the following notice:

> "On Wednesday, 2nd March, was married at St Pancras Church, Middlesex, Thomas Coutts, Esq, to Miss Harriot Mellon. The charitable disposition of this lady entitles her to the good wishes of all. She is the daughter of Mrs Entwistle of this town, and is now the mother-in-law of the Dowager Countess of Guildford."

Harriot had, for some time before her marriage, been living at Holly Lodge, Highgate, which was always her favourite residence. Mr Coutts's health still remained in a very precarious state, and his wife nursed him most tenderly; indeed, her care is said to have prolonged his life considerably. Mrs Entwistle's health, however, had been for some time failing. "The improvement in their daughter's fortunes," says the latter's biographer, "even before her marriage, brought a great accession of ease to Mr and Mrs Entwistle." But the dark shade of ill-health clouded the ease and enjoyment which after so many years of ups and downs, the Entwistles, *père et mère*, at last experienced. Despite everything that Mr Coutts's money could buy, Mrs Entwistle's health gradually failed, and she ended her eventful life on the 6th of May 1815, in her sixty-third year.

The *Cheltenham Chronicle* in an old notice gave a glowing account of the many charities of Mrs Entwistle. She had a very grand funeral, which it was sad that she could not have herself witnessed—it would have pleased her much, and sadder still that she did not live to see her daughter in her last role—a Duchess.

Thomas Entwistle, on whom his wife's temper had been some restraint, now made many low acquaintances in Cheltenham. This worried Mrs Coutts very much and as he was very fond of fishing, she offered to settle him (with an annuity of £500 a year) in a very pretty cottage on the banks of the Thames. Entwistle, however, had retained few of the aristocratic prejudices of the Fleetwood Havershams, and preferred the lower High Street in Cheltenham and his lowly friends. There he remained, incessantly worrying his stepdaughter for money, which she continually supplied until his death, which occurred only four years after that of his wife.

On Mr Entwistle's death, Mrs Coutts placed in the Parish Church at Cheltenham a handsome white marble tablet to her mother and stepfather. A stone was placed in the churchyard to mark the place of interment, and at the head of the grave, Harriot, then a Duchess, erected another monument in 1832 to her mother only.

> "This Tablet
> was erected to the memory of
> Mrs Sarah Entwistle,
> by her affectionate daughter
> Harriot,
> Duchess of St Albans,
> Sept. 31st, 1832."

The Duchess wanted to place this tablet against a wall which divided the churchyard from private property. But it was reported in Cheltenham that the owner demanded such an exorbitant sum for his permission to allow its erection, that the Duchess put it at the head of the grave. She was told, however, that as the tablet was to be put on the consecrated side of the wall, the owner of the property had no right to make such a claim. Both stones are now against the wall. Many of the stones in the Parish Churchyard are now far away from the graves they were intended to mark.

Mr and Mrs Coutts lived on very happily together and frequently entertained the Royal Family and all the other great people of the day at Holly Lodge. Harriot was very tactful and lived on the best of good terms with her stepchildren. She lavished the greatest care and attention on the aged banker, who, in return, left the whole of his property, including the Bank, to his widow on his death in 1822. After this she seems to have taken a great interest in the Bank, and spent much of her time there, signing papers and carrying out other duties required of the head of a great firm.

In September 1815, Mrs Jenner's long illness came to an end in Cheltenham, and the disconsolate widower retired to Berkeley, where he had spent more and more time as he grew older, there to pass the evening of his days. The peace of the little town of Berkeley and the leafy lanes, full of bird and animal life, were much more attractive to Jenner than were social pleasures. Cheltenham had always seemed to him "too gay" to use his own words. Had it not been that the climate suited his wife, the great doctor would not have spent so much time away from Berkeley.

On the 10th of August 1815, the *Cheltenham Chronicle* announces the arrival of the Ex-Queen of Würtemberg, the wife of Jérôme Bonaparte, "a lady rendered peculiarly interesting by her beauty and misfortunes."

The Duc d'Orléans, afterwards Louis Philippe, King of the French, with his wife, Marie Amelie, daughter of King Ferdinand of Naples, and their children, arrived at the Spa on the 13th of July 1816. The Duke had, at the time, a residence at Twickenham, whence he often made excursions with his family for the good of their health and also in order to educate his children by showing them different places. They lived at Cheltenham for about three months, and appear to have occupied the present Cambray Pavilion during part of their stay, possibly only while the Duke of Wellington was at Cambray House.

During their stay in the town their Royal Highnesses entered familiarly into the society of the place, visiting and being visited by many of the residents, who were invariably received by them with marked civility, when as the invited guests of the exiled Prince they appeared at the weekly breakfasts given by him to those whom he honoured with his friendship or acquaintance. The Duc d'Orléans also patronised most of the fashionable amusements of the day, and was, with his uncle, the Comte d'Artois, a frequent attendant at the bazaar sales when these took place at the old Assembly Rooms, thirty years ago one of the fashionable lounges of Cheltenham. "We well remember," says a writer in the *Looker On*, "being there when their Royal Highnesses were present and attracted considerable notice; the peculiarity of their costume; the little cocked hat and long queue, generally arresting the immediate attention of strangers. On this occasion a pair of plated telescope candlesticks were put up for sale, the fluent auctioneer expatiating according to custom upon their excellent quality and manufacture. There were several bidders, the Comte d'Artois was one, and outbidding his opponents, the lot was knocked down to him for ten shillings. Handing over payment in the silver tokens of those days, His Royal Highness received his purchase from the porter and putting a candlestick in each pocket, walked leisurely away, apparently well pleased with his purchase."

An interesting anecdote of Louis Philippe was related by His Royal Highness the Duc d'Aumale at the seventy-second anniversary of the Royal Literary Fund Dinner, held at the Freemasons' Tavern:[*]

> "I cannot pretend to be thoroughly acquainted with your literature, but if I know
> something of it I owe it to two circumstances. The first that I was educated by a
> father who had been an exile as I am now, who had found on your shores the same

---

[*] See *The Times*, May 1861.

hospitable shelter, and who both knew and loved your country, your language, the great work of your literature, as well I suppose as any foreigner ever did or can. I remember that in the earliest days of my life, when he was himself free from all political responsibility, in the happy and quiet evenings of Neuilly, he used often, after having shown to his children the engraved portraits of celebrated men, and told their deeds, or plates which commemorated the military achievements of our countrymen, to take down from the shelves of the library some huge folio volume of Boydell's *Illustrated Shakespeare*, a copy of which he had bought himself at the Auction Room at Cheltenham, and give us an outline of the finest scenes of your great dramatist, reciting occasionally some of the beautiful passages which had remained engraved in his wonderful memory. That was my first impression of English literature, and one which will never be effaced from my mind, for it is connected with one of my earliest recollections of the best of fathers."

In July 1816 it became known in the town that the Duke of Wellington's physicians had ordered a course of the Cheltenham waters in order to repair the ravages wrought upon his iron frame by the late long campaign. A public meeting, with Colonel Berkeley in the chair, was convened, and ample funds were at once forthcoming, so that triumphal arches and functions might be got up, but "the immortal Deliverer of Europe" stole a march on them, and arrived with his Duchess and two sons and a suite, before the flowers and flags and fireworks and things were ready. The reception committee, which included Colonel Berkeley, Lord Clarina, Sir W. Cunningham, Sir Arthur Faulkner, and Mr Luke Reilly, therefore, received the hero after the event. Three arches were erected, which spanned the entrance to Cambray, one over each footpath and the other across the road, extending from Mr Notcutt's, the chemist's shop, on one side to Mr White's, the grocer's establishment, on the other.

The Duke stayed at Colonel Riddell's house in Cambray, afterwards called Wellington Mansion, which had in 1814 and for some time previously been leased to Sir Edward May, a jewel amongst tenants, who had spent £8000 on the premises.

Nothing was mentioned in the newspapers but Wellington and Waterloo, and one tale was told of two gentlemen (whose Waterloo medals showed them to be military) "who were introduced to each other at a party a few nights ago, when one of them said to the other: 'I think, sir, I had the pleasure of meeting you at the Duke of Richmond's ball, but we probably met about that time at Napoleon's *Grand Rout*.'"

The *Cheltenham Chronicler* fairly extended himself over the Wellingtons. "If any event," he chanted, "could have risen the Duke and his engaging Consort in our estimation, we should have found it in their affability and kind condescension towards the numerous and at times intrusive marks of individual esteem and unrestrained expressions of joy."

At the theatre, the Duke and Duchess sat in the box fitted up a few years since for the Prince Regent. "The Duchess and her two sweet boys arrived first, and was conducted to the box by Mr Watson (our worthy manager) and Mr Cooper, who were fully dressed!!! At the beginning of the second act appeared His Grace, accompanied by Lord Lynedoch, a foreign nobleman, and Dr Christie. A burst of joy and exultation came from every quarter of the theatre, and God Save the King was sung by the whole dramatic corps led by the Miss Halfords and Mr Jones."

On another occasion the Duke and Duchess attended some affair in the old Assembly Rooms, at which six hundred persons were present. "Since the ball a few years since," said the *Chronicle* man, "which the Prince of Wales honoured with his presence, never was seen such a constellation of beauty, rank and fashion as at the Assembly Rooms on Wednesday evening. His Grace was dressed in mourning, with the collar and star of the Garter, and round his cravat was a superb collar of scarlet enamel, set in gold and diamonds, being the collar of some foreign order of knighthood."

' The *Chronicle* for 22nd July 1816 says:

"A very interesting ceremony took place on Monday on the lawn of Wellington House (lately Cambray House).

Colonel Riddell having intimated to the illustrious hero that he wished to have some remembrance of his visit, suggested the planting of a British oak before the lawn of his mansion. To this the Duke readily assented: 'I instantly went and gave my gardener directions to prepare the ground. I also employed two men to have the plant carefully removed from the Regent Gardens, hating obtained permission from Mr Haynes, the proprietor, so to do. At eleven o'clock I waited on His Grace to have the time it would be most convenient to him to superintend the planting. His Grace replied, "Directly, if you please." I had no time to lose; called at the Regent Gardens, gave orders for the tree to be removed to the lawn, and secured some of the best fruits the town could produce; these were sent to my gardener in baskets, accompanied by Miss Ballinger.

'I met Miss Costello with her Mother, and she had left at my house a few days previous a volume of her Poems, and a few very complimentary to the Duke on his arrival in Cheltenham. I thought it would be a good opportunity to present both her and the book. I requested her to go and wait my return at Wellington Gardens, and I had a silver salver, on which I placed a few seeds, and two cruets filled with oil and wine.

'Everything being ready, His Grace, attended by the Duchess, their sons, the Marquis of Douro, Lord Charles Wellesley, and their nephew, Master Gerald Wellesley, Lady C. Bathurst, Lord Apsley, etc, came to the lawn, and the ceremony of planting the oak commenced. The Duke, on the tree having been put in the earth, poured therein the oil and wine, and threw in a few seeds; the same ceremony was performed by the Duchess, and the rest of the noble attendants. His Grace took particular interest

Miss Foote, as Maria Darlington
in *A Roland for an Oliver.* From
the painting by G. Clint, A.R.A.

in directing the planting of the tree ; and when sufficient earth was put round the
plant to make it firm, the Duchess concluded by pouring water on its roots. This
being done, the opportunity offered to present my young friend to His Grace and his
illustrious Consort; her book and verses were graciously received by the Duke and
the Duchess, with an affability peculiar to herself, complimented her on her turn for
poetry. The fruits were now presented by Miss Costello and myself.'"

Miss Louisa Stuart Costello became a fairly well-known author and actress. She
presented her poems to Tom Moore also.

"In conversation the Duke remarked that the time coincided with that when
the cannonade commenced at Salamanca. His Grace consented to remain till the
gardener had finished planting the tree, and the turf replaced round the stem. The
Duke observed it was a fine young plant, and he hoped it would thrive. I said, 'Under
such happy auspices it could not do otherwise.' The sun, that had not been visible
for some days, made its appearance, and was hailed by all present as a happy omen.
Thus ended the ceremony of planting the Waterloo Oak at Wellington House."

The great event of the Duke's visit in 1816 was the opening of the "New Grand
Assembly Rooms," which became the centre of Cheltenham's social life. They

were situated in the High Street, and many Cheltonians well remember the building, as it was only pulled down at the very end of the nineteenth century to make way for the fine local branch of Lloyds' Bank. At one corner of the building was Williams's famous Library, well known to book-lovers all the world over. In this book-shop was kept a weighing-machine, still preserved in the Municipal Museum, in which all the celebrities or nonentities of the day who frequented Cheltenham were weighed. The great day of the opening of the Assembly Rooms came at last. This is how it struck the scribe of 29th July 1816: "The most sanguine expectations could not have been more amply gratified than on Monday night, the Ball announced for that evening under the auspices of the Duke and Duchess of Wellington was honoured beyond all former precedent. The truly superb Assembly Rooms contained upwards of 1400 personages of distinction in Society, whose splendid attire, aided by the magic influence of the scene, gave it an air of enchantment. About 10 o'clock the Duke, accompanied by his illustrious Consort, arrived. A burst of congratulation was instantly diffused amidst the charm of swelling melody. They returned the greeting with pleasure and complacency. He wore no decorations except his star and the Duchess was similarly unaided with ornaments."

On Wednesday, the 31st, the Duke left for Lord Bathurst's seat at Cirencester. His Grace gave "our clergyman," Mr Phillips, a large sum of money to be distributed among local charities. Two days later the Duchess followed, and Cambray House was reoccupied by the Duke of Orleans, who seems to have temporarily vacated it for the use of the victorious General. So ended the second of the five "Cures" undergone by the Iron Duke at the Gloucestershire watering place.

In October 1816 Bonaparte's celebrated military carriage taken at Waterloo, together with its curious contents, was to be on view for a few days near The Crescent. It was to be drawn by the same horses, and driven by the same coachman, as when it was the property of the Emperor.

The previously mentioned Royal Crescent had been built in about the year 1809 on the site then known as the Church Mead. Shortly before it was finished some carpenters had left shavings about, and No 5, which belonged to Mr Jessop, caught fire, through the ignition of these shavings. It was at No 15 in the Crescent that Mr Jervis, the Incumbent of Cheltenham, had resided for many years. In 1821 Dr Denman (afterwards Lord Chief Justice), one of the Counsel for Queen Caroline, had visited Cheltenham, on which occasion the Incumbent, being a King George's man, had refused to allow the bells to be rung. The populace, however, met Dr Denman at Charlton Kings, and, taking his horses from the carriage, dragged him through the town to his lodgings at No 5 Crescent, from the balcony of which house he addressed the people for three-quarters of an hour. The mob then proceeded to the Church, and, arming themselves with weapons from the site of the subsequent Public Offices, burst open the belfry door and regaled their visitor with a merry peal. On the same evening the street lights were put out, and afterwards the mob attacked Mr Jervis's house, broke the windows and did other damage. As Sir Matthew Wood was Queen Caroline's principal backer, and Wraxall, the Regent's historiographer, spent much of his time at Cheltenham, it was no wonder if public opinion ran high in the town. No 8 Royal Crescent was bought on 26th February 1861, as a Parsonage House "to the Parish Church of St Mary's." Shelley's son-in-law, Mr E. J. Esdaile, was on the committee which arranged for the purchase of the house, and contributed £20 to the fund raised for the purpose. In February 1863 the Rev. E. Walker, then Incumbent of Cheltenham, resigned his Perpetual Curacy into the hands of the Bishop, and was formally appointed by the patrons and instituted by the Bishop to the Rectory of Cheltenham. The Rectory of Cheltenham had been purchased from the lay proprietors for £500, with the object of having it vested in the hands of Simeon's Trustees, the patrons of the living.

The great Edmund Kean was in Cheltenham in 1816. On 12th September of that year the *Cheltenham Chronicler* says that Kean's second appearance will be as Bertram in "The Devil to Pay." The scribe adds: "Last Tuesday Kean appeared in Richard III. Were we to point out the natural or physical defects of this gentleman, the labour would be unprofitable and unpleasing; his voice is harsh and inharmonious, reminding us of Lady Macbeth's description of the raven that croaked the fatal entrance of Duncan under the battlements—and his figure must not be critically dwelt upon; his great mind, however, peers through his eye and irradiates his countenance. Lose sight of his face, his acting deteriorates; his flexible and influencing front is the index which marks the rich volume of his passions. To illustrate the beauties of his acting, the effect would be pleasing, yet superfluous, for he manifestly has so many singular and excelling traits that a review of these would infinitely repay the labour. In various instances he caught the mind of his audience by surprise, which was admitted in repeated plaudits. The savageness of a corrupt mental agony was dreadfully characteristic in the dying scene—the grave was forgotten—he seemed deified by revenge; the terrific glare of his eye and his convulsive mutterings indicated nothing but ambitious hate.

"On 19th September Kean terminated his engagement at our theatre. He filled the last scene of Sir Giles Overreach with an appalling grandeur, and gave vent to the fullest extent of ambition, pride, avarice and hate imaginable. His Hamlet was received with frequent bursts of applause, with alternate pauses of perfect stillness, the offerings of public praise to Mr Kean. Though we cannot bestow so complete an encomium on his portrait of the Danish Prince as on some other characters, yet it is displayed on such high lines of originality as is to be deservedly prominent.

"In all probability Mr Kean will again visit us before the termination of the season. Never was an actor so indefatigable in his theatrical tours, more deserving, or better rewarded. He has as little sleep as Mina—the guerilla chieftain—travelling from port to port night and day; only tarrying to take the reward of his conquests."

XII

1819–1824

*Mr Fotheringham, MC—King George IV—The Cheltenham
Steeplechases—"The Berkeleys and the Cravens of the Chase," and
Colonel Charretie—The Struggle for Supremacy between Francis Close
and Colonel Berkeley.*

Mr King died in his seventieth year in October 1816, and it was decided to elect a
successor who could give all his time to Cheltenham, for though the arrangement
whereby Mr King had combined the duties of MC at Bath and Cheltenham
had at first proved satisfactory, because Bath was a winter and Cheltenham a
summer resort, Cheltenham had grown into a considerable residential town, and
throughout the year there was scarcely ever any diminution of the fashionable
company; there was, as an old guide-book has it, "an unbroken chain of
elegant enjoyments, delight and gaiety." Mr King's successor was Mr Alexander
Fotheringham, who held the office barely three years, dying under tragic
circumstances on 22nd July 1820. The story is vividly told in the local paper. "His
accomplished lady" had "expired after a short but severe illness on the previous
Sunday and at the very moment when the hearse arrived to convey her remains
to the grave, his widowed heart gave way, and he died in convulsions in less than
half an hour." Mrs Fotheringham's funeral was postponed, and on the Tuesday
following, husband and wife were "interred together at Prestbury in the same
vault wherein five of their children had in one year been laid." With so many
afflictions, no wonder his widowed heart could bear no more.

There was considerable competition to fill the vacancy, five candidates soon
appearing on the scene. The aspirants who had the most support were Mr Marshall,
the MC of the Kingston Rooms at Bath, and Captain Clough, MC of the Isle of
Thanet, who ruled over Society at Ramsgate and Margate. The election campaign
lasted several weeks and each of the candidates issued his election address as he
would have done in a political contest. Feeling ran very high in the town between
the supporters of the various candidates. This led to manifestos and rejoinders,

which make very amusing reading. Mr Marshall had seen ten years' war service in Holland, France and the Netherlands, but had been compulsorily retired from his regiment, the 1st Foot, on the general reduction of the army at the close of the Napoleonic wars. He made an appeal to the subscribers of the Assembly Rooms, on the ground that he was the father of a numerous family who "looked up to him for support, and were dependent on his exertions." "The cause is not my own," he wrote, "it is my children's." Captain Clough replied that he could have made a similar appeal, but considered that it would be undignified to do so, and added, "My opponents have presented themselves before you as objects of your compassion and regard."

When the great day came, the contest between Mr Marshall and Captain Clough proved very close, but the former's supporters were keen enough to come from Bath, Clifton, and even London, to vote for their man. These out-voters won the day for Mr Marshall, who was triumphantly declared the victor by 228 votes to 200.

We give below an account of Mr Marshall's Investiture:

"The Countess of Haddington having taken the Chair, Mr Marshall, supported on the right by Colonel Berkeley, and on the left by Mr Scott, was introduced and preceded by Mr Kelly, proprietor of the Rooms, bearing the insignia on a velvet cushion, conducted through a most numerous and fashionable assemblage, by the Chair of the Lady President, to whom he was presented by Colonel Berkeley in a most kind and appropriate address, marked by those gracious and excellent impulses which are ever conspicuous in his character.

The Countess of Haddington, on investing Mr Marshall with the insignia of his office, expressed the satisfaction it afforded her, and a reliance upon the zeal with which his duties would be discharged by Mr Marshall, who seemed nearly overpowered by his feelings, but briefly expressed his gratitude."

George IV had lost the esteem and respect of many of his subjects, especially of those who sympathised with Queen Caroline, and the journeys which he undertook at this time to various parts of his dominions were possibly made with the idea of recovering some of his former popularity. In the course of one of these progresses he visited Cheltenham after a tour in Ireland, arriving there on 14th September 1821.

The *Cheltenham Chronicle* gives the following account of this flying visit:

"His Majesty advanced at a rapid rate in his green travelling carriage, and was met about the distance of half a mile on the Gloucester Road by a large party of our townsmen on horseback, and each decorated with the patriotic exclamation: 'God Save the King!'—a salute which His Majesty the King felt and most graciously acknowledged by his own peculiarly expressive and often repeated bow, an honour which in his progress through the town our sovereign repeatedly conferred in the kindest manner on several individuals whom he observed prominent in their manifestations of regard; and highly gratified was the look with which the Royal Eye contemplated the various balconies, in which groups of ladies of the first fashion and respectability displayed their fascinating forms. His Majesty, who, we rejoice to say, looked in excellent health though somewhat pale from the effects of his long voyage and journey, was dressed in a long military frock-coat, and sat uncovered, his sealskin cap lying on the seat beside him; on his left hand sat Lord Graves and on the opposite seat we observed, as we thought, Lord Francis Conyngham and Colonel Quentin.

At a few minutes past two o'clock the royal equipage, escorted by nearly one hundred gentlemen, riding before it and all around it and gaily decked with their large blue favours, cheering and cheered by an immense crowd as they galloped along, passed through the Charlton Gate, and halted, while Mr Marshall, who rightly anticipated the point of 'vantage-ground,' and had made his arrangements most judiciously, approached adorned, with the insignia of his office (accompanied by the Rev. C. Jervis as chairman of the meeting and Mr P. Kelly, one of the proprietors of the Rooms), and made an obeisance to HM, who immediately lowered the window, and was addressed by our excellent Master of the Ceremonies. The King was pleased to receive Mr Marshall in the most gracious and affable manner, and made the following kind reply: 'I thank you ... and am too much fatigued to allow of my making a longer stay in Cheltenham. I am not, however, unmindful of the kind attention I have received when last here, and SHALL CERTAINLY MAKE A POINT OF PAYING CHELTENHAM ANOTHER AND AN EARLY VISIT.'

During his reply His Majesty was almost unceasingly saluted with the warmest expression of duty and of love, and at the close the popular feeling found utterance of 'God bless the King!' It reached his ear. It touched his royal heart; his eyes at all times animated, were lighted up with joy, he crossed his arms upon his breast and bowed on every side to his subjects, to his people, to his friends ... All was hurried, it is true, but it was the hurry and the eagerness of affection; there was no parade, but there was that pleased alacrity which no premeditation could supply. Our King felt and acknowledged it all, he seemed proud of himself and his subjects as he moved along—

'Whilst hearts and hands of freeborn men
Were all the guards around him.'"

The Duchess of Buccleuch, the Honourable Mrs Brudenell, Sir William and Lady Sarah and the Misses de Crespigny and Lady Throgmorton were in Cheltenham at the time, and so was Sir Isaac Heard, the Garter King-at-Arms, who, indeed, spent a good deal of his time in the town.

The King failed to make the promised return visit, though the local paper announced that he would come the following year. In the last years of his life he was very much of an invalid. The death of his brother, the Duke of York, in 1826, to whom he was sincerely attached, affected him greatly, and he was seriously ill for a time.

In 1818 some races had been held on Nottingham Hill, and in the following year a meeting about the establishment of annual races was held in Cheltenham, with Colonel Macleod of Colbecks in the chair. Colonel Fotheringham, the Master of the Ceremonies, said that Colonel Berkeley was prepared to help on the movement in every way.

On the Wednesday before 26th August 1819, and in the two following days, the first of the regular annual race-meetings was held on Cleeve Hill, the Duke of Gloucester, who by this time was almost a resident, subscribing a hundred guineas to the race funds. His Royal Highness was probably living at this time in St George's Place which, like the lower High Street, was a much more fashionable locality in 1819 than in after years. Dr Jenner lived in St George's Place; and here also William Archer, the grandfather of the famous Fred, had a pretty little cottage, in which the greatest of all jockeys was destined to be born. William Archer, at the time of the earlier Georges, did a thriving business in letting out "double" horses for ladies to ride about behind their squires or grooms on pillions. The front of his cottage may have been somewhat altered, but the yard at the back retains, or did retain, some of the aspects of an old posting place. Archer's son, also named William, was destined in after years to live at a great local sporting rendezvous, the King's Arms at Prestbury. The second William Archer married Emma Hayward, the dark gipsy-looking daughter of the landlord. A writer in a local newspaper, published in 1895, says:

"The village hostelry, the King's Arms, or Head, I can see to this day. I can see the landlord (Mr Hayward) in his old-fashioned cut-away blue coat, with brass buttons, drab breeches and gaiters, and can picture his daughter standing at the door. Many's the chat I have had with her." Mr Hayward was churchwarden at Prestbury for more than forty years; and the family had probably been there for a long time before his day. The Haywards were highly respected, and were thought to have good blood in their veins. From them, so some say, Fred and Charlie Archer got their aristocratic looks. The King's Arms was in the old days a sort of Club for sportsmen and the haunt of many celebrities of days that are gone, while their headquarters in Cheltenham was the Plough Hotel, though for a time the Imperial was very fashionable.

After the Cheltenham races became an annual fixture most of the races were for some years flat races, but eventually the meeting was wholly given up to steeplechases and hurdle races, and so famous did the Cheltenham Races become that at length the winners of the. Cheltenham Grand Annual were penalised in the Grand National. Colonel Berkeley supported the famous race-meeting at Cheltenham from its commencement in 1819, giving a thousand pounds a year towards its maintenance, and acting as one of the stewards. Despite this princely financial support, it cannot be said that he was much of a racing man, though his principal associates, his cousin—and some said, his evil genius—Berkeley Craven, Major-General Thomas Charretie, and Mr Fulwar Craven of Brockhampton, were well known on the turf.

Of the sporting celebrities who haunted Cheltenham and Prestbury in old days one of the most famous was Major-General Thomas Charretie, better known as Colonel Charretie, who, in his time, came second only to Colonel Berkeley in the sporting life, and perhaps also in the social life of Cheltenham. He also bulks largely in the early history of steeplechasing. Born in 1784, Colonel Charretie was a year or two older than Colonel Berkeley, and probably led the latter into many of his wild orgies and escapades. He doubtless often helped the younger man to paint the Spa of Cheltenham red, and certainly was seldom missing from Berkeley Castle when high revels were being held. Little is known of his extraction except that he was an Irishman by birth and must have had private means, or he could not have joined so expensive a regiment as the 2nd Life Guards, in which he became a Captain in 1812, remaining in that regiment till exchanging to the half-pay list in 1816. He became Colonel on 10th January 1832, and Major-General on 9th November 1846. Charretie had entered the 22nd Light Dragoons on 9th June 1804, as a Cornet, had been promoted to Lieutenant, 6th February 1805. We are told that Charretie was at Vellore at the time of the mutiny there in July 1806, when two hundred of the men of the King's 69th Regiment were amongst those massacred by insurgent native troops, and when the survivors were rescued by the gallant Gillespie. Probably Charretie was attached to the 19th Dragoons and took part in "Gillespie's Ride." Charretie, on 25th December 1807, became a Captain in the 46th Foot, the South Devonshire Regiment, and on 23rd January 1812, Captain, 2nd Life Guards. He served under Wellesley in the Peninsular War, was present at Barcelona, Pamplona, and other engagements. Subsequently at the Battle of Waterloo he is said to have led his troop of Life Guardsmen with considerable dash and daring against the French Cuirassiers, though there is no official record of this.

His recorded connection with Cheltenham begins on 10th July 1815, when, about a month after Wellington's great victory, in St Mary's Church, Cheltenham, Lieutenant-Colonel Charretie married a girl then resident in the town, "Miss Margaret Anne Burges, only daughter of John Henry Burges, Esquire, of Parkanaur, in County Tyrone, Ireland." He himself was described as "of St Mary-le-bonne in the Parish of Westminster." The ceremony was performed by the Right Reverend and Honourable the Bishop of Derry. Charretie and his wife were constantly in Cheltenham, staying sometimes at the Plough, at others at 7 Lansdown Place, 6 Exmouth Street, and other houses, and at the time of his death he had a residence in Bryanston Square. A great man in Cheltenham Society, as he was in sporting circles generally, Charretie frequently attended the local balls, when he usually wore the uniform of the Berkeley Hunt, that great pack which in old days had hunted the country between Hyde Park Gate and Gloucestershire. A local newspaper, on 15th June 1839, describes a duel which "took place last Sunday, between Colonel Charretie and Mr Sanguinetti, on the Old Racecourse at Prestbury." He took a lively interest in local affairs, interesting himself, amongst other matters, in Cheltenham's water supply.

Another great sportsman, as well-known on the turf generally as he was in Cheltenham, was L. C. Fulwar Craven, Esquire, of Brockhampton Park, who may fitly be described as the last of the Cheltenham Dandies. The print reproduced here is undeniably attractive to us latter-day Georgians, and invites inquiry as to who and what was the comfortable-looking old gentleman in the comfortable clothes. Diligent questioning of old inhabitants and aged rustics produces nods and winks and knowing looks. Evidently Fulwar was a gay old boy, a roystering survivor of the Regency, with the faults, as well as the qualities, of that lively era. He was born in 1782, being the eldest son of the Reverend John Craven, of Barton Court, Hungerford, and Chilton House, Wiltshire, by his wife, the heiress of Sir Jemmett Raymond. He was the grandson of the Honourable Charles Craven, Governor of Carolina in the reign of Queen Anne, and the great-grandson of the second Lord Craven. As a young man he held a commission in the 1st Royals.

Mr Craven was a patron of all sorts of sport, which, in those days, consisted principally of racing and coursing, cock-fighting, shooting, and pugilism. He never cared for hunting, in which respect he differed from his brother Charles, who was a master of hounds for a great number of years in Sussex. It was as a racing man that Fulwar Craven became most famous, and in that respect he almost ranked with Lord George Bentinck, Jack Mytton, Squire Osbaldeston, the fourth Duke of Grafton, and the Duke of Rutland, as one of the great patrons of the turf in his day.

In 1839 Mr Fulwar Craven nearly succeeded in winning the Derby, when his mare Deception, winner of the Oaks for him, two days later, ran second to Bloomsbury.

"The Craven," as Fulwar was habitually called, was a well-known figure in Cheltenham for over fifty years, as familiar indeed, to the *habitués* of the High Street as the High Street itself. He was remarkable for his wonderful attire, and his high yellow gig. He always wore beautifully flowered waistcoats and a white beaver hat, of which the beaver was unusually long. A great friend of his was Mr Prescod of Alstone, who drove about in a blue or a yellow chariot. The equipage of Mrs Thornley, wife of the owner of Lilleybrook, was also very gorgeous, and between its back wheels ran one of those spotted carriage dogs, which Bob Chapman called "Damnation Hounds."

Fulwar Craven loafed about the town with all sorts of queer characters and would hobnob with anyone. Many tales are told of him. One day, when he was driving in his inevitable yellow gig into the town, he met a sweep with all his brushes and implements. "Jump up behind," said "The Craven." "Like this, with all my things?" questioned the sweep. "Never mind, that doesn't matter. Jump up," replied old Fulwar. The sweep had a brush in one hand and a shovel in the other, and every moment he clapped them together with a "Ting, ting !" "The Craven" drove on, and soon he met an organ-grinder with his hurdy-gurdy. He stopped again and cried to the hurdy-gurdy man, "Jump up behind," and made him turn the handle of the organ as he drove on to the Royal Hotel—then much as it is to-day. On reaching the hotel yard Mr Craven shouted, "Ostler," and on that familiar's appearance he ordered him to "help these gentlemen down with their luggage." A guinea each to the sweep and the organ-grinder must have constituted a very satisfactory end of the episode.

Amongst the famous sportsmen who frequented Cheltenham in the Georgian days, Berkeley Craven should not be forgotten: the handsomest, the cleverest, the most dashing and the most unfortunate of all the Berkeleys and Cravens who haunted Cheltenham in the Georgian days.

The Honourable Henry Augustus Berkeley Craven was born on the 21st of December 1776, son of the sixth Baron and first Earl Craven by his wife, a sister of the fifth Earl of Berkeley, and, therefore, the aunt of Colonel Berkeley and his brothers. This lady has left behind her an autobiography in which she pluckily undertook the difficult task of whitewashing herself in the eyes of posterity, for whose good opinion she had a tremendous craving. She occasionally, in her diary, notices her children in a casual sort of way, and once she remarks that, in the year after the birth of her son Berkeley, Lord Craven gave her a lottery ticket, with which she won a valuable prize. This sporting event seems to have fixed in the memory of the beautiful and volatile Countess the date of her son's advent into the world.

If Lord Craven was no paragon, Lady Craven was not in a position to throw stones, but he seems at first to have been very much in love with his wife who, had she cared to do so, might perhaps have made a decent member of society of him. After one or two false starts, however, Lord Craven deserted his wife and announced that he did not want to see her any more. She, thereupon, with an air of injured innocence, went abroad and soon wrote to her now unappreciative husband to tell him that she had found a comfortable home at the Court of the Margrave of Anspach, who, as he had a wife of his own, had adopted her as a sister! Lord Craven seems to have said nothing, and what he thought we have not the means of knowing. Lady Craven sat tight and waited, and in due course the Margravine died, and subsequently Lord Craven himself. By this time, the Countess's virtuous brother, the Earl of Berkeley, husband of Mary Cole, was getting seriously annoyed with her, and neither before nor after the death of Lord Craven, which was followed by a marriage between his lordship's widow and the Margrave, would he have anything to do with his sister. Lord Berkeley had been appointed guardian of the young Cravens by the late Earl, but when Lady Craven had first left Lord Craven she had taken the youngest boy, Keppel, abroad with her, and had refused to give him up. The other children were brought up by Lord Berkeley. Grantley Berkeley tells us that both Berkeley Craven and his brother Keppel spent a great deal of their time in Cheltenham.

The Assembly Room (the scene of Byron's proposal of marriage to Miss Milbanke).

At the age of eighteen Berkeley started upon a military career of sorts, being appointed Captain of an "independent company of foot," and in 1825 he had become a Major-General. He married, in December 1829, Mademoiselle Marie Clarisse Tribhault.

When Berkeley's mother and her second husband came to England (having sold the principality), Queen Charlotte would not receive them at Court as her cousins, nor, indeed, as anything else. The Margravine, therefore, started a sort of Court of her own at Brandenburg House, Hammersmith. She had many portraits of herself painted, but she vainly tells us that not one of them was nearly good enough. The Margravine, who had also been given the title of Princess Berkeley, was very proud of Berkeley Craven's looks, and called him "An ornament to Society."

The year 1824 was a turning-point in the history of Cheltenham, for it marked the beginning of the end, so far as the Berkeley regime was concerned. In that year the affair of Maria Foote brought Colonel Berkeley into considerable disrepute, though perhaps on the whole he might have behaved much worse. In that year also the Reverend Francis Close became assistant Curate at the new Trinity Church, and two years later, his fiend, Mr Simeon (who had bought the presentation to the living in 1816), appointed him to the Perpetual Curacy of Cheltenham, where he was to reign as an almost absolute monarch for many years, in fact, until he became Dean of Carlisle in 1856. He was, indeed, the forerunner of the Victorian era, so far as his future parish was concerned, and his coming was heavy with menace to the Georgian age, and presaged the decline and fall of the Berkeley empire at the Spa, though at present the Curate was merely a speck in Colonel Berkeley's bright heaven of blue. The Colonel's now splendid establishment of hounds and horses was looked upon as a godsend to the town, and gave a powerful impulse to its mercantile interests. When it was pointed out to him that when the hounds were at Berkeley, Cheltenham had no outdoor sport to offer its visitors, he organised staghounds, and provided the red deer, making Craven Berkeley, MP, the first master.

Colonel Berkeley was, however, ceasing to be the little tin god he had been in his younger days. His female associates were flaunted so openly as to shock Society. Nor was the establishment at German Cottage near the High Street the only one he kept in the town. Another expensive hobby of the Colonel's, apart from his association with various actresses, was the stage. He spared neither time nor expense in bringing down the best dramatic talent from the metropolis, and often the whole cost of the entertainments fell upon him. In his dramatic ventures he used to perform with the best professionals in the country, and excellent amateur actor as he apparently was, one cannot place too much weight on the appreciative notices in the local press, as the critics used up all their epithets in praise of him and his fellow-amateurs, often having nothing left for their distinguished professional *confrères*. He would tour the country with his brothers, Maurice and Augustus, John Austin, Dawkins, and others. At this time he lived in the society of actors and actresses, and often had one of the latter under his charge. By his patronage he undoubtedly secured theatrical fare for Cheltenham, almost equal to that provided on the London stage, and during the slump in theatrical enterprise, the town lost a very considerable asset.

One of the most notorious of Colonel Berkeley's theatrical associates was Mrs Bunn, an actress, formerly Miss Somerville. There is a great deal about this lady in Grantley Berkeley's *Memoirs*.

In the summer of 1815 Colonel Berkeley had met at Cheltenham, Miss Maria Foote, the fascinating actress, who was considered to be one of the most beautiful women of her day. She was then a young girl in her teens and Colonel Berkeley performed at her Benefit at the Cheltenham Theatre. She lived with Colonel Berkeley several years and bore him two daughters, for whom he subsequently provided liberally. In time came the inevitable quarrel, and they parted, but Colonel Berkeley made his late *inamorata* an allowance of a thousand pounds a year. In 1824 the new *Cheltenham Journal* severely criticised Colonel Berkeley's conduct towards the actress and made uncomplimentary references to his mother and the circumstances of his birth.

Miss Foote was not the ill-used martyr that the article implied, and the tone of the newspaper attack naturally filled Colonel Berkeley with wrath. When the editor made uncomplimentary remarks on the ladies at the Berkeley Hunt Ball, Colonel Berkeley found it a good excuse for getting his own back. He proceeded with Mr Robert Carr Hammond and Lord Sussex Lennox to the editor's house in Northfield Place, and there horsewhipped him. This affair was the subject of one of Robert Cruikshank's best-known caricatures. Robert Hammond is seen standing by the door to prevent anyone coming to the assistance of the editor (a Mr Jasper Judge), while Lord Sussex guards the fire-irons, which might have made useful weapons. However justifiable, it was a cowardly business, as Mr Judge was taken unawares and was quite unable to defend himself.

The editor brought an action against Colonel Berkeley and obtained £500 damages. The lady who was the original cause of the trouble was not inconsolable. Soon afterwards a Mr Haynes made her an offer of marriage, which promise he failed to keep. Miss Maria brought a breach of promise action and was awarded £3000 damages. Subsequently she became a countess, as the wife of Lord Harrington.

The young clergyman, Francis Close, who, as has been said, had been appointed to Cheltenham, was the man who sounded the death-knell of Georgian Cheltenham. The ban he subsequently placed on the famous race-meeting and on all theatrical enterprises was largely responsible for the winding-up of the town's business as a pleasure resort and a fashionable spa. There were other causes at work, such as the popularity of foreign watering-places, which had been inaccessible to Englishmen during the Napoleonic wars, and the increased facilities for more extended travel by the laying down of railroads. But to Francis Close much of the credit—or blame—is due for hastening the decline and fall of Cheltenham as a resort of the *beau-monde*. It is true, however, that he was not only a destructive force, but also a builder. His opponents, and they were numerous, were ready to admit that it was largely as a consequence of his energy and enthusiasm that Cheltenham became famous as an educational centre. During his "reign" too, the town grew in population from 19,000 to 40,000 inhabitants.

"The Power of the Church," says W. E. Adams, the author of *The Memoirs of a Social Atom*, who for several years worked in the office of a Cheltenham journal, "was probably never more remarkably demonstrated anywhere than it was in Cheltenham during many years of the middle of the nineteenth century. As a matter of fact, the history of the town, for all that period, was the history of a single clergyman."

Francis Close was born in 1797, his father being a parson. But his was more of a martial than a priestly family, for his three brothers were soldiers, as were two of his four sons, a third holding a commission in the Royal Navy. In a memoir of this notable divine it is said that at one time he had a strong inclination to go to sea—an early passion which he had learnt sitting on Admiral Cornwallis's knee, and listening to the inspiring tales of sea life related by the Admiral, who is described by William Hickey as "a veritable Trunnion, but more of a brute than Smollett made of his hero."

The earnest wishes of Francis Close's mother alone restrained Cornwallis from taking the boy to sea with him, but the taste for salt water remained, and in Close's boyhood his boating propensities displayed themselves on the Thames, and afterwards, when at Hull with his tutor, he always made the journey to London by sea, for the pleasure of the voyage; and on one occasion he was nearly lost in a gale of wind off Yarmouth. This taste for the water followed him to college, where, having no taste for mathematics, he devoted his leisure hours chiefly to aquatic adventures.

It will scarcely be believed that at this time there was not a six- or eight-oared boat on the river. Mr Close did much to recommend the practice of rowing and sailing among the gownsmen, and a story is still current among the barges of how Mr Close cut the towing-line of a train of barges which were coming up the river, and drove them all on shore, because they would not give way and would have capsized his boat. Often was he seen in later life going down the Channel in an open boat, with only two or three of his own boys for a crew; and the coast between Portsmouth and Plymouth was as familiar to him as the King's Highway.

Francis Close was educated at Merchant Taylors' School, and at St John's College, Cambridge, and in his college days he came under the influence of Simeon, the great evangelical leader, who found in him just the sort of enthusiastic young man he needed. While Close was at Cambridge he also made the acquaintance of a Staffordshire family named Arden, which resulted in his marriage with Miss Annie Diana Arden. Shortly after leaving college he was ordained, and after holding two or three curacies for short periods he came, as has been seen, in 1824, as curate to Holy Trinity, Cheltenham, then but recently built, and the only other church in the town besides the beautiful old Parish Church of St Mary's. The handsome young clergyman soon became extremely popular, and two years later was appointed, by Mr Simeon, Incumbent of Cheltenham.

It was only three years before battle was joined, and the Berkeley family began to sit up and take notice of the young man who dared to pit his will against theirs, and though it was a long time before Mr Close really gained the mastery, the Close Season set in at the Spa.

The Cheltenham Annual Races were in full swing in 1827 when Mr Close launched his campaign against them. In this year he preached his first sermon "On the evil consequences of attending the Racecourse." This tirade was subsequently printed, and ran into many editions. It was being hawked about the streets when John Parry, the younger, wrote *Dolly Dubbins's Diary*, in which that imaginary young lady is described as going to the Parish Church in order to hear Mr Close preach on his pet subject.

Francis Close cannot have known much about actors and actresses, but at least he knew well, as did all Cheltenham, that not at one house in the town only did Colonel Berkeley keep his notorious theatrical associates, of whom there were several, though Miss Foote and Mrs Bunn were the best known of them.

It was not until 3rd May 1839 that the pride of Watson's heart, the Cambray Theatre, was burnt down, but even now Mr Close was injuring all theatrical enterprise in the town, and this was hard on the many respectable actors and actresses who played in Cheltenham.

The grand stand on the racecourse was eventually broken up and sold for firewood, and subsequently, when flames licked up the theatre, Mr Close exercised his overpowering influence, with the effect that no regular theatre was established while he remained in the town.

XIII

1824–1826

*Sir Walter Scott—Yates—Terry—Macready—A Gretna Green
Romance—A Bard of Butterflies.*

In July 1824 Frederick Henry Yates, then a celebrated actor, and the father of
Edmund Yates, became manager of the Cheltenham Theatre.

Yates was born in 1797. Educated at Charterhouse, he obtained a post in the
Commissariat Department, served under Wellington in the Peninsular War and
was, it is said, present at Waterloo. From 1818 up to 1825 Yates had chiefly acted
at Covent Garden, but in March 1825 he and Daniel Terry bought the Adelphi
Theatre for £25,000. In November 1823 Yates married Elizabeth Brunton, a
well-known actress, and a member of an old theatrical family.

Sir Walter Scott's sister-in-law, Mrs Scott, lived in Cheltenham, and in 1826 the
great man himself came on a visit to the Spa, possibly with the object of spying
out the land for his friend, Daniel Terry, the actor, who, like Scott himself, was
at this time financially embarrassed. A Cheltenham journalist's account of this
exciting event reads: "Sir Walter is certainly what may be called a plain man; but
there is an air of benignity, combined with intelligence in his countenance, which
renders his appearance very pleasing. We were glad to see him look so well, and
long may he live to enjoy that universal applause which he so deservedly merits.

"He arrived on Tuesday, the 21st November, and remained only two days with
us. He spent the greater part of his time in the company of his sister-in-law, Mrs
Scott of Oxford Street."

Daniel Terry, Scott's intimate friend, was born at Bath in or about 1780. As soon
as he left school was apprenticed to an architect, with whom he remained for five
years, then becoming an actor. After playing in the elder Macready's company he
returned to his former profession, which he finally abandoned when he joined
John Kemble in the north of England. Kemble's company broke up in 1806, and
Terry, while playing in Liverpool, attracted the attention of Henry Siddons, and
soon became manager of the Edinburgh Theatre under his new acquaintance.

At this time Sir Walter Scott was greatly excited about the production at this theatre of a new play by Joanna Baillie, niece of the great surgeon, John Hunter, in which Siddons and Terry played, much to the contentment of The Wizard of the North. Terry, of whom all Scott's literary friends appear to have been very fond, was introduced to the poet by the Ballantynes. A warm friendship soon sprang up, and Terry adored his famous friend so much that he began unconsciously to imitate him.

Lockhart says of Terry: "His small, birdlike features had acquired, before I knew him, a truly ludicrous cast of Scott's meditative frown; and to crown all he habitually affected his tone and accent so that, though a native of Bath a stranger could hardly have doubted that he was a Scotchman. The handwriting of the two men was almost exactly alike. One of Mathews's best caricatures was of Terry's sober mimicry of Scott." By 1811 the intimacy had made rapid strides, and when Scott bought Abbotsford, Terry's architectural advice was invaluable to him. Even after he had made a great success at the Haymarket, Terry continued to visit Scotland almost every season, and was very much at Scott's service as architect of the improvements going on at his new estate.

On the 18th of September 1813 Terry performed the part of Leon in "Have a Wife and Rule a Wife" at Covent Garden—his first appearance there. Except for summer vacations at the Haymarket and frequent migrations to Edinburgh, Terry remained at Covent Garden until 1822. About this time the actor, who had been previously married, took as his second wife, Elizabeth, daughter of Alexander Nasmyth, the painter. Their son, Walter, was naturally Scott's godson, and their daughter was christened Jane. When, in conjunction with Frederick Yates, Terry took the Adelphi Theatre, both Scott and Ballantyne became security for him for a considerable amount, which Sir Walter eventually had to pay. Terry's friends were doubtful as to the success of the undertaking, and it was after a visit to the Adelphi that Scott calve down to Cheltenham, of which he and Terry had possibly heard a good deal from Yates.

Colonel Berkeley still greatly patronised the Cheltenham Theatre and Mrs Yates's aunt, Louisa Brunton, had married Lord Craven. Whether or not this connection with the Berkeleys and Cravens helped Yates it is impossible to say, but it seems strange that two such well-known and even celebrated actors as Yates and Terry found it worth while to become, even for a short time, managers of the Cheltenham Theatre.

Mr and Mrs Yates determined that their son, Edmund, should not be brought up to their own profession. He became a journalist and novelist, and far more famous than his parents had ever been in their dramatic vocation; indeed, they are probably best remembered to-day as his parents.

The *Cheltenham Chronicle* of 26th April 1827 thus proudly heralds arrival at the theatre of "that admirable and clever comedian Mr Terry, whose talents are well known and appreciated in the theatrical world."

Possibly Yates came down to make some of the arrangements for his friend, as well as to give his "inimitable entertainment in Cheltenham," which he did on the 15th of May. In "Reminiscences or Scenes from Life," Yates imitated, amongst others, Kean as Richard III and Young as Hamlet.

The local dramatic critic on 22nd May 1827 notices the play of "John Bull" and Terry's "Job Thornberry," which was magnificent. "The admirable manner in which he performed his trying scene with John Bull, and his interview with Peregrine and his daughter exhibited a degree of feeling which we only expect from the best actors of the day. The whole business of the farce in 'The Wedding Day' seemed to devolve upon Terry, Miss Penley and Miss Cooke. On Wednesday, 4th June, 'The Hypocrite' was performed, Terry was Dr Cantwell and Liston had little to do. Mrs Daly and Miss R. Penley are valuable additions to our company. The amusing farce was 'XYZ,' with Liston as Neddy Brey, Esq.

"On Thursday we were given 'Sweethearts and Wives,' with Liston as Billy Lackaday, Terry as Admiral Fraulelin, and Miss R. Penley as Eugenia. The audience were sent home laughing to their beds. Every wrinkle and dimple filled with frolic and good-humour. 18th June. 'Guy Mannering,' dramatised by Mr Terry with Miss Penley excellent as Meg Merrilies. On Thursday, a fine tabby cat caused much amusement by coming on the stage. Mr Terry was Mr Hardcastle in 'She Stoops to Conquer.' 'The Honeymoon' was to be performed on Tuesday, 8th July."

The Close Season was now, however, setting in with frosty severity, so that probably Terry did not make nearly so much money in Cheltenham as he had hoped. Indeed, nothing had really gone well with the theatre since the death of the elder Watson. It was much harmed by Mr Close's hatred of the drama, and would have long been in a bad way but for Colonel Berkeley and his amateurs.

Terry's health, too, was failing, and not many months after he left Cheltenham he died, a broken man, worn out by illness and debts and by the difficulties of existence generally.

In 1825 Macready, the great actor, had been in Cheltenham. The *Cheltenham Chronicle* says: "Mr Macready's Virginius stands alone in the solitary pre-eminence of genius. It is perfect. Acting cannot go beyond it. No acting of his that we have lately seen can approach it."

The *Chronicle* of 14th October 1826 has the following story: "When Mr Macready lately visited Cheltenham, one of the performers, addressing himself to the tragedian in the green-room, observed that the robbery recently committed in the Treasury of the Birmingham Theatre was a severe calamity. "It might have been!" said Macready, with an air of mystery. "Might have been! Surely, Mr Macready, the loss of £200 at such times as the present may be considered a serious calamity. But, pray, sir, do you not think it was actually so?" After a considerable pause, during which 'Each list'ner held his breath to hear' the solution of the apparent enigma, 'The mighty master' raising his eyes from the carpet upon which they had been bent as if in deep study of its pattern, drew himself up with peculiar grandeur and answered, 'I played for them.'"

William Charles Macready was born on the 3rd of March 1793, in the parish of St Pancras, London. His father, said to have been an Irishman, or of Irish extraction, was the manager of a provincial company, and the lessee of several theatres.

Macready was intended for the Church or for the Bar, and at the age of ten was sent to Rugby. He had visited Cheltenham as a child in the year 1798, concerning which visit he writes in his diary: "The interval of several weeks between my translation from one school to another was passed in Cheltenham. My journey there differed somewhat from modern travelling. Leaving London with my father about noon by the Long Coach (a sort of clumsy omnibus), reaching Oxford about midnight, to supper in the kitchen of the Inn (on beef which I remember my father indignantly denounced as of *mauvaise odeur*), we arrived in Cheltenham in something less than twenty-four hours. This populous and handsomely laid-out town was then little better than one long street, with a few intersecting smaller ones. The Well Walk, as it was then, now called the Royal Old Wells, was crowded in the early morning with visitors parading up and down after their daily doses of the waters. My inevitable tumbler was very unwillingly taken, and a little aviary, near the little theatre, belonging to a Mr Watson, makes up the sum total of my recollections of the place."

When he was about seventeen years of age, his father's business affairs became embarrassed, and the son took up the management of the theatrical company in the hope of helping to straighten matters out.

In June 1810 at Birmingham he had made his first appearance as an actor, and his success was so great that the company was saved from ruin, and thus Macready's career was settled for him. He went on from one success to another.

In 1860 Macready settled in Cheltenham and from that time until his death lived at 6 Wellington Square. He became very religious, talked little about the stage, interested himself in local affairs, and on one occasion wrote a letter to the *Cheltenham Examiner*, in which he suggested the provision of a public library for the town of which he had become an inhabitant.

The late Miss Alice Urch said: "I taught Nevil Macready when I was little more than a child myself, and the first day I began to give him lessons, I took him out for a walk, when the child remarked, 'No one will believe you're my governess, they'll think you're my sister.' I remember also that on that first day I was there, a wasp settled on Mr Macready's face. We watched it crawling right across his wide forehead, and he never moved a muscle, so that, of course, it didn't sting him. Mr Macready was not exactly handsome; very fine-looking though. Mrs Macready was always very kind to me. She realised that I was very young, and always contrived that I should see all the celebrities who came to Wellington Square. I remember one day Dickens came to dine with him, and Mrs Macready came and said: 'My dear, when they are coming out from dinner, look down over the staircase and you will see Mr Dickens. It's always nice to be able to say you have seen such people.'

"I looked down as she told me, but I can't remember much about Dickens's looks; except that he had on a black velvet coat. Miss Hogarth used to come there, too—Dickens's wife's sister; the one you heard talked of a good deal. She had a very sweet face."

Miss Urch continues: "I went to see the Macreadys lately in London, and Gordon, Sir Nevil's boy, came to the station with me, and we passed Hogarth Square. For old times' sake I went to see the picture of Mr Macready in the National Portrait Gallery, when I was last in London. It is a splendid likeness of him. Mr Macready, of course, made money, and acted for money, but it always took a second place with him. His art was everything to him, and he made a sort of religion of it, giving it of his very best. There was nothing done for show nor effect; it was just the best possible. I remember when Irving died, and there was so much —well, sort of puff and advertisement about him, Mrs Macready said: 'There was nothing like this when Mr Macready died,' meaning I suppose, that Macready was such a much greater man, and somehow didn't need people to be fulsome about him. He had just done the very best he could. The first Mrs Macready came of a theatrical family, I believe, and yet her children never showed the slightest desire to become actors and actresses. Cyril Maude is said to have told Nevil Macready that if he had gone on the stage, he himself would have been nowhere. Yet *Nevil's* mother had nothing to do with theatrical folks. Mr Macready *never* advised people to go on the stage, and never seemed to want to talk about it.

"There was one old lady who used to stay with them. I can't remember her name, but I think she held some office in Queen Victoria's household—used to look after the Queen's pet birds, or something of that sort. Macready lost his voice almost completely; I expect from having strained it so much when he was acting, and one day he spoke in a very low voice, and I think the old lady thought he was piling on the agony. 'William,' she said, so sharply, 'William, I am sure you could speak louder if you liked.' Oh, no, he didn't say anything. He just smiled. He had such a nice smile, and such kind eyes. I never heard him called William by anybody else."

Macready died on 27th April 1873, aged eighty years.

Off the stage as well as on, in Cheltenham, there were doubtless many romances connected with the Spa, which culminated before the mock parsons of Gretna Green. Yet no other one created so much stir as did the elopement in February 1836 of Ann Hicks, the plain heiress to more than one large estate, with an Irish adventurer. The story of her short-lived romance and its sequel is amusingly related by Mrs Hicks Beach in her clever book entitled *A Cotswold Family: Hicks and Hicks Beach*.

The unfortunate heroine of the Gretna Green romance was the only child of Sir William Hicks and of Lady Hicks, who had been a Miss Chute of The Vynes, a well-known Hampshire property and, as Lady Hicks's brothers and sisters were all childless, her daughter Ann was regarded as the heiress to this estate with its splendid mansion-house.

Before the death of his father in 1801, Sir William Hicks' had been living in a house on the outskirts of Cheltenham, called The Belle Vue, now known as the Belle Vue Hotel. The house was then "truly rural," and possessed a considerable garden, alongside the London road, while in front the grounds, on which no other houses had as yet been built, sloped down to the willows of the Chelt, by which Byron had declared that he had sat down and wept when he remembered Georgiana Cottage and the gloriously beautiful Lady Oxford. Sir William Hicks kept on his Cheltenham residence after he succeeded to Witcombe, and spent part of each year there, for he was Chairman of the Cheltenham bench, and, as the old files of the *Chronicle* show, took a considerable part in the public affairs of the town.

It was between Witcombe and Cheltenham then that Sir William's only child grew up. In due course she came out at the Cheltenham balls and assemblies. She was no beauty—in fact, she was a replica of her plain father, only without his stutter—but at the balls she was not without partners; her wealth and social position made that impossible in the scheming, worldly little watering-place. Nor was she without suitors, though none met with any response until an Irishman, William Lambart Cromie, came upon the scene, who had haunted every ball or other festival to which Ann had gone. Ann's heart was probably easily won, but her parents did not at all approve of her Irish suitor, whose family, although he was heir to a baronetcy, was by no means distinguished.

Ann was so captivated as to be ready to disobey her parents, and rumours of rebellion evidently got abroad. The *Cheltenham Chronicle* for 22nd February 1826, said: "It is rumoured in the fashionable circles that the only daughter of a worthy baronet in this neighbourhood is about to receive the flowery wreath of Hymen from the hand of a late wily visitor of good family connections."

The following week a far more stirring announcement was possible. "A great sensation was excited in the town last week by the sudden disappearance of Miss H————, daughter of Sir W. H————, and sole presumptive heiress to more than one large fortune. The young lady took the road to Scotland by a circuitous route, accompanied by Mr Cromie, to whom, according to a letter received from her, dated Carlisle, she has been united by the Gretna parson." Three weeks afterwards the eloping couple were remarried in the more orthodox fashion in Marylebone Church, and the parish register states that "these parties have been heretofore married to each other in Scotland." Sir William was terribly, though, of course, impotently, angry and never forgave his daughter, but Lady Hicks soon determined to make the best of a bad job. All she could do at the time was to get her little Ann a first-class lady's maid, before the erring couple set off on a continental honeymoon, which came to an abrupt conclusion when Paris was reached. Lambart Cromie and the first-class lady's maid disappeared, and left the poor little bride stranded in the French capital. Sir William, on hearing the news, could do no less than set forth immediately for Paris to rescue his daughter, who meekly and shamefacedly returned with him to renew her quiet life at Witcombe. Cheltenham and its gaieties were for her now things of the past. Sir William and his lady gave up The Belle Vue and for the rest of her life Ann Cromie lived in seclusion at Witcombe, with no more exciting incidents to vary the monotony than the occasional visits of relatives. She had, moreover, by her social *faux pas*, lost all chance of succeeding to her uncle's property in Hampshire.

Little is known of the later life of Lambart Cromie, except that he died in a lunatic asylum, and that for some years previous to his death, Ann visited him there annually. In 1827, he had reappeared in Cheltenham; and Ann, who had been spending a wretched eleven years under the parental roof, seems to have been prepared to return to her husband much to the consternation of her parents and other relatives. Three years later he was there again, and his little wife wrote to a cousin, "I am going to Cheltenham to-morrow, where Lambart will arrive to-day, and look out for a house for us in the meantime, to save the trouble of going to an hotel first and then moving; I have not the least idea how long we shall stay there."

Sir William took drastic measures which apparently were effectual in putting a stop to a reconciliation. He made a will by which he practically disinherited his daughter if she ever lived with her husband again, or if her husband died and she married another Irishman!

In 1834, Sir William died, being survived only five years by Lady Hicks. Lady Cromie—her husband had by then succeeded to the baronetcy—now came into her own, and as the mistress of Witcombe, was at last a personage in the eyes of the world. At first she took an interest in the estate and built a school and school-house for the villagers. Subsequently the lonely lady took up religion fervently, and much-needed improvements to the manor house were shelved in order that large cheques might be given to her ardent friend, the Rev. Francis Close. Whatever his enemies might say about him, the famous Incumbent of Cheltenham was a man of big ideas, ecclesiastical and educational; and most of these he succeeded in carrying out. But much money was required for their fulfilment, and one of the sources he tapped, and that frequently, was the Mistress of Witcombe. Thus quietly, in her secluded home, this victim of a Georgian tragedy, lived on retaining, it is true, her Georgian prejudices—and all the customs of her Georgian youth. Indeed, it was not until 1885 that this link with the Georgian Era passed away; and the story of her romance became more than ever a memory of the dim and far-gone past.

A very different marriage from poor Anne Hicks's was the wedding, in the presence, as the bride remarks, "of all the rank, fashion and beauty of Cheltenham," of Haynes Bayly, the poet, and Helena Hayes. This fashionable function took place at St James's Church, on 11th July 1826, and was thus announced: "Married at Cheltenham by the Rev. John T. Becher, Prebendary of Southwell, Thomas

Haynes Bayly, Esq, of Mount Beacon House, near Bath, to Helena Becher Hayes, only surviving daughter and heiress of the late Benjamin Hayes, Esq, of Marble Hill, in the County of Cork."

Haynes Bayly, already a well-known poet, was born at Bath in October 1797, and was thus twenty-three years of age when his Helena acquired him. She wrote his life, expressing her stupendous pride in him in two pretentious volumes with covers of dunducketty greenish-brown in which THB's "Muse" or "Pensive Muse," however she might feel at the moment, is always honoured with a capital M. while The Poet is thus described with the definite article, both also with caps. His *Lyre* also, for he knew no lower case, no minor chords, and it is a very splendid *Lyre*, is depicted on the cover of each of the two volumes, mounting on eagles' feathers, and supported by a pedestal. And what more do you want? "The young poet," says Helena, "was nurtured in the lap of luxury. He was generally considered an idle boy, though, strictly speaking, he did not merit this censure." He dramatised a tale when seven years of age, and he wrote a poem "To a Friend" in a child's round hand. Haynes Bayly proceeded in due course to Winchester, where he edited a school newspaper "containing all the proceedings of the masters and pupils of that celebrated establishment." At seventeen years of age he was summoned home by his father, who wished him to follow his own profession of the law. The boy, however, had taken a great dislike for the law. "A profession too dull for his versatile genius. Fascinated by the muses, he wished to wear only their silken bands." Haynes Bayly, senior, however, scorned this chilly attire for his son—one thinks he must have been the old Nathaniel Bayly who had dealt with William Hickey—and Thomas's next idea was to become a clergyman. He soon, however, dropped this scheme and desired to become a poet only.

When at St Mary's Hall, Oxford, an incident occurred which was "highly creditable to Mr Haynes Bayly." A girl who, like himself, lived in Bath, and of whom he knew but little, wrote to ask him about the health of her brother, who was a college friend of Haynes Bayly's. "Her anxiety for a consumptive brother, who left off writing home, led her thus to overstep the bounds of propriety."

The brother died. Haynes Bayly had looked after him during his long illness, and had "closed his eyes in peace," while the sister, although Helena evidently thought her a forward young minx, did not apparently venture to come to Oxford, though why the poor boy was so much left to the ministrations of Haynes Bayly does not transpire. After his friend's death, the poet visited the sister and the rest of the family in Bath, and soon became engaged to the girl, but Mr Haynes Bayly did not rise to the occasion, and flatly refused to provide for Thomas and his intended bride. The lovers "were both too wise to think of living upon love, and after mutual sighs and tears, they parted, never to meet again." Haynes Bayly, junior, was, for a time, inconsolable and as usual, had recourse to his ink-bottle. He let off steam with "Mournful Reflections" about the brother, and with "May Thy Lot in Life be Happy " about the sister. After that he felt much better.

Rosa soon afterwards married someone else, and her former sweetheart wrote: "Oh, no, we never mention her," and "The Sonnets to Rosa," amongst which latter collection of songs is the charming "Isle of Beauty," which Mrs Haynes Bayly expurgated, perhaps because she did not approve of the sentiment, "Absence makes the heart grow fonder," when addressed to her predecessor in Thomas's affections.

The opening lines read as follows:

"Shades of evening close not o'er us,
Leave our lonely bark awhile!
Morn, alas! will not restore us
Yonder dim and distant Isle.
Still my fancy can discover
Sunny spots where friends may dwell;
Darker shadows round us hover,
Isle of beauty, fare-thee-well."

After his parting from Rosa, Haynes Bayly went for a trip to Dublin, was received in the first circles, and shone in amateur theatricals. Here he wrote "Isabel," which created a great sensation, and soon afterwards Balfe gave the young poet a good advertisement by composing the music for one of his ballads.

In 1824 Thomas returned home. Mrs Hayes's *soirées* in Bath were frequented at that time by the talented, the young and the gay, and the hostess's daughter, Helena, asked one of her suitors to bring the song-writer to one of her mother's parties. When she had thus scraped an acquaintance with the handsome poet and had found out that he was *épris,* Helena did not find him—or says that she did not—exactly what her imagination had portrayed, so that she begged her mother to leave Bath for Paris; which she did, when Helena promptly wished herself back in Bath. Haynes Bayly now wrote two poems in praise of "Helena's Worth and Loveliness," which she transcribes at full length in her book, and he wrote a new one henceforth on each of her birthdays.

After nearly a year, Thomas discovered that he had at last found favour in the eyes of Miss Hayes, and gave her a little box which, so he said, contained something alive, and begged that it should be opened in his absence. It contained no mouse, but a little ruby heart, and he followed up this gift with a letter "so full of wit and fun," that Helena subsequently inserted it at full length in her *Memoir* of her husband. There was, apparently, plenty of money, so that Mr Haynes Bayly, senior, probably thought that his changeable son had done as well for himself as could have been expected. Settlements were made and the marriage took place as before related.

The first poem composed by Thomas after his marriage was "I'd be a Butterfly," in which, as poor Helena sadly remarks, he foretold his own early decease:

"Oh, folly caught me as I slept
Upon a lilac spray;
And spurned me when his hand had swept
My golden down away.

Alas! alas how very brief
Is pleasure's brightest ray.
The sun that warms the summer leaf
Will hasten its decay."

Haynes Bayly at the time of his marriage had a rising reputation as a poet, and he "visited and corresponded with several persons of high rank." Doubtless he had other friends who moved in less exalted circles but these, with the exception of Theodore Hook, his friend for better for worse, Helena does not mention. This brilliant and sometimes unscrupulous writer was greatly attached to the poet whose beautiful wistful face looks out on us from the frontispiece of the first of Helena's absurd volumes, and makes her readers see for themselves that there was something in the man after all.

One of the best-known of Haynes Bayly's poems is "The Mistletoe Bough;" he also wrote "Lilla's a Lady," "She wore a Wreath of Roses," "Come open your Casement, my Dear," and many other old-world tunes.

The best of Haynes Bayly's plays was "Perfection," which was performed by Madame Vestris and her company before "a house crowded in every part."

Thomas Haynes Bayly died, aged forty-two, at No 430 High Street, Cheltenham, on April 22nd 1839, and was buried in the cemetery at the bottom of the town.

Mrs Morgan, an admirer of his poetry, put up a tombstone over his grave with a butterfly on it; and she planted a willow, which "hung mournfully over his grave." Helena Bayly, his wife, was left very badly off and a fund was got up for her. Theodore Hook wrote the inscription on a tablet put up in St James's Church to Haynes Bayly.

XIV

1823–1828

Colonel Riddell—The Last Three Visits of the Duke of Wellington —
Henry Thompson—Pearson Thompson—Mr Fortescue—Major Agg, etc.

Colonel Riddell had had many excitements at Wellington Mansion since the
Duke of Wellington's visit to Cheltenham in 1816. He had protected the Waterloo
Oak by railings and had laid the first stone of the Wellington Obelisk on the
lawn beside the tree, when Lord Hill and other fashionable people were present.
This stone was laid in May 1817, and the Colonel then intended "to throw a
commodious arch and bridge (instead of the present dangerous one) over that
part of the Chelt which divided his property from Lady Mary Lindsay's."

In 1818, he was making a new carriage drive from Cambray, through his own
land into the road at its extremity, thus forming an improved ride into the New
Bath Road, and a more beautiful entrance into Thompson's and the Sherborne
Spas. The road, in passing over the Chelt, was to be thrown over the Chelt by an
eight-foot stone arch, with an iron palisade. After passing the arch it was to take a
sweep to the right of the Oak and Obelisk.

On 11th June 1822, Colonel Riddell had a great Waterloo Party in his garden,
when amidst a great peal of bells the Wellington Road and the delightful grounds
were thrown open to two hundred guests. Six girls, neatly attired, bearing baskets
of fruit and preceding an excellent band of music, walked in procession from the
Colonel's new cottage to the charming lawn in front of Wellington House.

He also kept up his medical interests. We read: "At the Mansion House,
Colonel Riddell, of the East India Company's service, waited on the Lord Mayor
to inform him that he had a sovereign remedy for the typhus fever which seemed
prevalent in the Metropolis. The Lord Mayor said that he was happy to hear it,
and begged the Colonel would not delay so important a communication. 'If I
had your authority for its introduction, my Lord Mayor, I am confident that the
contagion would soon depart.' The Lord Mayor said that he did not himself know
much about fevers, but why did not the Colonel call the attention of the Medical

Faculty to his specific.'The Medical Faculty! If I cured a whole hospital of patients the physicians would take no notice.' 'You must advertise in the newspapers,' said the Lord Mayor … Finally the Colonel went away without mentioning his specific, or saying that he would follow the advice just given to him."

After inheriting his Enfield Estate from his mother, Mrs Mockler, Colonel Riddell took less interest in Cheltenham, and had been little in the Spa for some years when he died in 1825. Nevertheless, he and Pearson Thompson and John Boles Watson had done much for Cheltenham "by the purchase and development of land, when the town must have been considered in embryo."

Colonel Riddell's residence has long since passed away. The obelisk erected on his lawn in honour of the Duke of Wellington's visit to the hero-worshipper's house, was pulled down in 1862 and carted away for building materials and its site was converted into Mr Pipe's nursery gardens. The Salvation Army buildings overlooking the Chelt stand in part of what was once the great man's garden, and the Colonel himself, who was such a feature of Georgian Cheltenham, is not so much as a memory with most of the town's present-day inhabitants.

When the Duke of Wellington next visited Cheltenham Spa, Colonel Riddell does not appear to have been present to welcome his idol, and it seems as if Wellington Mansion, the original Cambray House, had then been sold. Wellington evidently did not come to Cheltenham for the races, for he reached the town on 26th July 1823, just after the big summer race meeting which always attracted so many fashionable people. The Duchess did not accompany him on this occasion.

"At a late hour on Saturday evening His Grace the Duke of Wellington arrived in Cheltenham and continued peals of the joy-bells announced the event. Georgiana House had been taken for his temporary residence; Wellington Mansion, which His Grace was very desirous of again occupying, being previously pre-engaged; but on Monday evening His Grace removed to Cambray House, which had been most politely tendered to him by Mr Baynham Jones."

The Duke was then a Cabinet Minister, holding the office of Master-General of the Ordnance. He had lately come under the administration of Mr Canning, and had begun his conflict with his political leader. Wellington was too strong a man not to make mistakes and enemies, but in Cheltenham his popularity continued unabated, and from time to time the most imposing figure of his age was continually seen in the High Street, in the churches, in the Well Walk, in the local places of amusement. He was doubtless the most splendid advertisement the Cheltenham waters ever had, for with characteristic thoroughness, he applied the healing streams both inwardly and outwardly. The Cheltenham people were for once fully alive to their luck in having the great soldier so often in their midst, and everybody was always anxious to see the eagle-faced victor of Waterloo leading his simple life among the veterans of his campaigns.

(27th July.) "At eight o'clock on Sunday morning, the Duke went to the Old Wells and drank the waters, which were presented to him on a new and handsome piece of plate by the proprietor, Mr Chambers, whom His Grace was pleased to recognise in a most condescending. manner. He then proceeded, accompanied by Mr Marshall, to the Montpellier and Sherborne Promenades.

(28th July.) "On Monday evening the Rooms were honoured by the presence of 'The Great Captain of the Age.' On this occasion, Mr Marshall, MC, most agreeably surprised the illustrious soldier, for at his entrance, which was announced by a full military band playing 'See the Conquering Hero Comes,' he beheld the floor chalked out most handsomely, and in the centre of every circle was inscribed 'Talavera,' and in the midst of the room was "'Talavera," 28th July 1808,' the anniversary of that eventful fight was thus announced to the Commander who on that day five years before so signally defeated the French. It will be seen that the Marquis of Headfort and several of the nobility are among our arrivals. The Dukes of Beaufort and Buckingham are, we hear, daily expected."

An announcement of the MC's Ball which the Duke desired to take place during his visit, and the editorial comments appear in the *Cheltenham Chronicles* of that time.

"The Duke of Wellington having in the kindest way expressed to the MC his express wish that his ball should take place during His Grace's stay in Cheltenharn, Mr Marshall begs very respectfully to announce that it will be on Monday next, the 11th inst. Tickets to be had at Mr Marshall's house (28 Winchcombe Place), at the libraries and also at the Spa."

(1st August 1823.) "The brilliant display of beauty and fashion at the Assembly last Monday evening has probably never been surpassed by anything of the kind hitherto noticed in the annals of gaiety and amusement. His Grace the Duke of Wellington honoured the joyous scene with his presence, and Mr Marshall has every reason to be proud of this demonstration of respect and good feeling and deeply indebted to our illustrious hero for the kind suggestion which induced the gratifying change in the appointment of the Ball."

The New Grand Promenade. "On Tuesday evening the new and truly grand Promenade at Bettison's library was opened for the first time under the patronage of the Duke in commemoration of His Majesty's birthday. At 9 o'clock nearly 700 Fashionables assembled, and every individual appeared highly gratified and delighted. The sparkling effect of the lamps, and the various ingenious devices, contrasted with die steady glare of the gas lights, was admirable. At a little after 9 o'clock, the entrance of His Grace the Duke of Wellington was announced by a fine military band playing 'See the Conquering Hero Comes.' The fireworks which were excellently arranged and of the first order, added much to the attraction of the evening."

(17th August 1823.) "His Grace the Duke of Wellington, after having attended service at the New Church, left Cheltenham on Sunday afternoon. The Duke sent his donation by the Master of the Ceremonies, to be added to the collection made that day at the Parish Church, in aid of the funds of the Dispensary and Casualty

Ward ... We are most happy to learn that from the very great benefit which His Grace has derived from the Cheltenham Waters, and the perfect restoration of his health, consequent on their use under the direction of Dr Coley, there is every prospect of the return of the 'Illustrious Hero' to this scene of health and pleasure."

Only a few months elapsed before the Duke of Wellington, on 14th April 1824, was again at the Spa for a cure. The *Chronicle* of 22nd April 1824, describes the Winter Ball at the Assembly Rooms on the preceding Monday evening. It was honoured by the presence of the Duke of Wellington, accompanied by Lord Apsley and Sir R. Arbuthnot, and was, besides, most fashionably and numerously attended, "a mark of attention and respect with which His Grace appeared much gratified, no less than by the pleasure which was depicted on the features of all around. Dancing was kept up with great spirit.

"The Duke left on Monday, the 24th of April, much improved both in health and appearance."

Mr Baynham Jones had a beautiful daughter, Bessie, who never married, despite countless admirers, one of whom was the Rev. Francis William Fowler, grandson of the old Vicar of Elmstone Hardwick, and another, later, was Major James R. E., of Dadapoor, Marrickville, Sydney. The following quotations are taken from a letter from Miss Chester Jones, Miss Bessie Jones's niece, to Miss Mary Humphris:

"... Now about the Duke of Wellington ... all I can tell you, *for certain*, is that the Duke, when looking for a house to spend some weeks in at Cheltenham took a fancy to Cambray House (which my grandfather built for himself, and moved into in 1817). Grandfather on hearing this from the (Duke's) Agent immediately offered it to the Duke, and he occupied it for *several* weeks, I cannot say how many, in the year 1824. The house then was nearly new, and well-furnished, and my dear grandfather, at one day's notice, turned out of Cambray House, with his wife, eight children, two servants and a governess into a private house in the High Street (afterwards a tailor's shop, and now a part of the Royal Hotel). The gardener and one housemaid only they left in the house as, of course, the Duke brought his own servants. To that housemaid we are indebted for little mementoes of His Grace, as whenever the barber came to cut his hair she managed, the moment he left his dressing-room, to carefully collect the hair cut, which I now possess. He used to read his letters in the garden (then a large one) under dear Aunt Carrie's favourite cherry tree, with a seat under it and all the seals, franks, etc., he threw down were also carefully collected by this maid. In entering the dining-room he had to pass daily a statue of himself as a young man, which he said was a very good one. This I have. At the end of his visit he called on dear grandmother in the High Street, and sat an hour with her, which Father remembered *well*, as he was then ten years old, and the only child present. The Duke took him on his knee and called him a 'good boy,' which much amused Father, at the time, as he was a veritable '*Pickle*,' but it was a true verdict for all that!!

I forgot to say that when the Duke received a message from his Agent to the effect that the house was quite at his disposal, he called on Grandfather on the following (I believe) day, which was Sunday, and told him that he 'should not think of turning any gentleman out of his house,' which Grandfather, I am told, quietly replied, with somewhat soldierly brevity, which I think pleased the Duke, 'Your Grace, we shall be out Wednesday evening, and the house at your disposal Thursday morning,' which it literally was, as in three days he had had all the ceilings whitewashed, and the rooms cleaned."

On 14th August 1828 Mr Marshall, the MC, received a letter to say that the Duke of Wellington would arrive in the town on the following day. He slept the night on the 15th at The Plough, and the next day went to Mr Marshall's house, The Priory. During his stay in Cheltenham from 15th August to 31st August, the Duke regularly went to the Royal Old Wells every morning soon after 7.30 to drink the waters and generally promenaded up and down the elm-tree avenue for about twenty minutes. After his second glass he usually mingled with the company at the adjoining Montpellier.

At about half-past eight, the Duke would go homewards, sometimes turning into the shop of Mr Abraham the optician, then adjoining the Pump Room, where he would look at the barometer and speculate with the old gentleman as to the sort of weather that was to be expected. On other mornings he would look in on Mawe's Museum, a building which occupied the site of the subsequent Montpellier Exchange. The victor of Waterloo would return to The Priory by nine o'clock for his plain and simple breakfast and would then read his dispatches and letters and reply to such letters as needed answers. When he had finished with them, the Duke would mount his horse and ride out for an hour or two, generally unattended, except for his servant, but occasionally accompanied by friends, who sometimes started with him from his own door, and at other times joined him in the course of his ride.

At four o'clock every day, His Grace visited the Montpellier Baths in the Bath Road, and there remained in a warm bath for an hour when he read the newspapers. He usually brought eight or nine of them with him, and one was kept open by means of a frame stretched across the bath, so that its illustrious occupant could glance over the contents of his paper. From the Baths, the Duke returned home to dinner. He seldom went out afterwards, unless some very particular friends should invite him, or unless he thought it his duty to patronise one or other of the public amusements which, however, he was not very fond of doing.

On Thursday, 19th August, he honoured the Promenade Ball, held at the Montpellier Rotunda. There is an account of this ball in the *Cheltenham Chronicle* of 28th August 1828:

"The Promenade Ball on Thursday last (21st August) was crowded at an early hour with fashionables, in consequence of the general expectations that His Grace the

Duke of Wellington would honour the Assembly with his presence. The most splendid preparations had been made for such a distinguished visit. At nearly ten o'clock the approach of His Grace was announced by the music striking up, 'See the Conquering Hero Comes,' and, in truth, we never heard this beautiful semi-chorus from Handel's 'Judas Maccabaeus' played with a more inspiring effect.

His Grace was received by Pearson Thompson, Esq, the proprietor of the Montpellier Spa. His Grace remained in the assembly for about an hour, during which he conversed frequently with Sir Thomas Lethbridge and General Sir T. Brown, to whom he expressed himself delighted with the novelty of ladies dancing in their Promenade costumes and hats, and later after the Duke had retired, dancing continued with unabated spirit until nearly two o'clock.

The Duke of Wellington, the Duke of Manchester, the Duke of Bedford, the Marquis of Worcester, and many others were at the Spa.

The arrival of His Grace was announced by three distinct and enthusiastic cheers from the populace assembled in front of the vestibule, when the Duke, with the Princess Esterhazy and her daughter, were ushered into the room by Mr Marshall, the Master of the Ceremonies, and their entrance was hailed by every mark of respect from the numerous assembly. The Princess danced with Colonel Dumaresq.

Shortly after his arrival the dance recommenced. His Grace was decorated with the Insignia of the Garter and appeared in excellent health and spirits."

Madame Vestris made her first appearance in Cheltenham this season about the 25th of August as Letitia Hardy in "The Belle's Stratagem," and Harriet Arlington in "The £100 Note." We are told that "the delightful roundness of voice and flowing melody by which this accomplished artist is so celebrated were never heard to greater advantage, while the bewitching playfulness of her manner in the volatile Harriet, and the careless gaiety with which she sung the snatches of old ballads, gained her the same enthusiastic applause which her acting and exquisite singing so richly merited in the play.

"His Grace the Duke of Wellington has been pleased to honour Madame Vestris by bespeaking the play of 'The Rencontre' and the farce of 'The £100 Note' in which that talented actress performed yesterday before a numerous and brilliant audience, who demonstrated their satisfaction by repeated and enthusiastic bursts of applause."

Madame Vestris was an exceptionally beautiful woman as well as an accomplished singer and actress.

A celebrated Mr Eulenberg came to Cheltenham and had the pleasure of performing before the Duke of Wellington, who was pleased to express his high admiration of the captivating and enchanting powers of the Jew's-harp. The Duke of Wellington left Cheltenham on Sunday afternoon the 31st August.

The *Chronicler* remarks that the Duke of Wellington has kindly and impartially patronised every amusement, and that the urbanity and condescension of his manners have gained him the esteem and affection of the townspeople.

As Pittville Pump Room is Joseph Pitt's monument in Cheltenham, so is Montpellier Spa the monument of Pearson Thompson who, like Pitt, and more completely, ruined himself by building speculations.

The Montpellier Pump Room had been opened in 1826, and soon became one of the most fashionable places of amusement in the town, as well as one of the favourite Spas.

Henry Thompson, Pearson Thompson's father, who died at "Hygeia House" in 1820, was, according to the *Morning Post*, the man "to whom Cheltenham was to a great degree obliged for the celebrity of the Springs, and for the most admired improvements of that fashionable place of resort."

Pearson Thompson, after the failure of his speculations, emigrated to Sydney, Australia, in 1850. On mounting a stage-coach, shortly after his arrival, he was joyously greeted by the driver, and looking up he discovered in him an old servant, who had been in his employ for many years in Cheltenham. Mr Thompson died in 1870 at Castlemaine, Victoria, Australia.

Mr Fortescue, who lived at Suffolk Hall, was related to the Duke of Wellington, as is the present member for Cheltenham, Sir James Agg-Gardner. Major James Agg's sister had married Mr John Gardner, the owner of a brewery in Cheltenham, and a partner in a bank, afterwards the County of Gloucester Bank, and since absorbed by Lloyds'. At Mr Gardner's death, as Sir James Agg-Gardner tells us in his *Reminiscences*, he left the brewery and his name to Major Agg's youngest son, Sir James Agg-Gardner's father, who had married Miss Eulalie Northey. One of Miss Northey's sisters married Lord Boston, another married Mr Pratt Tynte, and a third became Lady de Sausmarez.

Sir James Agg-Gardner says in *Some Parliamentary Recollections*, that after his father's death much of his family life in Cheltenham centred in his house of his great-uncle, Mr Fortescue, who had established himself in the town in the thirties, and remained there until the late sixties. After he became an octogenarian he married Miss Eager, a lady of considerable talent and attraction, who belonged, like himself, to an old Irish family. Mr Fortescue had gone out to India with his relative, Lord Wellesley, and under his auspices had obtained a post in the Civil Service, which he filled for many years. Sir James Agg-Gardner has a beautiful family portrait of the blue-eyed, black-haired, handsome Duke of Wellington, painted by an Academician named Rowe. Mr Fortescue returned to England, broken down in health, and with only one lung, but thanks to the Cheltenham climate he lived and hunted for many years. He died in London at the age of ninety-six, the victim of a street accident, and his sister, Sir James Agg-Gardner's grandmother, readied a similar age. The Fortescues belonged to the Irish branch of their family, of which Lord Clermont was the head.

Very constant visitors to Cheltenham were the famous brothers, Sir Charles and Sir William Napier. They were the sons by her second marriage of that enchanting Lady Sarah Lennox, who had captivated George III, when she became, for the time being, a hay-maker in the grounds of Holland House, Kensington. His family managed to prevent the marriage, and after her hopes of becoming Queen of England were blighted, the fair hay-maker of Holland House married Sir Charles Bunbury, winner of the first Derby, and brother of the caricaturist, Harry Bunbury. Harry had married Goldsmith's "Little Comedy," and Colonel Gwyn, who came to Cheltenham with George III, had married her sister the "Jessamy Bride."

Sir Charles Bunbury was much taken up with his racehorses; so much so that it is said that when he lay dying, he tried again and again to speak, and the watchers at his bedside at last managed to hear the words:

"Depend upon it, Eleanor is a damned good mare."

Sir Charles was perhaps not so fond of Lady Sarah as he was of his horses. At any rate, the marriage turned out badly, and Lady Sarah bolted with Lord William Gordon, son of a half-sister of Lindsay Gordon's great-grandmother. Eventually the high-spirited lady married again and became the mother of the famous Napiers, and she herself is believed to have been a visitor to Cheltenham.

On 21st September 1848 Sir Charles Napier arrived in Cheltenham and took up his abode in Imperial Square. He brought with him his horse, a little Arab, which he had ridden during most of his Indian battles, and mounted on which he was daily to be seen in public.

Amongst the officers who had served under him, and who were then in Cheltenham, were Colonel Willis, his Adjutant-General, Major McMurdo, his son-in-law and Quartermaster-General, who was with him throughout his Indian campaigning; Colonel Lloyd, commanding his Artillery; Major Leslie, commanding the Horse Artillery, who had commanded it so gallantly that, at the especial command of Lord Ellenborough, it was now known as Leslie's Horse; Major Poole, of the gallant 22nd Regiment, the regiment led into action by Napier himself; Captain Tait, commanding the regular Horse; Colonel Harrison, who commanded the Light Company of the 50th Regiment (Sir Charles, then Major, Napier's own regiment) at the battle of Corunna; Captain Richardson, who served with Sir Charles in the Peninsular and America; Colonel Clark-Kennedy, who so gallantly captured the French Standard at Waterloo; and several other officers. On 5th October a public dinner to Sir Charles Napier was held at the Queen's Hotel, at which Lords Ellenborough, Northwick and Dunalley, and between eighty and ninety Indian officers were present.

Sir Charles Napier, while at the Spa, was painted by the local artist, Mr Williams. The late Colonel Cunliffe-Martin said that the painter used to tell him how Napier described his campaigns while he painted.

In March 1849 the news arrived in Cheltenham of the disastrous battle of Chillianwallah on the Jhelum, in which the British, under Lord Gough, met with severe reverses, having twenty-six officers killed or wounded. Amongst the officers who fell in these disasters, was Brigadier Pennycuick, and there were many others well-known in Cheltenham.

Sir Charles Napier was one day up in town at the Horse Guards when it was suggested to the authorities there that it might be some slight consolation to Mrs Pennycuick if Sir Charles would take back with him to the widow the medal, etc., to which her husband had been entitled. He did not suffer two hours to elapse after his return to Cheltenham before he found an opportunity to discharge the mournful duty which he had undertaken.

On hearing the bad news the Duke of Wellington immediately applied to Sir Charles Napier to take command of the Indian Army, and it was in that letter the Duke addressed to Sir Charles the memorable words: "If you don't go, I must."

On 13th March 1849 Napier left Cheltenham, accompanied to town by Major McMurdo and other members of his family. A number of his friends were on the platform and cheered him heartily. Amongst these were Captain Sir Richard O'Connor, RN, Colonel Clark-Kennedy, General Hunter, Colonel de Courcy, Captain Robertson, Captain Phipps, Captain Kirwan, Mr Stewart, Captain Iredell, Mr Fortescue, Mr Hennessy, Mr Wightwick, Mr Kieller, Captain Cox, etc, etc.

XV

1830–1837

George IV—Charretie—Fulwar Craven—Berkeley Craven—Colonel Berkeley—Francis Close.

George IV died in his sixty-eighth year, in May 1830. It is said that, like the Cheltenham *roué*, Colonel Berkeley, he repented him of his evil doings and was thoroughly in earnest in his religious feelings. Some of the good people of Cheltenham thought otherwise. On the night of the King's death a terrible thunderstorm raged and there was a great smell of sulphur. They said that the King's soul was going to its own place with an appropriate accompaniment.

In his Brighton days the Prince Regent had taken a fancy to a clergyman named Carr, nephew of William Hickey's friend, the Rev. Robartes Carr, and had given him preferment and eventually a bishopric. He it was who ministered to the King on his death-bed, when the monarch made an edifying end, despite the thunder-claps, the waterspouts, the lurid lightning and the alleged sulphur.

Almost at the same time as the King, William Hickey, that great chronicler of the Georgian era, both as regards London and Calcutta, appears to have died in London. Berkeley Craven had backed Gladiator to win the Derby of 1836, and when the Epsom race was won by Bay Middleton, Mr Craven shot himself at his house in Connaught Place, Edgware Road. His death caused a great sensation, not only in the West of England, but in the sporting world generally. He had backed the Yorkshire filly, winner of the Oaks, and had he waited for that race Mr Craven would have had enough money to have tided him over his difficulties. With Berkeley Craven one of the great sporting figures, well-known in Cheltenham, disappeared.

In the year of Waterloo, Tommy Coleman had first begun to organise steeple-chasing and in 1831, what is called the first St Albans Steeple-chase had taken place. Mr Tom Pickernell's father, well-known in Cheltenham, had taken up steeple-chasing enthusiastically, and Colonel Charretie, always in search of some new excitement, had sent some horses to be trained for the new sport which, he foresaw, would be both fashionable and fascinating. Colonel Charretie's friend, the renowned Mr Osbaldeston, was a great man at St Albans in the beginning of cross-country racing, and in 1834 the event had become an annual fixture. Charretie was invited to officiate as umpire, but when the day came he was so ill as to be unable to leave Cheltenham.

The famous Napoleon-Grimaldi match took place at Dunchurch on 6th April 1833, and aroused great interest on account of the celebrity of the riders and the fame of the horses concerned. Squire Osbaldeston steered Grimaldi, while Captain Becher, the great horseman who was destined to give his name to Becher's Brook in the Grand National of 1839, had the mount on Colonel Charretie's champion Napoleon.

"During the match," says *The Field,* "the river Learn had to be jumped, and the horses and their riders were for a few seconds lost to sight. Mr Osbaldeston, however, first reached dry land, and the famous grey won by a length and a half, but was objected to for going on the wrong side of the Rags. Mr Dench of Dunchurch and Mr Crommelin (possibly Commeline) could not get at the rights of the matter, and it was referred to the Referee, Mr Robins, whose decision was in favour of Napoleon." Colonel Charretie, however, in this instance, showed a desire to remove his own rather than his neighbour's landmark, and said that rather than any unpleasantness should arise between such old friends as himself and "The Squire," he would consent to the stakes being drawn—a proceeding which gave general satisfaction to all parties.

On the 3rd of March 1842, some Cheltenham friends presented to that famous sportsman, Major-General Thomas Charretie (usually known as Colonel Charretie) a splendid silver vase, "an exquisitely beautiful specimen of the workmanship of Messrs Martin & Company." At a dinner held in honour of this gallant officer a sort of anthem was sung by Mr Sapio, and the admiring townspeople joined in the chorus. In the same year Charretie, then fifty-two years of age, was concerned with the other men (chiefly old bachelors, though he himself was married), who frequented the Imperial Hotel, in getting up the Imperial Steeplechase at the Cheltenham Races. Like Lindsay Gordon, who would "make people talk about him if he died in the Cheltenham Brook," Charretie loved to be eccentric, and as the grey Napoleon was probably the best horse he ever owned, he felt justified in making one of his famous bets. This was that he would win a shooting match, win the Imperial Steeplechase, and play the role of the Duke of Gloucester in "Richard III" all on the same day. The Colonel was, of course, a first-class shot, which made him a welcome guest at shooting parties and gave him yet another source of income at pigeon-shooting matches.

A subscription was got up in order to pay the expenses of a dinner after the Steeple-chase, to which Mrs Joseph, the liberal landlady of that establishment, added five pounds. The following list of entries for the great event was published:

Mr Robinson's	Imperial Tom
Mr Holmes's	Great Western
Mr Pearce's	Drover
Capt. Lindsay's	Snooks
Mr Lee's	Miss Reeves
Mr Disney's	Cherito
Mr Sander's	Baggot
Mr Coglin's	Sanson
Mr Warrener's	Smike
Col. Charretie's	Napoleon

Alas! the famous Napoleon for once let his master down, and the great race was won by

1. Mr C. Robinson's Imperial Tom well-named as the event proved.
2. Colonel Charretie's Napoleon.
3. Mr Lee's Miss Reeves.

After the Steeplechase it was announced in "Fashionable Changes" in the *Cheltenham Journal* that Colonel and Mrs Charretie had left Wolseley Terrace for London. The Spa appears to have been deprived of his stimulating presence until the 24th of October, when the Colonel returned alone to the Plough Hotel. The same newspaper said that the "Close Season" had, indeed, fairly set in, and adds: "The grand stand has disappeared from Cleeve Hill and its materials have been sold by auction. The County of Gloucester Races seem about to be transferred to Tewkesbury." Gorhambury, owned by Colonel Charretie, and backed by him to win a large sum of money in the Derby of 1843, could only get second in that race to Cotherstone, but in the same season won the Queen's Vase at Ascot.

Passionately fond of shooting, Charretie took a great interest in the introduction of breech-loaders, in favour of which he was most enthusiastic. There is a good deal about this famous sportsman in Blew's *History of Steeple-chasing*, and in the local newspapers as well, for Cheltenham was very proud of him, and the sporting world generally watched his hectic career with interest.

The *Field* says of Charretie:

"Of his nous in dealing with men we will now give an illustration. And the illustration is the account of Charretie's adventures as a poacher. He very often went out shooting on some other people's property without an invitation, and once he hired some shooting near North Mimms. The Marquis of Salisbury's keeper saw the trespasser and pointed him out to his master—'There he is on your lordship's land again.' Lord Salisbury was so much annoyed with the Colonel that he dismounted from his favourite cob, surveyed Charretie with cold contempt, and ordered his man to warn the uninvited guest off his land, and should he refuse to go, to shoot his dog. 'Very well,' replied the Colonel, 'you shoot my dog; I'll shoot your pony.' The keeper was as good as Lord Salisbury's word, and Colonel Charretie was as good as his own, for, 'as soon as the dog was a corpse, the pony was fit for the kennel.' Turning to his assailant the Colonel told his assailant that should he shoot Charretie's remaining dog, the poacher's other barrel was for the keeper, and as there was no disbelieving such evidence as that given by Lord Salisbury's defunct steed, the keeper thought that discretion might be the better part of valour. It is said that Charretie's next piece of bluff was to send Mr Osbaldeston to Hatfield with a demand for 'satisfaction.' However, the matter was satisfactorily arranged—at least for every one but the departed pony and dog—and there was no further bloodshed."

One of Charretie's bets was that he would learn the whole of the *Morning Post* by heart for one particular day, and it is said that he triumphantly declaimed the contents of that issue of the newspaper, not forgetting the advertisements. General Charretie died on 24th January 1866.

Captain Charretie was staying in Cheltenham in 1841, who may have been related to the General. This was possibly Captain John Charretie, who married Miss Anna Maria Kirwan, an oil painter and miniaturist.

At Cheltenham races in 1834 Mr Fulwar Craven and Colonel Gilbert, as stewards of the meeting, issued a notice that thimble-tables would not be allowed on the course. It must, however, have been a disheartening job to try to put down any form of gambling, when Major-General Thomas Charretie had just arrived at the Plough, prepared as usual to make a bet on anything that walked the earth on four or on two legs. Lord Segrave, better known as Colonel Berkeley, was also at the Plough, and the Duke of Gloucester was in the town. Even the demure damsels of those days were bitten with the racing fever, and a rhyme on the races was published which included the lines:

"Go tell the young ladies
To put on their bonnets,
The carriage is just coming
Round the door;
To shut the piano and throw
Up their sonnets,
And leave for a season Haynes
Bayly and Moore."

The Cheltenham Race-course of those days was on the top of Cleeve Hill, with the grand stand quite close to Mr Craven's beautiful country seat. It was from Mr Craven and Mr Cartwright that Black Tom Oliver secured much of the necessary financial support for his training stable at Wroughton, for which place he eventually more or less gave up Prestbury.

This race meeting of 1834 was destined to be the last attended by His Royal Highness the Duke of Gloucester, Lord High Steward of Gloucestershire, and the kind and constant friend of Cheltenham Spa. The Duke, besides going to the races, rode about the town as usual, entertained his friends, and underwent his annual cure at the Spa, and when he left for Bagshot it was understood that he had derived great benefit from the waters, but despite this reported improvement, he died in November of the same year. "His interment," says the *Morning Post*, "took place on Thursday, in the Royal Chapel of St George's, Windsor. His Royal Highness, the Duke of Sussex, who, in spite of the remonstrances of his physicians and friends, was determined to act as chief mourner at his brother's funeral, feeling it his duty to do so. He arrived at the Castle in a close private carriage about noon. Detachments of the Life Guards under Colonel Lygon of the 2nd Fusilier Guards, the illustrious deceased's own regiment, commanded by Colonel Lockwood, reached Windsor at an early hour ... At Bagshot House, where, as it is well known, the Royal Duke breathed his last, his name will live so long as goodness and virtue hold any empire over the minds of men."

During the funeral the bells of St Mary's Church, Cheltenham, rang a muffled peal, and the local paper remarks that "An Address of condolence to Her Royal Highness the Duchess of Gloucester lies for signature at the Assembly Rooms. It expresses the regret of all classes of the inhabitants at the melancholy event." Thus Cheltenham took a last farewell of that prince, who of all the royal family had done most for the welfare of the town. For twenty-seven years he had paid her an annual visit, often extending over months, and he had forwarded her interests faithfully in so far as it lay in his power to do so.

To return to old Fulwar Craven. He was a great practical joker, and was ever playing some trick or other on his intimates. He had no mean capacity for port wine, but not to the extent of his contemporary, the famous Jack Mytton; it was, nevertheless, conceded that he could hold his own in this respect with most people. We have plenty of evidence that he was very open-handed and generous. Thus the *Cheltenham Journal* of 27th April 1846 records that "Fulwar Craven, Esquire, lost in the streets of Cirencester between £40 and £50 in notes, and gave half to Sergeant Frape of the Police Force who found it." In his last years Mr Craven was not much seen in Cheltenham. Doubtless he felt out of things in those mid-Victorian days. The men who wore bright fancy waistcoats, practised mad practical jokes, drank their three bottles and flung reckless guineas to all and sundry who might take their fancy, had passed away, and he preferred to remain in the seclusion of beautiful Brockhampton. Mr Craven died in 1860.

Sir James Agg-Gardner said that Mr Craven's daughter and heiress married Mr Colquhit Goodwin, who assumed the name of Craven, and that their daughter married Mr George Vansittart of Bisham Abbey, Berkshire.

As the despotic ruler of Cheltenham, Mr Close was now fairly in the saddle, and he rode about the town, the acknowledged ruler of the place. The daughter of his old churchwarden remembers how one day Mr Close rode up with a note for her father, and did not get off his horse but handed the missive through a window to the children, who were looking out at him.

The day of "The Berkeleys and the Cravens of the Chase" was drawing to a close, though they had put up a good fight, and died hard. Grantley Berkeley says of the Incumbent: "Like the legend of 'The Little Jackdaw and the Abbot,' Mr Close then 'cursed us sitting, he cursed us walking,' he cursed the theatre, and seemed willing it should take fire, but he did not make us 'bald.' The playhouse was, however, burnt down, the tide of womankind set in with a run upon the new preacher, and his church was filled to overflowing. Ladies said enthusiastically to their male visitors on Monday, 'You should have *seen* Mr Close in his pulpit, yesterday. He looked so beautiful, and his action was *so* grand!' 'Seen,' I used to reply, 'I hope you don't go to "look" instead of to "hear" him. I have seen Mr Close, and think it would do him good to attend to the theatre, if only to learn a better method of delivery. When he clasps his hands together, he looks as if he were squeezing a lemon into a punch-bowl, and not as if urging a plea to Heaven.'"

The Close Season, however, went on; endless pairs of slippers were worked for the parson, and presented to him as if he had been a centipede; a house was built and furnished for him at the expense of the female members of his congregation, and it was said that they also worked him a study carpet, a square of which was supplied by each admirer.

A devoted admirer wrote of Mr Close:

"There he is, with somewhat rolling gait, half-sailor-like, trudging down Bayshill, carrying his Bible in a leather case with a loop handle, his little wife on his arm, to St Mary's ... Passing between the limes of the old Churchyard he hurriedly bows to some of the better known of the congregation with perhaps a heartily spoken word, then bobs beneath the low porch of the tiny little vestry door."

Francis Close was a builder, and almost every existing educational and religious or charitable establishment in the town was either evolved from his fertile brain or was put on a sounder basis by his organising capacity. He built six new churches in Cheltenham, and the Grammar School had fallen into a state of decay, and had very few pupils, but Close lived to see it with three hundred. He took an active part in the foundation of Cheltenham College, and "laboured most intensely" to establish the important Church of England Training College for teachers in primary schools. The Ladies' College was not one of his works, and he also did much for the Hospital, although that institution owed much to Dr Charles Fowler, whose portrait is in the board room, and to others. At the time in which it was built the Hospital was thought to be a model of what one of its size should be. Mr D. J. Humphris,

Mr Close's churchwarden for many years, was the architect of the Hospital, of the old College Chapel, and of many other buildings in the town, and there are still in existence engravings from water-colour drawings by hint of the College and the Hospital. His son, H. D. Humphris, wrote and illustrated *The Principles of Perspective.*

D. J. Humphris's sister, Caroline Tucker, was the wife of the Rev. W. Guise Tucker, the head of the naval chaplains, whose life and letters she published. W. G. Tucker's father was the Rev. J. Tucker, Rector of Hawling at the time of his death, and who had had a school called Ham House, Charlton Kings, in rather a remote place, but which, even in early Georgian days, was quite extensively advertised. A paragraph in the *Cheltenham Chronicle* in 1825 says that the famous Robert Stephen Hawker, Vicar of Morwenstow, and subsequently author of the lines:

> "And shall Trelawny die, and shall Trelawny die?
> Then thirty thousand Cornishmen will know the reason why"

was formerly a pupil at Ham House. The Grammar School usually gets the credit for Hawker, but possibly he was at both schools. The Rev. W. G. Tucker's son was the late Major-General W. Guise Tucker, CB, RMA, called "Krupp Tucker."

To return to Mr Close and his works. In the thirty-two years of his ministry in Cheltenham he obtained thousands upon thousands of pounds for religious and scholastic purposes. Lady Cromie, and other rich old ladies, contributed largely to his schemes, and, indeed, many gave and gave willingly when Mr Close asked for help. In 1838 the congregation erected a house called The Grange, and presented him with the freehold. While Mr Close was thus enormously popular in Cheltenham, an admirer says, and with pride, that he was never universally popular, for he was too militant a man to seek every one's friendship. His tongue and his pen were powerful weapons with which he attacked every one and everything of whom and of which he disapproved. The late Miss Williams, and her sister, Miss Helen, sisters of Mr George Heather Williams, remembered Mr Close well, and Miss Williams said that one day "the Incumbent held up his Bible and asserted: 'I consider that every word, aye, every letter,' tapping it like this and this, 'in this Book is inspired.' Mr Close," Miss Williams went on, "had a very musical voice. Somehow he never struck me as being quite *genuine,* and then he was so inconsistent. He fought against racing and theatres tooth and nail, and yet his daughters went to all the balls, and his sons, I think, went into the Army and Navy, and it was told of them that they had had enough of the church in their youth and said so."

"Mr Close," Miss Williams added, "did not much approve of scientific research, and he would say 'The nearer to Science, the farther from God.'"

Mr Close once proclaimed a solemn fast-day and carried it out in the teeth of a protesting Bishop, of whom he made short work, yet he stopped the collections for the SPG on the grounds that that body was High Church. Church Congresses were anathema to him but he simply revelled in missionary meetings of sorts.

In 1856, after thirty-two years in Cheltenham, Francis Close, then a grey-haired man of sixty, left the town to become Dean of Carlisle. He preached his last sermon in St Mary's Church on 9th November 1856. About a thousand pounds was raised by the Cheltenham people, and to this his old enemy, Lord Fitzhardinge, contributed twenty-five pounds, so that apparently the adversaries had buried the hatchet.

The honour which had been conferred on Mr Close was well deserved, but he by no means regarded his new office as being one of comfortable retirement and dignified ease, and his energy, so long as he held the Deanery, was unabated. Indeed, no doubt he rattled them all up in Carlisle just as he had done with his congregation in Cheltenham, and he continued to labour zealously, especially in the cause of temperance, amongst the working-men of his new home. Tobacco, almost equally with drink, was an evil thing in his eyes, and he earnestly conducted a crusade against "My Lady Nicotine."

Dean Close, when past his eightieth birthday, made a second matrimonial venture with a widow from Liverpool, a Mrs Hodgson. He resigned his Deanery a year or two before his death, which occurred at Penzance on 17th December 1882. He had been away from Cornwall, but in the course of his last journey back to the sea he loved so well, he had stayed in Cheltenham at the Lansdown Hotel, but had not been strong enough to see more than a few of those who had been his devoted parishioners. He was buried at Carlisle, though Cheltenham would have been a more fitting final resting-place, for there this labourer had borne the heat and burden of the day.

On 30th July 1847 Sir Willoughby Jones defeating the Hon. C. Berkeley by a majority of 108 votes, had been returned for Parliament, and was the first Conservative Member for Cheltenham. After this, Earl Fitzhardinge wrote on 14th August, and declined his usual present of red deer to the Cheltenham Stag Hunt, and also claimed the hounds as his own property, requiring them to be sent at once to Berkeley Castle. Mr Theobald, thereupon, offered to undertake the Mastership of a new pack. This offer was accepted, and a committee, consisting of Messrs Fortescue, Gardner, Thompson, Skillicorne and Henley, was appointed to make arrangements for keeping up the sport as heretofore. In Lord Fitzhardinge's later days he turned more towards religious matters, and certainly in the months which preceded his death it is thought that he repented of many of the actions of his earlier life. He was much under the influence of the Congregational Minister from Cheltenham, Dr Morton Brown.

On 23rd February 1856 had occurred the accident to Lord Fitzhardinge which ultimately caused his death. While following the hounds in the Vale of Berkeley, his lordship stooped to avoid an overhanging bough, when the horse stumbled in a rut and the sudden check caused the rider to be thrown over the horse's head with considerable violence. Lord Fitzhardinge, however, luckily pitched on his shoulder, though it was at first feared that one or more ribs had been broken.

The carriage was sent for and his lordship was conveyed to Berkeley Castle, while messengers were despatched for medical assistance. It was hoped for sometime that Earl Fitzhardinge had not sustained any serious injury, but the shock to the system of a man past his seventieth birthday was too great, and he never recovered, though he lingered for some months.

On 10th October 1857 Lord Fitzhardinge died at Berkeley Castle, and was buried in great state, a ceremonial procession, almost like that with which kings are honoured, following the coffin, on which was the inscription:

> "William Fitzhardinge, Earl Fitzhardinge of Berkeley Castle, in the County of Gloucester, claiming as of right to be Earl of Berkeley by descent, and Baron of Berkeley by tenure. Born 26th December 1789. Died 10th October 1857."

In the procession, besides the inevitable mutes, walked the High Constable of Berkeley and other officials: The coronet of the deceased nobleman was borne by the Chief Steward, and four of his favourite horses followed, covered with velvet and plumes. Seven thousand people, it was said, witnessed the solemn scene. The High Bailiff of Cheltenham issued a notice, requesting shops to be shut, and the bells of St Mary's tolled heavily when Cheltenham's former king was carried to his last resting-place. All but Grantley Berkeley then forgot the frailties which a friendly local paper had said that it dared not catalogue, and only remembered Lord Fitzhardinge's apparently sincere repentance, his liberality, his kindness of heart and his great public services.

On 25th April 1880 the Hon. Grantley Berkeley died. A younger son of the fifth Earl of Berkeley, he was heir-presumptive to his brother Moreton, the chivalrous sixth Earl, who never assumed the title, as he believed that his elder brother William was legitimate. Grantley, on the other hand, did all he could to blacken the reputation of his own father and mother, and, had he outlived his elder brother, would certainly have used the title. In about 1865 the then Lord Fitzhardinge and the Honourables A. F. H. and T. Berkeley had published a pamphlet in which they affirmed that many of the statements made by the Hon. Grantley Berkeley in his *Memoirs* were untrue, and that written testimony to the Prince Regent's belief in Lord Berkeley's earlier marriage existed. Grantley Berkeley had married in 1824 Caroline Martha, daughter of Paul Benfield, son of a local surveyor, who had, years before, in 1764, gone out to India and had made a great fortune and lost it again, so that he died in 1810 as obscurely in Paris as he had been born in Cheltenham. He had been at one time Member of Parliament for Cricklade.

Grantley Berkeley's elder son, Swinburne, died in 1865, and his younger son, Edward, died in 1878.

One good point about Grantley Berkeley was his fondness for dogs. He describes in his *Memoirs* the first dog he ever had, a half-brother of the black bull-terrier which was Colonel Berkeley's constant companion in Cheltenham.

XVI

Doctor Boisragon—Pryse Lockhart Gordon and Harriet Mellon, Duchess of St Albans.

Doctor Boisragon was a great man in Cheltenham Society, as were his two sons, Theodore, who was the doctor's partner, and a talented musician, and Conrad, who studied in Italy, under the name of Conrado Borrani, and achieved some distinction as a professional singer in the forties of last century.

In his younger days, the elder Doctor Boisragon was much in request at balls and routs. On 5th April 1822 there was a grand fancy dress ball at the Spa, at which a reel was danced by the Doctor, and on the 22nd of January 1825 Miss Colmore gave a fancy dress ball at Charlton House which, from contemporary descriptions, appears to have been rather an arduous form of entertainment for the guests. Doctor Boisragon represented "a theatrical manager of the old school co-temporary with Garrick. Tate Wilkinson and the immortal Mara. Stirring genius. Ye powers! He was inimitable. His corrections of the text of young dramatic aspirants and his insinuating mode of procuring 'bespeaks' were quite irresistible."

The doctor's son, Conrad, was very good-natured in singing for his old friends at Cheltenham, and on 6th November 1841 the annual dinner of the Literary Society was held, with Doctor Boisragon in the chair. Borrani, with others, sang "Non Nobis, Domine," and after dinner, Conrad and Mr Evans sang several songs. On 10th November of the same year a complaint was made of an ill-natured letter in a local paper, which remarked that Borrani had substituted new songs for the ones which he had been announced to sing at a recent concert, the fact being that the accompaniments had not yet arrived. In another *contretemps*—at the performance of "Green Bushes" in Cheltenham—Miss Oakwell Smith said that she herself, as a small child, came to the rescue, when another child was missing or ill, whom Borrani had to carry across a mountain stream. The singer begged Miss Smith's father, who was a friend of his, to lend his little girl for the evening, and Miss Smith had the poster which advertised the evening's entertainment, and on which her

own name appeared. She said that her delight and excitement knew no bounds
when Conrad rushed across the plank with herself tucked under his arm.

In 1845, Borrani was singing at Drury Lane, and was very successful in what
was then Balfe's new opera, "The Enchantress."

But both Doctor Boisragon and his son, Conrad, despite their success in their
respective professions, ultimately lost a great deal of money. Indeed, Conrad is
said to have died in very straitened circumstances. Doctor Boisragon retired and
lived in Paris for some years, where he was on terms of intimacy with King
Louis Philippe until the dethronement of that monarch, and his flight, after the
Revolution of 1848.

After he returned from France, Doctor Boisragon lived for a time in London,
and later at Bideford, where he had purchased the beautiful cottage residence
in which "he breathed his last on the 26th of May 1852, and in his seventy-fifth
year." Mrs Boisragon had died in Cheltenham on the 13th of September 1840.

There was another famous doctor who spent a good deal of his time, in his
later years, in Cheltenham. This was Sir George Smith Gibbes, Bt, the great
Bath physician who was Mrs Piozzi's medical attendant and her great friend.
Mrs Piozzi herself visited Cheltenham in her old age and gave a grand ball. Her
nephew, Mr Salusbury, lived in the town. Curiously enough, another baronet
named Gibbes—Sir Osborne Gibbes—lived in Cheltenham.

Major Pryse Gordon, the author of the *Personal Memoirs*, unfortunately wrote
very little after he came to Cheltenham, and not much is known about his doings
there. He saw a good deal of Lord Northwick, who had a famous picture gallery at
his large house with the high wall round it, near the College, and where Nelson is
said to have once dined. After Lord Northwick's death, his famous and wonderful
collection of pictures was sold and dispersed, and to some extent the same thing
happened to the great Phillipps library also located at Thirlestaine House.

Major Pryse Gordon was on friendly terms with Mr Armitage, a member of a
family well known in Cheltenham, and he saw a good deal of Bulwer Lytton when
the latter was at the Spa. Gordon was a connoisseur in wines as well as in pictures,
and himself, at one time, owned a Vandyck, as well as other interesting works of
art. Amongst his intimate friends were Sheridan, Burdett, Horne Tooke, Dr Parr,
Dr Burney, Campbell, the poet, who came to Cheltenham to collect material
for his *Life of Mrs Siddons*, Professor Porson, Sir J. Mackintosh, Monk Lewis, John
and Charles Kemble, Dr Wolcott, Bannister, Sir M. A. Shee, George Colman, Sir
G. Lawrence, Northcote, Opie, Godwin, Curran, Perry of the *Morning Chronicle*,
Lord Erskine, etc.

Major Gordon took Scott and Byron over the field of Waterloo, and in his
wife's album both poets wrote their poems on Wellington's great victory. Pryse
Gordon's *Personal Memoirs* are often quoted by historians of the Georgian days.
Goding says that he died on and September 1845, at his residence in Cambray, but
a local newspaper gives a slightly different account of Major Gordon's death:

"Sudden death of Major Gordon.—It is with deep regret that we announce this sad event which took place yesterday at the Imperial Hotel—where Major Gordon had taken up his residence for the winter. He had been in indifferent health for some days, but not so much as to excite the least apprehensions, and had even been out before breakfast, of which he partook as usual. In the afternoon he was taken suddenly ill, and within two hours expired—the immediate cause of death being, it is understood, the rupture of a blood-vessel. There are few men more intimately known in society identified with Cheltenham than, from his very long and constant residence in the place, was the deceased, or one whose sudden death will be more regretted by the friends who knew him."

Harriot Mellon, as Tom Coutts's wealthy and attractive, if somewhat rotund, widow was, of course, a tremendous catch, and she soon had many exalted suitors—amongst them, it was said, HRH the Duke of York. In 1825, she had become very friendly with the Duke of St Albans and his sisters, and it soon became evident that the former was eager to form an alliance. He was about twenty years her junior, being only five-and-twenty when he proposed to her. She made him wait a year to give him a chance to change his mind, but though he was not blind to the material advantages of such a marriage, he seems to have been sincerely attached to her. He refused to allow her to make any settlements on him, and most likely was well aware that she would leave the bulk of her money back to the Coutts family. They were married by special licence in Stratton Street on 16th June 1827, the ceremony being performed by the Rev. Lord Frederick Beauclerk (of sporting celebrity) an uncle of the bridegroom. The pair were very happy together despite the disparity in their ages, and despite the Duchess's outbreaks of temper, which became more like her mother's as the years went on. But her two husbands seemed to have been spared her rages.

Harriot Mellon, in her latest role of a duchess, appeared in the town in all her glory in 1838, accompanied by the Duke of St Albans. They took a house in Suffolk Lawn, one of those substantial residences of which three had been built by three friends, James Allardyce, MD, Mr Sherwood and Mr Ingledew, all members of the medical profession, who had been, together with their neighbour, Mr Balfour, amongst the earliest of the Anglo-Indian settlers in the town, the most material contributors to its subsequent colonisation by the retired servants of the old East India Company.

When Harriot Mellon and her Duke came to live in Suffolk Lawn they went in for entertaining to a considerable extent; giving several musical parties, and entertaining "select parties" to dinner, at one of which Mr Dorn performed on the horn, and Mr Eulenstein on the Jew's-harp, while Mr Blatz was in attendance with his sleight-of-hand tricks.

They attended the theatre to see T. P. Cooke act, and Yates also appears to have been a star attraction there during the period covered by the Duchess's visit to the Spa. What memories Harriot must have had as she sat—the observed of all beholders; a duchess; the widow of the great Tom Coutts, and said to have had a royal duke among her suitors—in Watson's playhouse, where she had so often been one of the performers herself, and in the town in which she had had such varied experiences and in which her mother and stepfather had gone through so many vicissitudes. Her patronage of the theatre was evidently much appreciated. "Since Colonel Berkeley retired from the stage," remarks the *Looker-on*, "the Cheltenham Theatre has met with but sorry encouragement. A happy change has come over theatricals here, under the patronage of Her Grace the Duchess of St Albans." *Poor* Mrs Entwistle to have died before this day!

The Duke and Duchess made short excursions in different directions during their visit, drove out each day to see some one or another of the interesting places in the neighbourhood; they patronised a fancy fair in aid of the Orphan Asylum and attended a public breakfast at Pittville at which Lord and Lady Rodney, the Countess of Camperdown, and Lady E. Duncan, the Earl of Moray and the Ladies Campbell, Lady Burdett and many other great people were present. Indeed, the town was full of fashionables, including the Duke of Gloucester, who then resided at 1 Lansdowne Place, the Duke and Duchess of Montrose, the Duke and Duchess of Hamilton, Lord Ellenborough, Lady Byron, with "Ada, sole daughter of my hearth and home," etc, etc. And the whilom Harriot Mellon was the centre of curiosity that August, and August was then the fashionable month in Cheltenham.

The Duke of St Albans, the King's Grand Falconer, astounded the villagers of Elmstone Hardwick and other places in the neighbourhood by going out on hawking expeditions in the country round the spa, with a cavalcade and all the pomp and circumstance of this old world sport. Who could have eyes even for the Duke of Gloucester and for ordinary dukes when his Grace of St Albans and Her Grace the Duchess provided so many excitements.

But alas! the town and theatre were to lose all this patronage and Tom Coutts's money was henceforward to be spent in Brighton. Some time before this visit an artist living in Cheltenham had executed a caricature group of various people including Harriot, then a duchess, whose representation amounted to "a somewhat laughable likeness of her rather portly figure." Some of the other persons caricatured were very angry and it was one of these who showed it to the Duchess, and made her exceedingly angry, too, by telling her she was being caricatured all over the town. The then Master of the Ceremonies heard that the picture had offended so many people that he sent for the artist and advised him to withdraw it from circulation. This was done and the broken stone on which the group had been drawn was sent to the Duchess together with all the impressions the artist could find. She was quite satisfied and sent back a liberal sum in compensation for his loss. Unfortunately, on the occasion of her visit in 1832, when she erected a second monument to her mother, some copies of the

Joseph Pitt, who laid
out the Pittville estate.
From a lithograph by
Richard Dighton

group had been found which had not been returned to the artist. Some friends
bought one of these and sent it to the Duchess. She believed the artist had gone
on selling the prints and had thus deceived her. She was furious as she always was
when she suspected deceit, and vowed that despite her love for the town and its
happy associations, she would never visit it as long as the unfortunate caricaturist
dwelt there, and this resolution, her biographer says, she never broke.

Early in June 1837 the Duchess of St Albans was at Mr Coutts's famous house,
No 1 Stratton Street, formerly next to Devonshire House and now, like the larger
house, a thing of the past. The Duchess became very ill; indeed, she had been for
some time in declining health. Her appetite was quite gone and her doctors were
afraid for her to see visitors lest they should excite her. She suggested being taken

to see Holly Lodge; and there, in Mr Coutts's pony-chair, she went all over the gardens and up the hill, for she felt that she was seeing it all for the last time. The dying Duchess made a progress through Highgate, taking exactly the same route Mr Coutts had taken on his last visit there. Then she asked to be taken back to Stratton Street, "to die on the bed where Tom Coutts expired." There she saw Lady Guildford, Mr Coutts's daughter, and said that Mr Coutts had appeared to her in the form of a little bird as he had promised to do. The Miss Burdetts saw her, and after them no one outside the house. On the 5th of August she recognised her husband and conversed clearly with him for a few minutes, and afterwards uttered no audible words, though her lips seemed to move as if in prayer. She opened her eyes next morning at eight o'clock and looked slowly round at her attendants, and pressed the Duke's hand. He had shown his devotion by sitting up with her for several nights. At twenty-five minutes past ten, on Sunday morning, 6th August 1837, held up by the Duke's arm, she peacefully breathed her last. She had always fervently desired to die on Sunday, because it was the day of Our Lord's resurrection. Sarah Entwistle and her daughter had always been prayerful, and, in a curious way, religious women. Harriot bequeathed the bulk of her fortune to Angela Burdett, one of Mr Coutts's grand-daughters, leaving the Duke of St Albans an annuity of £10,0000 a year, Holly Lodge, her residence in Piccadilly, and the use of the rooms at Coutts's Bank, and two thousand pounds worth of plate absolutely.

The *Looker-on* for 12th August 1837, gives an obituary notice of the Duchess of St Albans which is not correct as regards her early years and gives the idea prevalent in Cheltenham that Harriot Mellon first appeared at the Spa as a poor girl, whereas she was a well-known actress when the Entwistles came to live in the town. It may truly be said that her life was one long romance, and that one of its most romantic episodes occurred in Georgian Cheltenham.

On 11th January 1837, the Cheltenham Stag Hunt was established, and the Hon. C. F. Berkeley, MP, became the first Master of Hounds.

Now occurred the death of William IV who, unlike his immediate predecessors, had never visited Cheltenham, though a statue of him had been erected in the town to commemorate the passing into law of the Reform Bill.

Dr Henry Fowler had some friends about the Court, and thus it happened that his young daughter was present when in the courtyard of St James's Palace, the eighteen-year-old Victoria was proclaimed Queen, in June 1837. In Cheltenham, Queen Victoria was proclaimed by J. N. Stratford, Esq, the Deputy-Sheriff.

XVII

The Irish Invasion of Cheltenham—Curran—Chief-Justice Bushe—John Bushe—Sir Josiah Coghill, etc, etc.

From almost the earliest known records of the history of Cheltenham, the Gloucestershire Spa has had many Irish residents and annual visitors, such as Thomas Moore, the poet, and his great friend, James Corry, the blue-eyed Lord Strangford, who once haunted the British Museum, the eccentric Lord Howth, Charles Kendal Bushe, the Irish Chief-Justice, Curran and many others.

A Cheltenham bard writes of the Irish in his native town:

"For the churchyard's so small and the Irish so many
They ought to be pickled and sent to Kilkenny."

Philpot Curran, whom Fox made Master of the Rolls in Ireland, one of the greatest orators of his own or any age, came in his last sad days to Cheltenham, in 1816, and again in 1817, in order to consult Sir Arthur Faulkner. His great admirer, Charles Phillips, has left some account of Curran's visits to the Spa. Phillips himself was evidently a familiar figure about the town. On 7th October 1813, the *Cheltenham Chronicle* describes a duel "between Charles Phillips Esquire of the Irish Bar, attended by Colonel O'Neil, and —————— Henriques, Esquire, whose second was Major Pearce. After an exchange of shots the affair terminated and the parties shook hands before leaving the ground." This affair took place on the Winchcomb Road. On October 14th, the same newspaper reports that the fourth anniversary of the Gloucester Missionary Society was held, with Charles Phillips, Esquire, in the chair, and that he made a most eloquent speech. There was much commotion in Cheltenham and Gloucester over the duelling propensities of this eccentric supporter of missions, but Mr Phillips explained to the reporter that the affair of honour was quite unavoidable, even to a man of his own peace-loving disposition.

In the autumn of 1816 Phillips came to Cheltenham with Curran. Of this visit he writes:

"Sir Arthur prescribed for him a regime to which I am afraid he did not very strictly adhere. However, in the hospitable welcome of his house the mind diseased found at least a temporary remedy. The very appearance of friends who were deservedly most dear to him, revived his spirits. I remember on the night of our arrival, the news of the victory of Algiers was just announced in Cheltenham; it was, of course, yhe universal topic of conversation, Lady F expatiating on the barbarities of the pirates with all the feeling natural to a good heart and a refined intellect, appeared to regret that the fortifications had not been obliterated. 'Ah! my dear Madam,' replied Curran, who had been travelling for two days and a night without intermission, 'they have had enough of it—sufficient for the Day has been the evil thereof.'

I had introduced him to two very lovely and accomplished sisters, who have since gone to increase the treasures of the east. After spending an evening in the enjoyment of conversation but rarely to be met with, he said to me, 'I never saw such creatures; even to my old eyes it is quite refreshing to see the sunshine of genius flying over their beautiful countenances …'

At the hazard of turning my volume into a jest-book, I cannot refrain from giving a remark of his about this time, on an Irish gentleman who certainly preserved most patriotically the richness of his pronunciation. He had visited Cheltenham, and during his stay there, had acquired a most extraordinary habit of lolling his tongue out of his mouth. 'What can he mean by it?' said somebody to Curran. 'Why, he means if he can to catch the English accent.'

In 1817, Curran again joined me in Cheltenham … His short stay in Cheltenham could scarcely be called existence. He constantly fell asleep in the day-time, and when he awoke it was only to thoughts of sadness. He was perpetually fancying things which never had any existence, and misinterpreting those which had. He told me he was dying; and, indeed, to show how firmly the prophetic presentiment was impressed upon his mind, the very night preceding his departure, he handed Lady Faulkner the following melancholy impromptu, written in pencil on a blank sheet of paper, which lay before him:

'For welcome warm, for greeting kind,
Its present thanks the tongue can tell,
But soon the heart no tongue may find
Then thank thee with a sad farewell.'"

A few weeks later he was dead. The *Cheltenham Chronicle* in its obituary column said:

"It will be within the recollection of many of our readers that on this spot the genius of Curran flung around the last flickering beams of his spirit, that beam that like a spark from the embers, preceded the extinction of the fire which had blazed from an imperishable lustre upon the declining glory of his country. The circumstances which gave rise to the last expression of wit that flowed from his lips was, we believe, the apprehension that he had felt a shock of the palsy. It occurred nearly at the period of his arrival on the last visit he was ever destined to pay to Cheltenham. He instantly consulted an eminent medical friend, and requested to have his pulse felt in order to ascertain whether his apprehensions were well founded; on being informed that he had no grounds for uneasiness, and that he indicated no symptoms of palsy, his countenance was at once illumined by that sort of dry-significant smile which was the harbinger of his wit; and he exclaimed—'O! 'Tis only a runaway rap, when I thought it had been a notice to quit.'"

In after years Curran's daughter, Mrs Elizabeth Odella Taylor, died in Cheltenham, at St Albans House. Her sister had been engaged to Robert Emmett, and it was of her that Moore wrote the poem, which begins with the line, "She is far from the land where her young hero sleeps."

Tom Moore, though not resident in the town, came here often, and probably knew the Spa well in 1812 when he expressed his satisfaction that Mrs Corry was ordered to drink the Cheltenham waters.

On 4th August 1825, Thomas Moore paid one of his frequent visits to Cheltenham, where his wife—the beautiful and charming actress, formerly Miss Dyke, whom he had married in 1811—was already staying. He writes: "I found darling Bessy in a snug little cottage, No 10 Suffolk Parade, or rather, found her at Lady Donegal's, whither she had gone to dinner. The Donegals are all kindness to her and her little people. Tom calling Lady Donegal 'Granny,' and all like the same family. I proposed that Bessy and Barbara should go to the play, when Young appeared as Hamlet, and the King and Ophelia were laughable beyond anything. Little Tom was much delighted.

"Went out with Bessy in the chair, I walked. Dined with the Donegals. In the evening Lord and Lady Kenmare and young Wilmot. Sung a good deal to them."

6th. "Went with Barbara and Miss Godfrey to see the humours of the wells before breakfast. Drove about afterwards with Bessy and Barbara. Called and sat a little while with Lady Kenmare. After dinner went to The Walks, Sir A. and Lady Faulkner being of our party, and I had to stand the glare of the night."

Bessy Moore did not care at all for Society, but she had a few very special friends—Lady Donegal and her nieces, the Miss Godwins, and Sir William Napier and his wife. Sir William did not live in Cheltenham, but he came there sometimes, and some of his relatives were often there. Between them and the Donegals the shy and retiring Mrs Moore was always sure of finding friends in the Garden Town.

Of 29th August, Moore, then back in London, wrote: "Walked into town, all in the rain, early. Worked a little. Went to Shoe Lane and to Longmans to get some money to send Bessy who means to leave Cheltenham on Friday." Moore was always gadding about amongst his fine friends, and he left Bessy alone a great deal, but she understood him well enough and knew that he was really devoted to her.

On one of his visits to Cheltenham, Thomas Moore was collecting material for his *Life of Byron*. Of this he writes: "Dined again at the Imperial with an old college acquaintance of mine, Peacock ... Went to a Mr Stewart's ... Found the Miss Strutts and a Miss R ———— a pretty piquante little girl, who mixed French and English in her talk rather amusingly. Went from thence to the ball, Miss R———— my companion. The Master of the Ceremonies had arranged that the band should strike up an Irish melody on my entering the room. Met ... among others the Belchers. Got hold of Mr Millet, another of the persons I came to look after; walked with him to his house; his wife, who is dead, was intimate with Miss Chaworth, and saw a good deal of Byron when he was a boy; said that Miss C ———— did not like Byron, nor did his wife, nor any of the girls."

Mr Millet was the fashionable portrait and miniature painter who had built the Imperial Hotel in Cheltenham, on the site of the present Queen's Hotel, out of his earnings as a painter and playwright, and let it for £500 a year.

William Jordan was one day with Millet when the latter saw bills of a play called "Aladdin." The miniaturist pointed out the advertisements to Jordan and said that he himself had once written a play of that name but had sent it to someone to see if it was any good, and had never heard any more of his MS. He asked Jordan if he would go with him to see this play with the same title as his own and they went together to the theatre. With growing excitement Millet watched the spectacle of "Aladdin" or "The Wonderful Lamp," and told Jordan that it was his own play. Mr Harris, who seems to have produced "Aladdin," afterwards sent Mr Millet a cheque for a hundred guineas, and apparently a great deal more money came in afterwards.

Millet's Hotel had later become the Imperial Club, and has been mentioned as the haunt of Colonel Charretie and his friends.

On 16th October 1827, Thomas Moore wrote in his diary: "Arrived at Cheltenham between two and three. One of the first persons I met, Colonel O'Neil: asked me to dine with him to-day at the Imperial: answered conditionally. After dressing, called at Williams the bookseller, to inquire after Mr Malpin, who was to be my introducer to some persons likely to be useful to me, he said, on the subject of Byron: not in Cheltenham but expected to-morrow. Called upon Lord Ashtown, who wanted me to dine with him to meet Colonel French. Dined with O'Neil: a *table d'hôte*; excellent dinner, more than twenty of the party, and almost all Irish; among others Mr Trevor the son of Lord Dungannon, and young Plunket, *the Plunket's* son. Mr Trevor mentioned Lord ———— going to a fancy ball at Florence as the hero of his own novel, Sir Something Maltravers, and as nobody of course had read the novel, nobody of course could make out his character, so that he was obliged to inform them, '*Voyez, regardez, je suis mon livre.*'

… O'Neil anxious that I should stop over Saturday to dine with his brother-in-law, Prescott (Prescod). I promised to do so …"

Mr Prescod, a Jamaica planter, lived at Alstone, in the ancient house burnt down some years ago by suffragettes. He left his property to his wife and after her death to Mrs La Terrière whom, as Mary Gurney, the Prescods had adopted.

Vice-Admiral Sir Josiah Coghill was one of the leading lights of Cheltenham Society. His delightful younger son, the late Colonel Kendal Coghill, CB, formerly Colonel of Queen Alexandra's Own 19th Hussars, was born in 1833, and was well over eighty when he died. A few years before his death he gave us some reminiscences of old Cheltenham for this book.

"I wish I could help you more with your work," he wrote, "but it is not in me. My life has been *acta non verba*, with a stronger belief in the sword than the pen. You make me feel like a cross-breed between *Old Mortality* and *The Last of the Mohicans*. I was very young in those days to which you allude but the names and faces are all quite familiar. Old James Corry was a character. A shortish man, with a comical semi-serious face, quite shaven, I never saw him acting but my family lived in Kilkenny before I was born and there were perpetual high-class theatricals there, which seemed, by the conversation in my day, to have been the object of life and creation. There was a regular Irish colony which migrated to Cheltenham every winter, such as my grandfather—Chief-Justice Bushe—Lord Muskerry, Tynte Pratt, Tiernay, Sheehan, Sir W. Osborne, Mr Rathbone, Mr Esmonde, etc."

There are many references in Moore's diary to his great friend, Mr Corry.

The late Major Connellan said that James Corry was born in Dublin on 8th September 1772; his father, another James Corry, was a member of a family of the County Monaghan, of which Lord Belmore is the head. The elder Corry married Miss Dillon, of the family of Lismullen, and had three children, James, Harriet and Eliza.

In 1798, James Corry, junior, married Maria, daughter of Thomas Sherrard of Marlay, agent over the estates of Lord Rokeby in the County Louth. She died in 1858.

"In 1805, his sister Harriet," says Major Connellan, "married Peter Connellan, whom Mr Corry had met as a Cambridge undergraduate, and there were two sons born of the marriage, of whom the elder was my father, also Peter Connellan. Mr Corry's younger sister, Eliza, married William Sherrard, his brother-in-law, in the same year. Peter Connellan died in less than two years after his marriage and his widow survived him nearly 55 years. In 1807, Mr Corry was induced by his friend Richard Power, who had seen him acting in private theatricals more than once, to join the Private Theatre of Kilkenny which had been instituted in 1802, and he appeared for the first time in October 1808, acting in 'The Rivals,' 'The Wanderer,' 'Macbeth,' 'Village Lawyer,' and 'The Midnight Hour.' He shone best, however, in farces, and though he proved a good all-round amateur actor, he confessed that neither tragedy nor high comedy best suited his powers. He continued to form one of the company until the theatre was closed in 1819. In 1816, he attended in Dublin, a complimentary dinner to Richard Power who had been ill, and my great-grandfather, Sir Robert Langrishe, occupied the chair, and made a speech which was highly praised. Corry was one of the best actors in Kilkenny Theatre, and wrote the best of the prologues and epilogues.

"After the theatre closed, Miss O'Neill, the actress, married Mr William Wrixon Becher, afterwards created a baronet.

"In 1829, Corry and his wife migrated to Cheltenham. They first lived at Rosina Cottage, Vittoria Road, and afterwards at 7 Spa Buildings. Later in the year Corry returned to Dublin to stay with the Leveson Gowers, and take a part of 'Mr Washington,' in a piece called 'First Love,' which he repeated at Bridgewater House the following Spring and again at Hatfield House; but though pressed by Lady Salisbury to undertake the same character at Whitsuntide, he declined on the ground of age, and his further appearances as an actor were confined to local theatricals amongst his friends at Cheltenham where, with Sir Josiah Coghill (an old acquaintance) and other friends, he was a familiar figure for nearly twenty years. His widow survived him about ten years, dying in 1858.

"His friendship with Moore produced a present of a Wine Strainer in 1825, and the MS of the graceful verses acknowledging it are in the possession of the writer …

"Mr Corry was a very able man, and worthy of a better post than the one which he had occupied (as Secretary to the Linen Board and Clerk of the Journals in the Irish House of Commons), and he was accused by his friends of hanging back. He was, however, a very agreeable member of society, very hospitable and an amusing companion, as well as a very generous and steadfast friend. He never had any children."

As an old man Mr Corry appeared for the last time on any stage at some theatricals in Cheltenham, and wrote and recited the prologue, in which he asked the audience sometimes in future to "Give old Sir Anthony a thought or two," and added:

"Years, many years, have gathered on his back.
Since last he revelled with his own dear Jack."

He died at his residence in Montpellier Spa Buildings, Cheltenham, on 11th January 1848.

Charles Kendal Bushe, a *habitué* of Cheltenham for many years, had been born in 1767 at Kilmurry, the ancestral seat of the family, which had been settled by Cromwell at Kilfane. A famous lawyer and orator, Bushe became Chief-Justice of the King's Bench in Ireland. The contemporary of Grattan, Flood, Curran, and Saurin, he had himself all an Irishman's wit and eloquence, and so brilliant was he that Grattan declared that he spoke with the lips of an angel.

Summer after summer, the Irish Chief-Justice visited Cheltenham where he gathered round him all the legal luminaries who visited the Spa. He was deeply interested in the famous Kilkenny theatricals, and after the death of their founder, Richard Power, Bushe penned in testimony to his worth and character one of the most eloquent tributes that have ever been written. Many of the Kilkenny players frequented Cheltenham and acted there in theatricals that were got up amongst the visitors and residents at the fashionable watering-place.

The relatives of Chief-Justice Bushe were constantly at the Spa, where they dispensed lavish hospitality to their fellowcountrymen and to many others.

Most of the Irish Colony in Cheltenham were sportsmen and delighted in the many free mounts which Lord Fitzhardinge placed at their disposal; doubtless this was the chief attraction which brought them to the town in such large numbers, many of them being as careless and impecunious as they were wild and unmanageable in the hunting-field. They were always sure of generous hospitality from their better-off fellow-countrymen resident in the town, amongst whom was Mr John Bushe, eldest son of the Chief-Justice.

Jack Bushe resided at the Spa during many years and managed at once to keep on friendly terms with both Lord Fitzhardinge and with his brother, Grantley— no mean feat! In 1829, Mr Bushe was master of the Cheltenham Harriers, which he had bought after the death of Dr Townshend, the sporting parson of Bishop's Cleeve. A writer in *Baily's Magazine* says:

> "In 1827 we find the well-known Johnny Bushe then lived at Cheltenham, and was a great man there; kept a pack of harriers, and hunted over the hills, and was a great man over walls, and at the same time Major Hamerton was going. Then there were great parties at Berkeley Castle amongst whom were the late Sir George Wombwell, Mr Colmore (father of the MFH), who always kept good horses; the Doynes of Ireland, one of whom, a big man, went to Melton; Dr Townshend of Cleeve and Mr Barnard of Whitefield were both good sportsmen and kept harriers, though perhaps of a little earlier date than the others mentioned."

Mr Bushe, on his father's death, came into the family estate of Kilmurry but sold it shortly afterwards. He married a daughter of the Earl of Listowel, with whom he does not seem to have lived very long. Lady Louisa Bushe was very charitable, and was one of the patronesses of the local Benevolent Asylum: Mr Bushe lived his last years in London, where he earned fame as a great whist-player and was one of the committee (including Hickey's acquaintances, Major-General Richard Smith and his son "Tippoo," and one or two other authorities on the game) who settled the laws of whist. He died an old man in 1870.

After Colonel Coghill had put up the new tablet to his father, Sir Josiah Coghill, who had been buried in Trinity Church so many years previously, he wrote: "It was very kind of you to 'ghoul' into Trinity Church to see my reminder that I once had a father. Of course, I was so young when he became such, that I hardly remember my entry into this sublunary sphere. I wish I could have given you more assistance, but all of those days are laying down their old stable jackets. I was much amused this morning on opening a very official registered letter to find it had only the papers about 'Ould Bushe,' which you had kindly returned. It looked like a death warrant or an arrest for High Treason or something terrible. The Riddell and Macleod of whom you speak must have been cherubims or firebrands in my time for I don't remember hearing them talked of. The ———— I did know, and I think he was the Irish MP. All these memories require digging for deeply in my subliminial. You ask for stories of grandfather and uncle Bushe. I had too much of the boy's terror of being hanged (and perhaps deservedly) by a Lord Chief-Justice to approach near enough to know his peccadilloes, loves or romances, which, if possessed, were wisely concealed under his scarlet and ermine robes. His son, John Bushe, of whom you wrote, was more careless and many of his he carried on his sleeve for crows to peck at, which the unco-guid did freely. Do you wonder after which of these worthies the descendant has taken? Which do you think would be more interesting as a study for your new book? I don't know that John Bushe ever kept a pack of harriers, but he was a well-known man in the hunting-field. A big man with an impossible riding leg; and the 'Bushe calf' became a proverbial reproach.

"He was a leading whist player in the London Clubs and I expect he was a gay lad as there were many puritan faces drawn while whispering went on about him. In 1852, while I was getting a leg-up to ride my first steeplechase I heard a rich Irish voice shout, 'Divvle a hand will throw that lad in his saddle but mine,' and I saw my uncle push his way to me, seize me unceremoniously and nearly throw me to the other side of my horse. He had come to India 'to shoot mee tiger.' The tales about him for which you ask were so whispered that I could not hear them, but he was a splendid and good fellow, who lived at The Albany all his later years. I enclose you a photograph of John Bushe. It shows the doggy, debonair look as much as to say, 'Ah, let the crows peck if it pleases them!' The baggy trousers were, I suspect, to conceal the enormous legs of which I wrote, and which, the Lord be praised, were not transmitted with the sins to the third and fourth generations."

His brother-in-law, Sir Josiah Coghill, Bart, Vice-Admiral of the *Red*, his wife, his nine daughters and two sons, managed to put in an extremely good time in Cheltenham. The Admiral had succeeded his brother on 21st May 1817, as third baronet. His Dublin residence was Belvedere House, and he was in his seventyeighth year when he died at Kenilworth House, Cheltenham. Sir Josiah had married first, Sophia, daughter of James Dodson, Esq, who died in 1811, and second, Anna Maria, eldest daughter of the Rt Hon. Charles Kendal Bushe,

Lord Chief-Justice of the Court of King's Bench in Ireland. "Respected by all who had the good fortune to know him, he was especially endeared to his more intimate friends and to his brother officers in both services. A rich fund of ready humour, and a hand prompt to follow the suggestions of a generous heart, were his characteristics." He was a most reckless driver of his own coach and was famous for his various mishaps.

In Cheltenham, Sir Josiah and his wife lived at one time in Lansdown Place and subsequently at Pittville House.

"Pittville," resumed Colonel Coghill, "was then a comparative *terra incognita*, but eventually outrivalled Lansdown, and from where the College is now, in Bath Road, to Leckhampton there was only the one house of Lord Northwick.

"However, I need not bore you with what I can see but cannot describe. It all makes me feel what a reincarnated spirit would experience on a return to Earth, and he would be glad to get back to his cloud once more and to take care in doing so in his fiery chariot that his brakes were strong enough to prevent his slipping back to the sulphur foundations

"I really hardly know what to write about my father as I was away from him so much as a school boarder, and only saw him in the holidays. The picture he has left in my eye is of a big jovial man, whose laugh might have been heard from Lansdowne to Pittville, and he was always entertaining old naval and military warriors of Nelson's and Wellington's day, whose whole conversation seemed to me to refer to 'Old Bony.' The names that come to my mind chiefly are Captain Frobisher, Captain Maunsell, Matagorda Maclean, Dr Æneas Cannon, and there were many others of his old comrades. Daily these old warriors used to haunt the Club which was in the then Assembly Rooms, and there they fought their old battles over again, and new ones over long whist and billiards."

Colonel Coghill resumes: "I don't know who could have heard of my having been born in Cheltenham. I was born at: Drumcondra, outside Dublin, which is now let as a Jesuit College, and I was baptized in the drawing-room there, as is shown in the baptismal register I possess. In fact my last sister was born there after me. In 1835 we made our *hegirah* from Ireland. Crossing in a packet boat from Dunleary, which had just been renamed *Kingstown*, we landed like a tribe at Birkenhead with our oxen and our asses and all that had been within our gates. Our family then was father, mother, ten unmarried girls and two young sons. All, or most of us, with nurses galore, were stowed into huge carriages and a mail coach, the latter driven by my father, who prided himself on steering a team of horses. I doubt if any company would have insured our lives with such a rollicking Jehu, who could steer a boat or a ship but not a team. We drove the whole way to Cheltenham, where we roosted till 1850. For years my father continued to drive his coach till it and the horses melted away and in '50 he followed their example.'"

"I often heard," said the late Major Connellan, "of Sir Josiah Coghill's four-in-hand experiences. When living in Kilkenny he invariably bumped a certain street

Wellington Mansion, the property of Colonel Riddell.

corner, which had to to be 'rounded off,' and remains to this day a monument of his reckless driving. He was a bluff old admiral of the old school, very good-natured but full of nautical and other expletives."

There was a place just above the Colonnade at Montpellier, Cheltenham, on the left-hand side as you go into the town where, Colonel Coghill said, Sir Josiah upset a coachful of little Coghills, but not one of them was hurt. In the public library at Cheltenham there is an art gallery round which Colonel Coghill walked one morning, looking at the collection of old prints, many of which are from caricatures by the famous Dightons; some being unnamed. "You say you don't know who that man is?" said Colonel Coghill. "Well, I think I do, he's my father." The librarian got wind of his arrival, and followed him round with a notebook and pencil, and Colonel Coghill put names to several of the other caricatures. "I think that one is Lytton," went on Colonel Coghill, "and that one in the group may be Dan O'Connor. That man with the whip is like one of the Berkeleys I think, one of those who were masters of hounds. Very likely it is Lord Fitzhardinge. Here is old Kirwan, the Master of the Ceremonies, and his old blue coat and buttons and things. But he used to wear silk tights. H———— there was half in and half out of Society. He didn't live alone."

"My mother's house in Lansdown," said Colonel Coghill, "was a sort of centre where all dropped in daily, but I was too young to be mixed up much in their lives. In fact, I was at the College from the day it first opened in Bayshill Terrace.

"A lot of lords of sorts used to blossom in Cheltenham, such as Lords Dunalley, Clancarty and De Sausmarez, many of the names I forget. Sir Bulwer Lytton was a leading literary tiger; he used to stay in one of those houses in Montpellier Terrace, the tall yellow one for choice (Beechworth Lodge) and he used to come across to our house and flirt with my mother, with whom he worked mesmerism daily. My mother had a regular Irish coterie always in tow as she was clever and amusing."

Bulwer Lytton was in Cheltenham in 1825 on the West of England tour on which he had set out because his mother objected to his engagement with Rosina Wheeler and he thought change of scene would do him good. At Cheltenham he found much material for sketches of provincial life and character, as seen in the genteel setting of watering-places that gave themselves the airs of Belgravia or Hyde Park. He had visited these resorts in childhood with his mother.

In 1825, he wrote to his mother from Cheltenham: "God knows that in spite of the great dejection and despondency of spirit, which makes me at times so silent, and at others so querulous, I do feel most utterly attached and grateful to you. Even now I have sacrificed much that is dear to me from the heartfelt desire that in all the great events of my life I may secure your approbation, and that in no event of it you may ever be ashamed of that kindness and affection you have shown me. God bless you—Mother—dearest Mother."

After meeting Miss Wheeler at the Spa, he writes to Mrs Wheeler: "I am detained in town a day or two longer than I had expected. My address will be Post Office, Cheltenham, etc." On his arrival in the town he writes to his mother, thanking her for having generously increased his income.

Lytton, although at this time writing to his mother of the sacrifice he was making in trying to forget Rosina, was not prepared to face the reality for, on receipt of Rosina's answer to one of his letters, in which she stated that she would not marry him, he hurried back to London and ardently implored to be accepted again as her lover. After explanations a complete reconciliation was effected, and on his return to Cheltenham he writes: "I give myself to the sweet hope that there is now nothing to bar the confidence and the commune of hearts."

On the 28th of January 1835, when husband and wife were fast drifting apart, Bulwer Lytton visited Rosina at Gloucester, and wrote to his mother: "Feeling deeply disappointed and, indeed, indignant at Rosina's manner. I drove to Cheltenham, meaning to proceed at once to town and arrange for our legal separation. While I was there Miss Green" (who was the confidante of both Lytton and his wife) "arrived, and represented Rosina as so ill, and, indeed, unhappy at my abrupt departure that I returned."

Lytton again visited Cheltenham, staying at the Belle Vue, then a hotel, in 1840, and he probably stayed in the town on several subsequent occasions.

Colonel Coghill writes: "Captain Frobisher often dined with my father who collected old sailors to dine. On other occasions he collected old Peninsulars as well as Trafalgar fighters, who lied and lied and lied and drank their two and three bottles!

"Captain Maunsell was another sailor character, who lived next door to Hamerton. I did not recognise his portrait in the Museum nor that of General (Matagorda) Maclean, perhaps from a pulpy memory. I sent my father's caricturish portrait to you, to satisfy the Curator of the Museum that I was not gassing, that he might compare and be satisfied. You will see that the two copies are alike even to the watch seals. I rescued my copy as a boy to take to India in 1880, as no one seemed to value it then, which is apparent from the broken edges, and had it framed, from which it had never been removed until to-day. We had and have several life-sized portraits by Williams which account for this watercolour not having been valued.

"Old Davis, librarian and proprietor of the *Looker-on*, knew more about Cheltenham in those days than any other man. Perhaps he had descendants to whom he communicated his knowledge. No, I don't write books, I leave that to field-marshals. As I write, the whole group of Peninsular and Trafalgar and Nile heroes who were knocking about Cheltenham then, seems to pass by me in file; old General Maclean, Sir Harry Smith, Frobisher, Maunsell. *The* character of the place was Captain Kirwan, the Master of the Ceremonies, the Beau Brummell of the town, who presided at all the public balls in the Assembly Rooms in 'tights,' silk stockings, blue tail coat, brass buttons, a cocked hat under his arm, and a blue silk sash over his shoulder. To maintain this dignity and for greeting every one every day, whether wet or fine with 'a nice day to-day,' he went round every house at the end of the season with a subscription book."

In May 1835, Mr Marshall, the Master of the Ceremonies, had been selected to superintend a series of Subscription Balls at the King's Concert Rooms, Hanover Square, under the patronage of HRH the Princess Augusta and the Landgravine of Hesse-Homburg. He suggested that he should keep on the direction of the summer amusements in Cheltenham and that another MC should be appointed to officiate at the Assembly Rooms Balls during his absence in the winter. This gave great offence locally, especially as Mr Marshall was understood to have implied that if one of his appointments went to the wall it would not be the London one. He was told bluntly that he couldn't be in London and Cheltenham at once, and that if he was not prepared to attend wholeheartedly to his business in Cheltenham he had better resign and leave his office for someone who could. Mr Marshall did resign, and there were only eighty people at his farewell ball, so angry were the Cheltenham people with their former MC. The step taken by the Master of the Ceremonies seems to have been an unwise one for himself and for "the children who were dependent upon him," for he was very unsuccessful with his London undertakings.

Again there was an election campaign with five candidates aspiring to the office. Marshall's successor was Captain (afterwards Lieutenant-Colonel) A. H. Kirwan, who had been identified for twenty years with the town and was extremely popular. The new MC had entered the 7th Fusiliers in 1813, and had served with them until 1829, when he had exchanged into the 66th Regiment, in which regiment he remained until his retirement on half-pay. Evidently he must have been something of a character, but he was much beloved by visitors and residents alike.

The temptation to quote the description of his initiation cannot be resisted:

"On Thursday evening last, Captain Kirwan was received at the entrance of the Promenade Room by the Earl of Moray and Mr Jearrad, Proprietor of the Rotunda, by whom he was conducted to Lady Burdett, who, surrounded by the Lady Patronesses, was seated on a raised dais, which had been erected for the occasion. Her ladyship in receiving Captain Kirwan, addressed him in a brief but appropriate congratulatory speech, after which he was invested with the Blue Ribbon. Captain Kirwan in his reply acknowledged the honour which had been conferred upon him after which the proceedings were closed with a flourish of trumpets, and the Band played the National Anthem."

In September 1835, a subscription was opened for "The MC's Medal," to which Tom Moore's friend, James Corry, was one of the subscribers.

Lieutenant-Colonel Andrew Hyacinth Kirwan died on 5th August 1872, at his residence, 8 Promenade Terrace, aged seventy-four years. He had held the office of MC for thirty-seven years, only resigning shortly before his death. No successor to him was appointed, and with his death the last link with the old Georgian days was broken.

XVIII

Some Victorians and Others—Cheltenham College.

The Rev. Archibald Boyd had, in 1840, become incumbent of Christ Church. He was described as "a different sort of man altogether from Mr Close, and not so overbearing. People said that Mr Boyd would drive men to Heaven, but that Mr Close would kick them there."

In 1842, as almost from the beginning of things in Cheltenham, the Spa was the resort of retired naval and military officers, for the most part of comparatively limited means. Some of them, together with Mr Close and other permanent residents, decided to found a proprietary college, which afterwards became a famous public school. One of these officers, who had a great deal to do with the college in its early days, was one of Wellington's old officers, Captain Robertson, RA, retired. His son, the famous Robertson of Brighton, was for some time Mr Boyd's curate at Christ Church. This young clergyman was afterwards described by Dean Stanley as "the greatest preacher of the century."

When Frederick Robertson died in 1853, he had published nothing but one sermon, two lectures, two addresses, and an analysis of "In Memoriam." But he had not long been dead before there arose an imperious demand for all that he had said or written … Mudie found his sermons as popular as novels. One is apt to think of the Rev. F. W. Robertson merely as the greatest preacher of his time, and as the friend of Lady Byron, with whom, though no doubt she deserves it, it is hard to feel a great deal of sympathy. But we should not forget that Robertson, apart from his real saintliness of character and from his great oratorical gifts, was a highly intellectual and fair-minded literary critic, who could thoroughly admire Tennyson's magnificent requiem even when he did not at all agree with some of the poet's views. The masterly analysis of "In Memoriam," shows us this clearly.

At the new Cheltenham College, Captain Adam Durnford Gordon, who had served in an irregular cavalry regiment in India, and was a very fine horseman and a noted big-game hunter, was given the appointment of Professor of Oriental Languages. He is nowadays best known to fame as the father of Adam Lindsay Gordon.

Colonel Coghill said: "Close behind the King's Walk on Bayshill the College first broke ground, then of the Do the Boys' Hall type, where more caning was applied than learning, and boxing was more prized than scholarship. I was at the College on the opening day, when Mr Litchfield, Captain Iredale and others, headed by Dr Phillips, opened the door in state and an oration was given to a crowd of us boys. Henry James claimed to be the first boy to enter, but we all claimed that also, so some of us economise the truth or, as one of the very respectable ministers would say, 'use terminological inexactitude.' There can be very few alive now who saw that opening day. The present Lord Loreburn and Lord Morley were quite new boys who joined years after. My chief reflection on those days is the gratification I felt in the expense I caused for new canes, with which I was constantly hammered for nothing. All I can claim of that place is the scoring on back and hands from an insensate headmaster who thought that talent should be driven in from extremities. He failed.

"When I was at Cheltenham College I was a boarder at The Priory for a long time. Why was I a boarder when my people lived in the town? *To get rid of me.* Then for a time I was at a house above the College, Boyce's house it was afterwards. I got a good many floggings there and everywhere. All undeserved! When I look round these houses here there seems hardly one in which I have not been flogged. The hall porter was a great institution. He wore a sort of uniform and held us across the table when we were getting flogged. They soon ran the first headmaster and then we had Dobson. He was always flogging me, but I don't know that I would mind having those days again. I lived every hour of them. I always thought when I had wings—if they allow them in the place below I'd come back and have a look at it all again. Perhaps as you say I shall have wings and be up above. They may discover there are some worse ones after all. But now I shall feel I have seen it all too lately and it ain't worth while to come again, perhaps. The chapel is rather fine inside. I find my memory plays me tricks. I made a mistake about where the Plough Hotel was and how we used to get across the yard to the old Assembly Rooms. I forget, and the College people forget me, except when there are subscription lists going round.

"I have to delve for the geography of the College playgrounds of prehistoric days. When I visited Cheltenham some years ago I found these places built over almost past recognition."

Before Colonel Coghill came to Cheltenham for the last time, and with a very severe cold he wrote: "I might come again perhaps on my way to town but perhaps by that time I shall be fitted with a pair of wings, or gone up in an Elijah's chariot and those who have brought me to Cheltenham will be criminally responsible and can sing, 'He lived in a hot climate, came to a cold one and passed on.'

"Years after I left the College I sang the Dean's Part in 'The Sorcerer,' in which the lines run, 'Peace, pray old Heart, why agitate the slumbers,' which I think to be very a propos of these disturbing memories of caning and masterly brutalities on my infant form. I refer to 1841. Many thanks for that amusing extract (from an old Cheltenham paper with an account of theatricals) throwing my mind back to primeval days ... I clearly remember my youthful blushes in those days—since worn out—on first facing an audience from a stage" (in a harmless little farce in some private theatricals, of which Sir Joshua Coghill was one of the promoters got up in aid of a local charity) "and my chief recollection about the theatricals is the antagonism raised by the parsons about them, so that Mr Boyd and Mr Close refused to have me confirmed about then as I was vowing to avoid the pomps and vanities of this wicked world. I remember the unctuous smile of Dean Close and the ferocious glare of Mr Boyd's game eye when telling me that the 'pomps,' which I was to forswear were so called from Pompey's theatrical displays. I suppose that we all have to talk rubbish in our day. Parsons were a power in those days and revelled in worked slippers, offered at their shrines by the faithful ... We acted in those days in the Assembly Rooms as The Well Walk Theatre of later days was a mineral spring drinking rooms then. I remember Shenton of Winchcomb Street well; also Sir William Osborne, Major Burns, Captain Todd, Captain Reveley, Captain Dodgson, etc., who all took parts. But all have passed on and can give you no more help than I regret I can ...

"You ask me who lived at 26 Promenade and gave theatricals there. That information is buried in the bosom of the gods. I don't know that Mr Gomonde ever took part in theatricals, though he sang funny simple songs to his own accompaniment, such as 'Fanny Grey.' It may have been Sir William Osborne or the Queer little Major ————, an Indian Officer, who lived in that house. But I was suffering too much from the complaint, long since cured, of excessive youth, to be in that swim ...

"Ought I to have crutches and slippers I only carried away from Cheltenham College two things, a broken nose, broken in the Sandpit, and the quotation of *Omne ignotum pro magnifico est*, which may mean the descent from an imagined pedestal ... This Sandpit was a hole in the top of the playground, at the end farthest from the town, from which material had been dug to build the villas up the road from Lord Northwick's corner house, in which the Tickells, Fords, etc, lived. In this Sandpit all disputes were settled, *vi et armis*. Many a maternal reproach I received on returning home with a pair of closed eyes, for I was very Irish, *ie* quarrelsome.

"Of course, when we were fighting in that Sandpit—Lindsay Gordon, I suppose, and Tom Pickernell, thought I don't remember them, and the rest—the masters couldn't see what we were doing below the surface. It was right in front of where the Gymnasium is now. There was a high hedge along here too where we all had our little private burrows. There were two walls, too cutting off the forbidden ground, part of the playground which didn't then belong to the College.

"In Suffolk Square here there were two large girls' schools, Miss Aldridge's and another. I used to get over the wall there. One day Miss Aldridge came up to Kenilworth House (when we lived at Pittville) to complain to my father. He stood there, champing his lips and trying not to laugh. At last he said, 'Damned young dog. He didn't get it from me. Where did he get it from?' I thought I was getting out of it very well. But on Saturday when I went home there were a lot of people there and my brother sat down to the piano and began to sing. And as I listened I recognised the poem I had written to the girl I had got over the wall to see. So I fell into it after all. The girl's name was Anna Matilda, and I heard the other day that she is a widow, and is still living in Cheltenham. Why don't l go to see her, do you say? Well, you see, I don't know her name. The College tart and bun shop was where the motor garage is in the Suffolk Road.

"As I walked up the London Road I saw that the public house near Cambray, next to Grosvenor Passage, was gone. I didn't remember the name, though something about Bluebells is running in my mind. Jimmy Edwards used to come there and box with us boys. I didn't so often go to that room down the town, but I could find my way all right to that passage by the Roebuck. I can't help thinking that Lindsay Gordon and I must have met at the College, but our lines led apart in very early days. I was at the College from its opening day until '49, and the next year started for India. Though our lives varied, our tastes ran together as 'The Cheltenham Earwig' (fern Edwards, the Middleweight Champion, known as 'The Earywig') was my teacher as well as Gordon's, and I haunted his rooms for education which I practised in the College Sandpit. I have no recollections of Gordon's having knocked me out of time there, though he probably did. Edwards called a fight a 'do-ment.' When he used to box with me he hadn't a thick head of hair like he has in your picture, but his head was nearly shaved. He used to say, ''it 'ard. 'Ere's my 'ead. 'It it; you can't 'urt it.' I remember the Griffithses of Marie Hill but I was too young to be in the hunting swim. Mr Barton ran the Stag Hounds then and I had a few runs with Lord Fitzhardinge's. Twelve years later I had a couple of seasons with Cregoe Colmore and Hugh Owen with the Cotswolds and then I went East again.

"George Reeves taught me to ride. Tom Oliver was a great steeple-chase rider and far too swell to teach the likes of me. He had a place at one time somewhere towards Alstone, where two roads branch off, one to the station. I think Oliver's place was on the straight one, the Gloucester Road, I suppose it is …

"Only the back part of the College buildings was built when I was a boy there … There was one boy, James Macpherson, who used to fight with me a great deal and years afterwards in India I was wounded and was carried into the hospital, when I heard a weak voice from the next bed, saying, 'Is that you, Paddy?' It was Macpherson, and he said, 'I'm dying of a broken heart. I've got nothing else to live for!' Just then one of the nurses stopped us talking and I collapsed and when I came round again I heard them hammering down his coffin. And *she* married someone else. Yes, I daresay if we had been let go on talking I *should* have bucked him up—and sent myself out.

"There was a much bigger boy who used to make me his sort of fag and bully me a bit and I swore when I was big enough I'd have his blood. Years afterwards in some fighting we were in a sort of gorge and W,——— the big boy, was behind and I thought he'd had time to run across. I saw he wasn't anywhere about and I didn't go back at once for I couldn't leave and after all I thought perhaps he had got across and if he was killed he was killed. But by and bye, I found him and they were still firing. He was hit and couldn't move and I got him on my back and crawled along, wriggling along the ground like a chameleon. I had to go back to my men and I left him lying on the ground and couldn't get him to a hospital then; I said I'd send an ambulance for him. Some time afterwards I was at a dance and I came across him and he had only one arm. He said, 'I have to thank you for saving my life!' I remembered how when I was at school I'd sworn to have his blood. And so I *had* had it—all over my jacket!

"There are still some of those armless ladies at Montpellier I see. We boys used to paint them red and blue and green and get flogged for it. I believe Dean Close objected to them because he thought they hadn't enough clothes on.

"Many thanks for the *Echoes* of a bygone past. As is correct for a newspaper one of them gives me the *news* or revives a fading memory of my heroism in the Crimea in '54. I had a vague idea that in that year I was helping to add a ruby to the British Crown in acquiring Burmah for it. I thought I had gone to Burmah in 1852–4–5–6 and got back to India in time for the Siege of Delhi.

"Perhaps the correspondent refers to my spirit, which may have been there while its tabernacle was visiting King Theebaw, *N'importe—ça m'est égal*, and I may in those elastic days of my youth have been, like Sir Boyle Roche's bird, in two places at once."

When Sir Josiah Coghill died he was succeeded by his elder son, Sir Joscelyn Coghill, who died some years ago. One of Sir Joscelyn's sons was the heroic Neville Coghill, who, with Melvill, saved the colours at Isandhlwana. King Edward, years afterwards, gave them the Victoria Cross posthumously.

Sydney Dobell was born 5th April 1824, eldest son of John Dobell, who was descended from the younger branch of an ancient Sussex family notable as cavaliers in the reign of Charles II. In 1844, Sydney married Emily Fordham, to whom he had been engaged at fifteen. The family had come to Cheltenham in 1829, and Sydney was subsequently for many years a member of his father's firm of wine merchants, carrying on business in Gloucester, Cheltenham and Tewkesbury. In 1848, when lodging at a small cottage on the slopes of Leckhampton Hill, Mr Dobell began "The Roman." He wrote more of it at Hucclecote and completed the poem at Coxhorne, Charlton Kings.

"The Roman," published in 1850, was received with a wonderful unanimity of applause, and the *Athenaeum* acclaimed the appearance of a new poet. In the spring of 1858, Dobell took Cleeve Tower, near the highest part of the Cotswolds, and with an enchanting view from its window. Ill-health for many years cut short his literary career, and practically all of his literary work was crowded into a space of six years.

One of Sydney Dobell's most exquisite poems was found in MS. after the death of the writer. It is:

"A Fragment of a Sleep-Song

Sister Simplicitie,
Sing, sing a song to me
Sing me to sleep.
Some legend low and long,
Slow as the summer song
Of the dull deep.

Some legend long and low,
Whose equal ebb and flow
To and fro creep
On the dim marge of grey
'Twixt the soul's night and day,
Washing 'awake' away
Into 'asleep.'

Some legend low and long
Never so weak or strong
As to let go
While it can hold this heart
Withouten sigh or smart
Or as to hold this heart when it sighs; No."

He spent the last part of his life at Barton End House, Horsley, where he died on 21st August 1874.

Mr Clarence Dobell was with Miss Mulock, in 1860, in Tewkesbury, when they took shelter from a shower in an alley in Tewkesbury, and saw the incident which afterwards was worked into *John Halifax Gentleman*, when a little girl came out of a house and gave a poor ragged boy a piece of bread.

During the ten years which preceded his death, Mr Dobell had, on account of ill-health, to a great extent withdrawn from literary and business pursuits. Carlyle and Charlotte Monte were amongst his friends and admirers and in September 1874 they visited Barton End House.

The elder of Sydney Dobell's two very charming brothers, Mr Clarence Dobell, was ten years younger than the poet, and he and his brother, Cyrus, only died a few years ago in Cheltenham. Mr Cyrus Faulkner Dobell used to hunt a great deal and could tell all sorts of stories about Fred Archer, while Mr Clarence Dobell had been one of the first boys at the College when Lindsay Gordon arrived there.

In about 1845, Alfred Tennyson came to live, or at least had his headquarters, with his mother at 10 St James's Square, adjoining St Gregory's Church, and directly facing the Great Western Station, which was built shortly after his arrival. Tennyson is said to have bribed one of the officials for temporary possession of a highly educated parrot, a pet of the railwaymen, which was wont to impart unauthorised information to travellers. This communicative bird was the source of much amusement to the Tennyson family, who were great lovers of animals and birds.

Mrs Tennyson, a handsome, bright, sympathetic, and rather unconventional old lady, seldom went out unless accompanied by two at least of three or four dogs which, with a monkey, belonged to the establishment. Mary and Matilda, the poet's sisters, were then unmarried. Mrs Tennyson's sister, Miss Fytche, and another more distant relative who acted as housekeeper, also lived at 10 St James's Square.

In an upper room, sacred from the intrusion of all save one or two special friends, most of "In Memoriam" was written. Sydney Dobell, Mr Dobson, Principal of the College, Mr Boyd of Christ Church, and his curate Robertson, all got to know Tennyson fairly well. The little room was not kept in very orderly fashion, for books and papers seem to have been quite as much on the floor and chairs as on the table.

"There," said the poet's son, "my father, pipe in mouth, would discourse to his friends, more unconstrainedly than anywhere else, on men and things, and what death meant. When the talk was on religious questions, which was not often, he spoke confidently of a future existence. 'Christianity,' he said, 'is tugging at my heart.'"

After his marriage Tennyson was not much at Cheltenham, and in 1853 Mrs Tennyson moved to Hampshire. In later years Mrs Tennyson and her daughter Matilda, made a lengthy stay, as did Mrs Alan Ker (Tennyson's eldest sister). Two of Tennyson's brothers died in Cheltenham.

One hears of Tennyson playing blind-man's-buff at a Christmas party in the town in 1848; how Robertson of Brighton and others met him in the house of a physician, probably Sir Arthur Faulkner, and how Tennyson got nervous or impatient when he saw that Robertson was expecting him to talk like an inspired prophet, and would at first talk about nothing but beer.

There is a good deal about Tennyson and other celebrities in the reminiscences of Dr Ker of Hadley House, Cheltenham, published in the *Cheltenham Examiner*, and there is an account somewhere of a day at Malvern, when Carlyle went for a long walk there with Tennyson and Sydney Dobell.

Several undoubted allusions to Cheltenham are in "In Memoriam." The verse about the sea where now the Long Street is, has already been quoted, and in the line: "The quarries trench'd along the hill," Tennyson obviously speaks of the quarries of Leckhampton Hill. Shakespeare complained of the "rough uneven ways," but Tennyson drank in the "Serenity" as Mrs Siddons had justly called it of the Cotswolds and their neighbourhood:

> "Calm and deep peace on this high wold,
> And in the dews that drench the furze,
> And all the silver gossamers
> That twinkle into green and gold."

The news of the various troubles in India naturally deeply affected the Cheltenham Military Colony. Lady Sale was in Cheltenham when she heard of the death of Sir Robert Sale, himself an old resident, at Moodkee in 1846. The accounts of the massacre at Cawnpore, in 1857, aroused such unbounded horror and indignation, that a subscription of £2000 was got up for the surviving sufferers.

Colonel Coghill came to Cheltenham not long before the Great War, was asked a question about Colonel Andrew Lang, and then drifted on from that to talk about some of his own experiences in the Mutiny.

He said: "I met a girl in India some years ago, and she said: 'Perhaps you remember my father, Lang of the Engineers?' Lang was a charming man. They were outside Delhi and didn't know what to be at. Shots were as thick as hail and no one could take observations. But Lang said, 'Oh, that's easily done!' and he dropped into the ditch and found out all about things under the hottest fire, and came back. And the next day when the same sort of thing happened and again Lang whipped off his sword and went across under heavy fire and made observations. It wasn't he who put the powder-bags against the Kashmir Gate. He was one of the party. Six men went up with powder bags under their arms. And the first was shot at once—they went across a narrow bit of plank—and the next was just fixing a bag when he went down. And so on. And the last was a sergeant, and he was just fixing the bags and managed to nail them on and set a match to them—and a little trumpeter was with them and after he was bowled over he sat up in the ditch and put his trumpet to his mouth and sounded the advance.

"Several years ago some of the Delhi Veterans gave me a silver cup and I didn't know what to say so I talked about the others and said if people knew what some of them in that room had done they would be covered with decorations as thick as Christmas trees. And I added, 'You needn't mind. I am not going to be personal—and one of the best of the lot is not here to-night.' And I told them about Lang. Some time afterwards Lang wrote to me and said, 'I have to thank you for the CB which I received by post this morning.'

"I was in India when the Mutiny broke out. We had just taken Burma. At the Siege of Delhi, we were well inside the city when orders came from the general a mile in the rear that we were to retire. We had lost a thousand odd men and sixty-three officers, and he saw the long procession of wounded being carried to the rear and he couldn't quite see what was going on, and so he gave the order to retire. But *our* general said, 'No, we can't retire.' And the orderly officer said, 'But if I can retire the general will say, "But why can't they"?' And we said, 'Nonsense, we'll just put you over the wall and go on.' Who was it who insisted on going on? Oh, well, we all did. We had been eight days getting there and we were inside. And *inside* we meant to stay. Of course, if we had gone back it meant that every white man and woman and child in India would have been killed. The general had sent word that unless Delhi was taken in twenty-four hours, he should have to give up holding out. And we *had* to do it. The general who gave the order to retire was old and though he had done very well up to then, he got panic-stricken and lost his head. No man ever had such a responsibility resting upon him before or since—the life of every white man and woman in India.

"What were we doing all that time? Well, that's a large order. What was *I* doing then? Why, *climbing up a ladder.* There was a great big sergeant on the ladder just above me, and a sword went through his cheek, and he fell over me on to my sword, so the first blood I drew was that of a white man. I threw him over on to the side and turned him on his face, so that he shouldn't choke. And just above me was Captain Jimmy Hay, the ugliest man in the Army, not a hair on his head or face. We could see his white head gleaming above us. And just as he got to the top a shot struck his knee and he was wild with rage. He stood there, with the shots falling like hail around him, and tied up his knee tightly and put a stone in to form a tourniquet, and all the while he wasn't looking at his knee but at the enemy and swearing hard. 'Wait till I get at you—you devils! You just wait till I get at you and you shall smart for this.' And then he was down among them and the crowd was too thick for him to draw his sword, but he cut and hit and slashed in all directions. And just then a bullet hit him in the mouth and it seemed as if that must be the end of him. And him, too, I turned over on his face so that he shouldn't suffocate in his blood—and went on. And later he was sent to the rear, carried by four natives on a door.

"After that we heard firing behind us and had time to ask what it was. And a sergeant said, 'It's that damned Hay. He ain't dead *yet!*' He was, as I said, being carried to the rear, where there was more fighting, and the four men who were carrying him, thinking he was dead or next door to it, dropped him and ran away. Then Hay got up, got into a little hut, propped the door open to make a sort of barrier and began defending the hut.

"And a few days afterwards, when I had to make a report about the number of dead and wounded, I went round to the hospital and thought of poor Hay. So I asked what had become of him and there, coming towards me, was a strange figure—Hay—bandaged all over, his chest tied up and on his head was a sort of bolster, tied in, more like a woman's waist than anything else, and very high. And on his chest was a placard, put there by himself—'Don't come near me, I stink!' His wounds had begun to suppurate. Was he greatly disfigured, do you say? Not a bit. You *couldn't* disfigure Hay. He was so ugly already. He only died a few years ago.

Charles Bushe, Lord Chief Justice of Ireland. After a painting by Charles Grey, A.R.H.A.

"I got some loot in Delhi. I found one rather queer thing. I was poking about in the Palace and in the dark in a sort of cellar I put my hand down a hole and felt a human arm. And it was a girl, and when I pulled her out she said she was in the Treasury, and had hidden there because it was the safest place to hide—and no one would come there. I explored round then and found she had been lying on a heap of lovely cashmere shawls. So I helped myself to them. Now we had been ordered to give in all we found to the Prize Fund. I had done that, and the Inspector-General helped himself to a lovely sword I had got, with diamonds and emeralds and rubies all over the hilt. He said, 'I'm just taking this as a souvenir!' And I remarked, 'That's exactly what I took it for, too.' So after that I sent in my conscience to the Depot and resolved to keep those shawls if I could. I thought they'd be so nice to send my people. I told Hodson of Hodson's Horse about them, and he said, 'I'll manage it for you if I can.' And one night I was in bed when I was awakened by a troop of horses clattering up the street. It was about half-past two in the morning and it was Hodson, and he said, 'I've come for those shawls.' So I jumped out and got my bath from under my-bed. The shawls were there. And Hodson made his men take off their saddles; they had blankets underneath to keep the saddles from galling, and we folded up a shawl in each blanket and put them on again. I must tell you that I had got them away from where I found them in the same way. I was the only cavalry officer, but I put some men on horses and got the shawls through that way. General Showers said, 'We don't want those horses,' and I answered then that the men were tired and it would be better to let them ride and tie. And he said, 'Well, don't do it again. We don't want to coddle them.' I sold the horses to the Commissariat and got the shawls so far on their way. Well, Hodson got them all safely to the gate and there we were stopped for the orders were very strict. 'This red-tape is too awful for words,' said Hodson. '*Get* off your horses, men. Oh, this sickening waste of a man's time.' And they searched and felt about but they found nothing, and at last someond said, 'We haven't had the blankets off.' '*Get* off your horses again,' ordered Hodson in a weary voice. 'This is a *little* too much.' Just then we heard firing. 'We can wait for no more of this damned nonsense,' said Hodson, 'come along.' We rode off and left them and got through. And it was another troop of Hodson's Horse *firing in the air! Clever.* Of course, he was, as clever as a schoolmaster. Well, he had his wife up at ———— and he sent the shawls up to her. She was very clever too, as clever as himself. And she got the shawls away and sent them home to my sisters.

"Another time Hodson rode in behind a cloud of dust, and the general said, 'What's this?' And Hodson said, 'It's a lot of the enemy's cattle. I've commandeered them. I thought they would come in handy for food.' The general said, 'Nonsense, man; we can't be driving about cattle.' 'Shall we let the Commissariat buy them?' asked Hodson. 'No, no! we don't want them,' replied the general. 'Turn them loose.' Hodson answered that that would never do, he thought. It would be dangerous to have cattle running about loose. The general said, 'Oh, well, *only* get rid of them. Turn them loose. Take them away. Get rid of them.' So Hodson took them away, and them too he sent up to his wife and the clever woman disposed of them at pukka prices.

"I caught a man by a well one day, and he swore he was a Bengali, but just as I was asking him questions, Hodson rode up. I said, 'This man says he is a Bengali!' 'Oh, no, he isn't,' replied Hodson. 'Here man, hold up your chin, and let's see what you're like,' and he whipped out his sword, and sliced off his head. I said, 'Oh, wasn't that rather summary?' 'Not at all,' replied Hodson, 'and just to show that I am right, have a look down that well.' The man's head had rolled down there, and with it were his arms and accoutrements, which he had just hidden there. No, it wasn't really cruel. It was a war in which quarter was neither given nor asked, It was bad luck for the man that Hodson came up just at the moment, for I don't think I could have killed him. I don't care for doing it in cold blood.

"We caught a man once, and Hodson asked him what he was, and he replied, 'A———— fighting man.' Hodson wouldn't let the men shoot him as he said it would attract attention. 'I'll just play with him a bit,' he said. He hadn't a sword, but a kind of rapier, and he just walked round the man, sort of fencing with him. And Hodson taunted him all the time and said, 'Call yourself a *fighting* man. Why, you're only a woman and not so good as a woman.' And at last when he got tired of it Hodson just made a sort of lunge and ran the man through. Oh, it was fair enough, the man would have killed Hodson if Hodson hadn't killed him.

"Yes, they were bad times in a way—and *very bad* for the people at home, who couldn't get news of what was going on sometimes for six months or more. But I don't think that sort of thing can ever happen again. The native regiments are broken up into different sects and peoples. They are not all Gurkhas or all Sikhs and so on—but there will be one company of one and one of another.

"That house with the blue letters on it in the Promenade in Cheltenham is where I mesmerised the ladies. Did I tell you about that: well, when I was down here for the hunting in the sixties, I went to see a mesmerist called McCarthy. And he said to the roomful of people that the power had gone out of him. He had been mesmerising a lady who was a very difficult subject. The man next me remarked, 'He's a fraud.' But I replied, 'Doesn't it strike you that a fraud wouldn't fail like that?' I was sorry for the man. He asked, 'Any of you who like can come again to-morrow night, and I'll see what I can do.' I went up to him and said, 'I think I can help you.' And I got hold of his thumbs and the power went out of me and into him, and he said, 'Thank God, it's coming back.' And he put quite a lot of them off and did all sorts of things, and they were all quite pleased. And the man who was sitting next to me was quite impressed, and we began to talk, and finally he said, 'Drop in one afternoon and have a cup of tea with me,' and I said I was hunting all the week and couldn't till Saturday and I'd come then.

"I went and I found a large crowd waiting. Seats all down a big room, which was quite full. And I asked, 'What's this? I thought you were going to be alone.' And the man answered, 'The fact is I told my wife and she told a friend or two, and they want to see something.' So I said: 'Well, I won't disappoint them if I can help it. Will any of them give themselves over to be mesmerised?' They replied, 'Oh, no, they wouldn't!' The man's wife said to him, 'You be mesmerised. We *must* do *something.*'

"He said he would if she would, and finally I put him and his wife and their daughter off in three chairs, facing the rest. Just then there was a ring at the bell. Three of the old tabbies of Cheltenham had come to call. And there were the host and hostess and their daughter asleep in all sorts of attitudes. I thought I'd better wake the wife up—and I did. But she wouldn't have her husband waked up at once. She said, 'Play about with him a bit.' So I did. I made him put his head down at her feet and then I waked him up.

"Oh, yes, I was rather a strong mesmerist, but now I go in for psychism."

Adam Lindsay Gordon, who became the national poet of Australia, had been born in the Azores in October 1833 and in 1842 had entered Cheltenham College, where his father was a master. Though he re-entered the College later he was only there for about a year the first time. During the next six years of his life his whereabouts are vague, except that he appears to have been in the neighbourhood of Cheltenham. For some three years Lindsay was at a school kept by the Rev. S. Garrard at Dumbleton, and he subsequently spent three years at the Royal Military Academy, Woolwich, and then a short time at the Royal Grammar School, Worcester, and, at eighteen years of age, he re-entered Cheltenham College in 1851. It was then that he and a younger boy, afterwards the great horseman, Tom Pickernell, began to haunt the boxing saloon kept by Jem Edwards, the unbeaten Middleweight Champion, in the Lower High Street, where once, by a fluke, Gordon knocked out "The Earywig" in a sparring match. Jem's grave is not far from Haynes Bayly's in the old cemetery at the bottom of the town, and on the stone are the words: "He that overcometh shall inherit all things."

The unfortunate college master, Captain Gordon, could not make his son settle down, either at Cheltenham, Dumbleton, Woolwich or Worcester, and the tradition is that he played truant from the College and also from the Royal Military Academy in order to ride in steeplechases.

At Prestbury, Lindsay met Tom Sayers who was training for a fight out at Tom Oliver's, and Gordon used to spar with Sayers to give him practice, although Sayers and the "Earywig " were naturally much more than a match for Lindsay, for all his courage.

Gordon was given his first mount on a race-horse by Tom Oliver when he rode in the trials at Prestbury Race-course, and as he dismounted the old trainer said to the delighted college boy, "There now, you young devil, you've won a race."

Black Tom gave Tom Pickernell *his* first ride also, but in a real steeplechase at Andoversford, and afterwards he remarked, "It's a good thing you didn't win, young Squire, or you'd have thought you could ride."

Lindsay Gordon rode in the Berkeley Hunt Cup Steeplechase in 1852 and 1853, in the latter year on Lalla Rookh or Louisa, then his own property, but without success. On 7th August 1853, he left England for Australia, never to return.

Several of the earlier pupils at the College remembered the gentle and kindly and extremely handsome Hindustani Master, and Captain Herbert Vaughan, RN, one of his pupils, treasured up a silver pencil-case which Captain Gordon gave to him, "not exactly as a prize, but as an encouragement to do better."

One of Gordon's poems, "By Flood and Field: A Legend of Cotteswold," describes a wonderful feat of horsemanship by Captain Louis Edmond Nolan, up by the Seven Springs. Ned Nolan, who appears to have been well known to Gordon, was the ADC who took the order for the Charge of the Light Brigade. He is thought to have seen that the General's instructions had been misunderstood, and to have ridden along in front of the advancing troops, vainly trying to turn them in the right direction, so that they should not ride through the fatal valley itself, but should skirt round it. He was immediately shot down, so that his thoughts and intentions can never now be known.

In "A Legend of Cotteswold," Gordon says:

"I remember the lowering wintry morn,
And the mist on the Cotswold hills,
Where I once heard the blast of the huntsman's horn,
Not far from the Seven rills.
Jack Esdaile was there, and Hugh St Clair,
Bob Chapman and Andrew Kerr,
And big George Griffiths on
Devil may care, And black Tom Oliver.
And one who rode on a dark, brown steed,
Clean-jointed, sinewy, spare,
With the lean game head of the Blacklock breed,
And the resolute eye that loves the lead,
And the quarters massive and spare,
A tower of strength with a promise of speed
(There was Celtic blood in the pair)."

This Jack Esdaile was Edward Jeffries Esdaile, of Cothelstone, Somerset, born 28th June 1813, who had married on 27th September 1837 Eliza Ianthe, only daughter of Percy Bysshe Shelley by his first wife, Harriette, second daughter of John Westbrook.

The Esdailes lived at that time in Cheltenham and Dr Ker in his reminiscences remarks that a greater contrast could not have existed than that between Shelley and his daughter, Ianthe, as Mrs Esdaile had strictly evangelical views, and was in no way remarkable, except as a good wife and mother. To her in her infancy Shelley had written the beautiful little sonnet "To Ianthe."

Jack Esdaile's son, the late Mr C. E. J. Esdaile, said of his father: "He was a very fine rider, but gave it up from conscientious scruples about '52. He succeeded to this property in 1866 and died in 1881. I cannot tell you more' of his riding than what I have been told. My father would hardly ever refer to his unregenerate days, but occasionally the old Adam would peep out in such a way as this: pointing to some hurdles which were the height of a deer park fence, once he said, 'Would your horse jump these?' I replied that I should not dream of asking him such a question. He remarked, 'I had a little mare once that would think nothing of them.' He had wonderful hands and could ride horses that very few would care to do. A famous jockey of those days who, I think, hunted with the Duke, observed to one of the field in a run in Somerset, 'No one could do that but Jack Esdaile.' The feat referred to was nothing very unusual for a Somerset man. It was, I am told, a quick descent of a very sloping covert into the road."

Mr C. E. J. Esdaile from his letters seemed to be much more interested in his father's riding exploits and in Lindsay Gordon's poetry than in the immortal works of his grandfather, Shelley. He himself was killed in the hunting-field.

George and Ned Griffiths were the sons of Mr Lewis Griffiths of Marie Hill. Lord James of Hereford thought that George Griffiths was really the man to whom Gordon referred in "A Legend of Cotteswold," but most authorities say that it was Ned.

Lindsay Gordon was a great upholder of Blacklock and his descendants, and would have rejoiced had he lived to see the victories and fame of Galopin, Galliard, the great St Simon, Persimmon, and the rest.

Bob Chapman was the famous Cheltenham horse-dealer whom people said King Edward privately visited sometimes at The Oaklands, Cheltenham. He ran away with Colonel Hogg's daughter and married her, and was a great man to hounds, who is said to have taught King Edward to hunt.

The La Terrières came to live at Alstone Villa in about 1860, when Colonel La Terrière (as he afterwards became) was about four years old. At four and a half years of age he was sent to a school in Cheltenham, kept by a Miss Hayward, and thence, after a year or two, was sent to a larger school, Miss Hill's, where there were some sixty boys, day-boys and boarders, including two Littledales, two Bevans, two Kerrs, three Bonds, a Money, Freckleton, Bax Ironside, Roddy Owen, brother of Hugh, and others.

At the age of five Mr La Terrière used to take his son out hunting, mounted on a little Shetland pony, called Toby, and he was blooded at Pegglesworth by Charles Turner.

"My father," he adds, "used to hunt till he was past seventy, and I used to go out with him whenever I came home for the holidays. He used to get Roddy Owen, a son of one of his best friends, and me into the field at Alstone on our two ponies, take away our saddles, and then make us go a lot of jumps he had there to practise horses on. The lessons he gave us were never forgotten by either of us I expect. It is a matter of sporting history, what Roddy* did in the riding line in after life, and I think at my best time I was quite up to the average as a horseman in the little I did between the flags and over hunting country. I never knew him in his prime, but I always understood from his contemporaries, The Giant (old Lord Fitzhardinge), Bob Chapman and others, that my father was about the best man to hounds of his day, and could ride a bad horse against anyone. He did a lot of riding between the flags too, though all I have as a memento of that is his old silk jacket, and the Oxford University Steeplechase Cup of 1841, which he won on a mare called Lancashire Witch.

"My father's brother, my Uncle Bill, went in for racing more than he did, but was in no way the horseman my father was. They were contemporaries of Adam Lindsay Gordon, whose poems I think the most human that were ever written, and his name appears with theirs in old records of the fifties."

Mr Hugh Owen, senior, and Mr La Terrière used to teach their boys to box, and at seven or eight years of age, young La Terrière one day, in a sparring match, knocked Roddy Owen into the fireplace, and cut his head open against the fender. The boys used to go and exercise their animals in the Christmas holidays at a Riding School, kept by Mr English who, like Bob Chapman, did a lot of horse-dealing. "I must not forget, either," adds Colonel La Terrière, "the family of Holmans. They were all well known ... a fine old sporting family. The two Owens, La Terrière and the two Archers, Fred and Charlie, sons of the steeplechase jockey, William Archer, were the small boys of the Cotswold hunt, of which Mr Cregoe Colmore of Moorend was at that time the Master. The Owens subsequently lived at Roderick House.

Frederick James Archer was born in St George's Place, Cheltenham, on 11th January 1857, in the quaint little Georgian Noah's-Ark-like house that is still standing, and where his grandfather, William Archer had kept a pillion-riding establishment in the far-off Georgian days. When William Archer, Fred's father, was a boy, there was a large piece of waste ground where the Gas Company now makes bricks, and also on the site where St Peter's Church now stands, and here pony and galloway races were held, in which William Archer, junior, is said to have competed, *in his pinafore*. When Fred Archer was three weeks old, William Archer succeeded his father-in-law as landlord of the King's Arms at Prestbury, and the family lived there for many years. Fred, as has been said, hunted from childhood, and soon the boy's feats of horsemanship amazed every one, it was said that he could jump the stiffest wall in the Cotswold country.

In 1868, William Archer took his eleven-year-old son to Newmarket and apprenticed him to Mathew Dawson, the great trainer. Fred Archer, George Stevens and Lindsay Gordon were all destined to die tragic deaths.

---

* Major R. Owen, DSO, won the Grand National of 1892 on Father O'Flynn.

Towards the end of 1870 the news reached his friends in Cheltenham that Lindsay Gordon had shot himself on Brighton Beach, Victoria, Australia, on 21st June of that year. He was thought to be the best amateur steeplechase rider of his day in Australia, and his fame as a poet was already established. It has been steadily growing since his death.

In 1871 George Stevens was riding up Cleeve Hill on his hack, The Clown, when his hat blew off and the horse was frightened, turned round and bolted down the hill at such a pace and on such a track that people said that no other horseman in England could have kept in the saddle. At length The Clown stumbled and fell, throwing Stevens over his head, so that the jockey struck a drain-pipe, fractured his skull, and died after a few hours. A stone marks the spot where this tragedy occurred.

Stevens won the Grand National on Free Trader, on Emblem, and Emblematic, Lord Coventry's twin mares, and twice on the Colonel. He was a quiet, unassuming man, highly respected by all who knew him.

No one else has ever won more than three Grand Nationals, and amongst those who won the great race *three* times were Tom Oliver, Tom Pickernell, and Jack Anthony, all connected with Cheltenham.

Fred Archer grew up, as is well known, to be the greatest of jockeys and the outstanding personality on the turf in his own or in any other day. He won the Derby on Silvio in 1877, Bend Or in 1880, Iroquois in 1881, Melton in 1885, and Ormonde in 1886, respectively, besides countless other important races. Weakened by fasting he shot himself when dangerously ill with typhoid or low fever in November 1886, and Cheltenham, Newmarket, and, indeed, the world at large were paralysed with horror when the news came. Archer was only twenty-nine years old at the time of his death, and his parents still survived. His elder brother, William Hayward Archer, had been fatally injured in 1878 in a steeplechase at Cheltenham at a time when the races were held first where the Cemetery Chapel now stands. His brother, Charlie, had on the previous day won the Cheltenham Grand Annual on Duellist.

The Dean Close Memorial School was founded in May 1886, a mile and a half from the centre of the town, in order to keep green the Dean's memory, and to instruct the young idea in the evangelical doctrines which he had upheld in his lifetime. The late Dean of Canterbury was one of those responsible for the foundation of this excellent school. Although, no doubt, missionaries and evangelical clergymen and temperance advocates and antitobacconists may have come forth from the Dean Close Memorial School, there are two outstanding personalities who were educated there, who come under none of the above-mentioned categories. These were Mr Jack Anthony the famous amateur rider, and James Elroy Flecker, the poet, the latter being the son of the Rev. W. H. Flecker, DD, first Headmaster of the Dean Close School, Cheltenham. Flecker's life, work, and tragically untimely death are too well known to require comment here. After long exile, when his heart often turned back to the hills and meadows of his home, he died in Davos on 3rd January 1915.

He lies buried in the beautiful cemetery at the foot of the Cotswolds where Cleeve and The Hewletts and the rest look down upon the quiet dead of the Cotswold Spa.

Cheltenham had felt the South African War severely as she has felt every war, since the Spa became a resort of retired officers. Her losses in the Great War were great and terrible.

The Public Library at Cheltenham contains a painting, with portraits of officers and non-commissioned officers, of a platoon the 5th Gloucesters marching through Hebuterne in July 1915. One of these officers is Mr Cyril Winterbotham who fell in the war. Mr Winterbotham belonged to an old and highly-esteemed family which has been for generations in the town, the late Mr J. B. Winterbotham being one of its best-known members. He and his wife gave two new bells to the Parish Church, and had the others re-cast, re-tuned and re-hung—a very delightful present to the town.

The 5th Gloucesters brought up a poet in the war, F. W. Harvey, from whose works Messrs Benn lately published a selection, and other books of his poems had previously appeared. "A Gloucestershire Lad" is one of the best known of Mr Harvey's poems, some of which are very charming, and he is a true son of Gloucestershire, with a deep sense of its beauties:

"I'm homesick for my hills again,
My hills again,
To see above the Severn plain,
Unscabbarded against the sky
The blue high blade of Cotswold lie."

And now, with the help of Mrs E. C. Willoughby and of Sir James Agg-Gardner, Captain Willoughby's wife and friend, this story of the Georgians and the rest has been brought to a close.

Quietly and unpretentiously as he had lived, E. C. Willoughby, almost at the start of the War, joined up as a private, and marched away up the Gloucester Road one day, with other recruits, to the railway station. His own share of this manuscript was left unfinished and even unchecked.

Less than a year later he was dead. On the heights of Chunak Bahr, where like the promised land, they could see the Straits and beyond spread out before them, the officers of the 7th Gloucesters, one by one, fell, killed or wounded, and the battalion fought on for hours without any officers. Young lads, most of them, who were new to the profession of arms, they fought on as steadily as the regulars of the regiment in that battle of old, when the two lines of the Gloucesters engaged the enemy front and rear, and were afterwards allowed to wear the regimental number behind as well as in front of their shakos, by which grand feat they earned the nickname of The Double Gloucesters.

Sir Ian Hamilton wrote on the 24th of December 1927: "I remember Captain Willoughby's sad but glorious death and I am glad to hear on Christmas Eve, twelve years afterwards, that his gallantry and self-sacrifice are going to be recorded."

But one cannot record here by name the gallantry and self-sacrifice of *all* the men who went forth to war from Cheltenham in the Gloucestershire Regiment, in the Royal Gloucestershire Hussars, in the Territorial Battalions (of which the 5th, 7th 9th and 10th Gloucesters were much connected with Cheltenham), or in other regiments, or who went down to the sea in ships—or above or below it in aeroplanes or submarines.

The Cotswold farmers, the citizens of Gloucester and Bristol, the townsmen of Cheltenham, Stroud, Tewkesbury, Cirencester and the rest, rose up and left their homes, their clubs and shops and offices and farms and did their duty until the going down of the sun, and alas, many of them did not come back. Some, like the gallant Colonel John Watkins Yardley, CMG, DSO, a well-known amateur rider, died *after* the war, worn out with hard service.

Since this story of old days was, as we and he thought, finished, Sir James Agg-Gardner, who went in and out amongst us doing good, has rested from his labours, and is not, in this world at least, because God has taken him, beautifully and peaceful, as one of his near relatives said, in his sleep. Perhaps he meant to do more things before he retired to rest, perhaps he was very tired, but that we do not know. At any rate he just loosened his collar and tie and lay down, as he often did, in his clothes, to rest awhile.

He was the lord of the manor and most of us, whether we knew him personally or not, who were born in Cheltenham, wherever we have lived since, have always regarded the very kind and shy and deprecating man with reverence and affection. We may have smiled at his shyness and his silence, but we really loved them and we loved him. It was the same at Westminster, where he perhaps had more influence than some of those who made many speeches, though he devoted himself and to a great extent his money to the tasks of helping his country, his party, the Primrose League, his constituency, and of making and keeping the House of Commons the best Club in the world. If he thought that the catering department was not paying well enough he gave dinners to his friends and thus kept things going.

Sir James Agg-Gardner's self-sacrificing kindness and his old-world courtliness of manner were perhaps his leading characteristics and of him it might have been truly said:

"He doeth little kindnesses,
Which most leave undone or despise."

He had two efficient secretaries but this did not keep him from answering very many letters with his own hand.

A clever man of the world and man of business, he was a shrewd and witty, if a kind and indulgent, observer of his fellow men. He may, like One greater than himself, have given help and advice to undeserving people who asked it, but one would think that he was not often deceived.

Of a friend of his own, of mature age, who got married and went to live in a highly respectable quarter of London, this confirmed bachelor remarked jestingly, "Silly ass," and when the other great friend to whom he was speaking said that the bride and bridegroom would be neighbours of his own, Sir James replied in his dry way, "Yes, a good many *notorious* people live there!"

It was characteristic of him that he cut out of his book of reminiscences the account of how, all on a day, his grandfather rode down from town and saved the Bank of Gloucester by pouring bags of money into it. Neither of the good deeds of himself nor of his family would he ever speak at all. The *Observer* of 12th August 1928 says:

"Sir James Agg-Gardner's death evokes in the *Manchester Guardian* an excellent story of how his great uncle's exertions saved the family bank at Cheltenham in the financial crisis of 1825. It was a case of rushing securities up to London by postchaise and bringing back the cash to meet an excited run, and the situation was saved, tradition says, with only five pounds to spare. This was evidently the basis on which Stanley Weyman built his novel of Ovington's Bank, one of his many faithful and fascinating pictures of England in the first half of the nineteenth century."

When on the outbreak of the war his parliamentary secretary was in camp at Felixstowe, Sir James went down frequently to visit him.

The best appreciation of Sir James Agg-Gardner, as the House of Commons saw him, was written in the *Evening News* when Commander Oliver Locker-Lampson reviewed his book, Some Parliamentary Recollections, in the *Evening News* of 19th December 1927, in the course of which the writer speaks of the stooping friendly figure of "not only the oldest but probably the most popular member of the House of Commons ... Sitting for the most part mute in a talkative assembly—mute, but oh so wakeful and watchful ... He was never rude, and yet never insincere in his life; he has always been unaware of class or any other false distinctions, and he could not be mean or self-seeking." Alas, his bodily presence will be seen no more, whether in the House of Commons or in his own town of Cheltenham, but his gracious spirit one will think, hovers in his own haunts, and his willing service may some day be put to higher uses when there shall be a new Heaven and a new Earth as well. We cannot help our grief and tears whether we knew Sir James Agg-Gardner much or little.

If this book should serve to help the town for which many Cheltonians fought and worked, and for which some of them died, it will not have been written in vain. It should be remembered, however, that the authors meant to write chiefly

Vice-Admiral Sir Josiah Coghill, Bt. Died 150. From a drawing by Richard Dighton

about the more or less forgotten Georgians, and that Lord James of Hereford, Lord Loreburn, Frederick Myers, Dorothea Beale, Adrian Wilson, Josephine Butter, and their contemporaries are well within the memories of living men and women and that Gustav Holst is in the prime of life.

Perhaps some Cheltenham men and women in foreign countries may read this book and say, as Flecker said of Cheltenham as well as of Greece:

"Oh, well I know sweet Hellas now,
And well I knew it then,
When I with starry lads walked out—
But ah, for home again!
Was I not bred in Gloucestershire,
One of the Englishmen!"